W9-CEV-884

Politics and International Relations of Southeast Asia

GENERAL EDITOR

George McT. Kahin

Burma: Military Rule and the Politics of Stagnation
    by Josef Silverstein

*Indonesian Foreign Policy and the Dilemma of Dependence:
From Sukarno to Soeharto*
    by Franklin B. Weinstein

Burma, 1975. (From the U.S. Department of State.)

BURMA

*Military Rule and
the Politics of Stagnation*

JOSEF SILVERSTEIN

WITHDRAWN

Cornell University Press | ITHACA AND LONDON

Burgess
DS
5304
.S55

c - 1

Copyright © 1977 by Cornell University

All rights reserved. Except for brief quotations in a review, this book, or parts thereof, must not be reproduced in any form without permission in writing from the publisher. For information address Cornell University Press, 124 Roberts Place, Ithaca, New York 14850.

First published in 1977 by Cornell University Press.
Published in the United Kingdom by Cornell University Press Ltd., 2–4 Brook Street, London W1Y 1AA.

International Standard Book Number (cloth) 0–8014–0911–X
International Standard Book Number (paper) 0–0814–9863–5
Library of Congress Catalog Card Number 77–3127
Printed in the United States of America
Librarians: Library of Congress cataloging information
appears on the last page of this book.

Contents

1980 SEP 03

Foreword

That broad area lying between China and India which since World War II has generally been known as Southeast Asia is one of the most heterogeneous in the world. Though it is generally referred to as a region, the principal basis for this designation is simply the geographic propinquity of its component states, and the fact that collectively they occupy the territory between China and the Indian subcontinent. The fundamental strata of the traditional cultures of nearly all the numerous peoples of Southeast Asia do set them apart from those of India and China. Beyond that, however, there are few common denominators among the states that currently make up the area except for roughly similar climatic conditions and, until recently at least, broadly similar economies and economic problems.

The political systems presently governing the lives of Southeast Asia's 300 million inhabitants have been built on considerably different cultures; the religious component alone embraces Buddhism, Confucianism, Christianity, Hinduism, and Islam. Except in the case of Thailand, the politics of all these countries have been conditioned by periods of colonial rule—ranging from little more than half a century to approximately four—each of which has had a distinctive character and political legacy. Even the nature of the Japanese wartime occupation, which covered the entire area, varied considerably among the several countries and had different political consequences. And after Japan's defeat, the courses to independence followed by these states diverged widely. Only through revolutionary anticolonial wars were two of the most populous, Indonesia and Vietnam, able to assert their independence. Although the others followed routes that were peaceful, they were not all necessarily smooth, and the time involved varied by as much as a decade.

Moreover, subsequent to independence the political character of these states has continued to be significantly affected by a wide range of relationships with outside powers. In a few cases these have been largely harmonious, attended by only relatively minor external efforts to influence the course of local political developments. However, most of these countries have been the object of interventions, covert and overt, by outside powers—particularly the United States—which have been calculated to shape internal political life in accordance with external interests. Thus the range of contemporary political systems in Southeast Asia is strikingly varied, encompassing a spectrum quite as broad as the differing cultures and divergent historical conditionings that have so profoundly influenced their character.

This series, "Politics and International Relations of Southeast Asia," stems from an earlier effort to treat the nature of government and politics in the states of Southeast Asia in a single volume. Since the second, revised edition of that book, *Governments and Politics of Southeast Asia*, was published in 1964, interest in these countries has grown, for understandable reasons, especially in the United States. This wider public concern, together with a greater disposition of academics to draw on the political experience of these countries in their teaching, has suggested the need for a more substantial treatment of their politics and governments than could be subsumed within the covers of a single book. The series therefore aims to devote separate volumes to each of the larger Southeast Asian states. All the books are to be written by political scientists who have lived and carried out research in one or more of the countries for a considerable period and who have previously published scholarly studies on their internal politics.

Although each of these volumes will include a section on the foreign policy of the country concerned, the increased importance of Southeast Asia in international relations that transcend this area has suggested the need for a few studies focused on the foreign relations of its major states. Thus the series will include this additional component.

Presumably one no longer needs to observe, as was the case in

1964, that the countries treated "are likely to be strange to many of our readers." But even though the increased American interaction with most of the countries has clearly obviated that proposition, many readers are still likely to be unacquainted with their earlier histories and the extent to which their pasts have affected the development of their recent and contemporary political character. Thus all those volumes dealing with the governments and politics of the area will include substantial historical sections as well as descriptions of the salient features of the present social and economic setting. In order to provide as much similarity of treatment as is compatible with the range of cultures and political systems presented by these states, the authors will follow a broadly similar pattern of organization and analysis of their political history, dynamics, and processes. This effort to achieve some basis of comparability may appear rather modest, but to have attempted any greater degree of uniformity would have militated against the latitude and flexibility required to do justice to the differing characteristics of the political systems described.

Josef Silverstein's volume on Burma is the culmination of his two decades of research and writing on various aspects of that country's politics and government. This has involved numerous visits there for research and university teaching, the first in 1955 and the most recent in 1972. It is appropriate that this study of the major Southeast Asian country most neglected by Western scholars should be among the first published in the Cornell series.

GEORGE McT. KAHIN

Ithaca, New York

Preface

On March 2, 1962, Burma's constitutional political system was displaced by a military dictatorship. The coup was swift, and the removal of all rival leaders was total. During the first decade of the "new order" the nation closed itself off from the prying eyes of outsiders as the coup leaders sought to transform the politics and the economy of the nation, the values and life style of its people. Foreign scholars and journalists who persisted in their efforts to record the changes taking place inside Burma had to rely on state-controlled publications that circulated outside the country, the statements of Burmese émigrés, bits and pieces of information in letters from friends still in Burma, and the reports of diplomats and the occasional journalists permitted brief visits to the country. While foreign scholars were denied access, Burmese scholars continued to work and to publish their findings mainly for their domestic audiences. All too few of their writings have been translated and circulated abroad. Because Burma's revolution did not "shake the world," no core of Burma-watchers exists on its borders, no priorities are assigned to the study of Burma, no crash programs support study of its languages and the training of scholar specialists. In the decade when the war in Vietnam, the political upheaval in Indonesia, the racial problems in Malaysia, the economic miracle in Singapore, and the troubles in the Philippines attracted world attention, and access to these countries was relatively easy, interest in Burma receded and few people continued to record and comment upon events within its borders.

It is unfortunate that the controlled revolution in Burma has not been studied in greater detail, especially by scholars interested in area politics, modernization, and social change. For here is a country that has experienced national disunity, revolt, secession, and low economic growth since it recovered independence in 1948; more important, here is a nation whose leaders, both constitutional and dictatorial, have sought to unite their people, improve the standard of living, and realize the modest goals of the independence movement by their own efforts and with domestic resources. While socialism has been the goal, the emphasis has been on the *Burmese* way to socialism; although new values and a new way of life are to supplant the old, the nation's social engineers have sought to create national unity and social harmony by finding a Burmese solution rather than importing one ready-made from abroad.

The importance civilian and military leaders have attached to preserving the nation's Burmese character requires consideration of those elements in Burma's past that persist into the present. This study will attempt to trace the roots of contemporary politics and to focus upon institutions and processes that represent continuity and change. Major attention will be given to the period of military rule in an attempt to define the limits and the depths of the controlled revolution.

This present work grew out of two earlier, less extensive examinations of Burmese politics and institutions: the section on Burma in George McT. Kahin, editor, *Governments and Politics of Southeast Asia* (1959) and the revised version of that section (1964). These studies were limited in both length and breadth of coverage. As a separate work, this book now explores topics more thoroughly and in greater detail. While some of the material appeared in the earlier studies in slightly different form, the new volume has been recast, viewing the period of military political dominance as part of a continuing historical development. Placing greater emphasis upon Burmese politics since the 1962 coup, I have relied upon data and information gathered in three brief trips to Burma in 1968, 1970, and 1972, and from other sources—newspapers, documents, interviews, and letters—accumulated over the past several years.

I hope that this study will make Burmese government and politics more understandable to any who have sought information and analysis and not found it. If this brief examination of a "do it yourself" nation stimulates others to study Burma in greater depth, or if it provides insights and suggests areas for comparison and contrast with other Asian nations so that better descriptions, more sophisticated analyses, and more informed understanding of Burma will result, it will have served a useful purpose.

This book is dedicated to my wife, Lynn, who has shared Burma with me from the very beginning.

JOSEF SILVERSTEIN

New Brunswick, New Jersey

BURMA

Military Rule and the Politics of Stagnation

1 | Sources of Burmese
Political Culture

Three outstanding geographic features have had a direct bearing on the political development of Burma. First, the country has a predominance of north-south valleys, mountains, and rivers. The major lines of communications follow the contours of the land, and Burma's chief cities and towns are located along a north-south axis in the interior rather than near the borders or the seacoast. Second, the country divides naturally into two distinct areas—the plains and delta, and the mountains. The political and cultural heartland of historic Burma was located in the valley watered by the Irrawaddy and Chindwin rivers and protected on three sides by a semicircle of mountains. The delta plain to the south of this area is the political and economic center of modern Burma. The 1947 constitution joined these two regions to form the political subdivision known as Burma proper, and the 1974 constitution divided the same area into nine states and divisions. Regardless of its political configuration, the area forms a natural region, and within it are located the seat of the national government and most of Burma's population, industry, and cities. The mountain areas, subdivided into five states, have little attraction for the plains people. Their relatively sparse population lives in a more backward state of social and political development than do the plains dwellers. Third, Burma always has been partially isolated from its neighbors, and the mountains have provided a land barrier to merchants and would-be invaders. Although Burma has a long seacoast, it lies outside the monsoon routes, and seaborne traders did not come to the country in large numbers.

Isolation contributed to Burma's inability to counter the rapid penetration of European traders and soldiers in the eighteenth and nineteenth centuries. Despite more than a century of contacts with the West through war, trade, and colonial rule, the sense of isolation and a desire to find solutions to local problems from within the Burmese tradition continue. The physical separation of peoples within modern Burma has contributed to the growth of differences among them in language, culture, and political consciousness, thereby continuing the persistence of separate identity and aspirations despite the strength of forces working to blend or submerge minority cultures with the ethnically Burman center. These elements—isolation and separation—will emerge more clearly after a brief review of the broad outlines of Burmese history and an examination of selective aspects of Burman[1] culture.

The Pattern of History to 1885

Burma's political history between the Pagan dynasty (1044–1287) and the British conquest (1824–1886) was characterized by endless struggles among at least four of the indigenous groups inhabiting the area of modern Burma and between them and their outside neighbors. The predominant groups in the internal struggle were the Burmans, whose home was in the Irrawaddy Valley, the Mons or Talaings, who lived in the south, the Shans from the north, central, and eastern parts of the hills surrounding the Irrawaddy Valley, and the Arakanese, whose home was the isolated western area that bears their name.

There were only three relatively short periods of political unification prior to the British conquest. The first began in the eleventh century when the Burman kings conquered their immediate neighbors and established the kingdom of Pagan. The two centuries of that dynasty, Burma's golden age, saw the flowering of an Indian- and Mon-influenced Burman culture,[2] evidence of which can still be seen in the ruins of the city of Pagan.

1. Although writers have used the terms Burman and Burmese in a variety of ways, most scholars since World War II use them as follows: Burman is an ethnic term identifying a particular group in Burma. Burmese is a political term including all the inhabitants of the country—Burmans, Karens, Shans, Kachins, Chins, Mons, and so on.

2. Gordon H. Luce, *Old Burma—Early Pagan*, 3 vols. (Locust Valley, N.Y.: J. J. Augustin, 1969–1970).

Theravada Buddhism became the religion of the Burmans of Pagan, influencing all aspects of their art and culture. The armies of Kublai Khan brought an end to Pagan in 1287, when they, in conjunction with the Shans, drove the Burman king from his throne and destroyed the empire.

The fall of Pagan marked the beginning of nearly two hundred years of Shan dominance in upper Burma. Powerful enough to dominate the leaderless Burmans, but too divided and quarrelsome to unite and establish a stable kingdom, the Shans established a royal center at Ava, and warfare characterized their period of ascendancy. Their chief internal rivals were the Mons of Pegu. During this period, many Burmans left their traditional homeland and relocated south and east in Toungoo.

The second unification of Burma under Burman rule began in 1486 and lasted until 1752. A new dynasty rose in Toungoo, subdued its neighbors, and re-established Burman rule in roughly the area incorporated in modern Burma. During the existence of this kingdom, the Burmans permanently subdued the Shans. In their wars with Siam, the Burmans were unable to gain more than temporary victories; the fighting between the two countries depopulated lower Burma as the people either fled from the wars or were taken prisoner and carried off to the land of their conquerors. By the end of the seventeenth century the vigor of the dynasty was spent, and Burma again became the center of quarreling groups. This kingdom, unlike its Burman predecessor, left no great cultural or architectural legacy.

The third unification under indigenous rule came in the eighteenth century, when a new line of Burman kings—known as the Konbaung dynasty—rose in the north in 1752 and forged an empire that lasted until 1886. Among its initial conquests were the Mons, who for centuries had been the Burmans' southern rival. The fall of Arakan in 1785 completed the Burman mastery of the south. The new dynasty engaged in numerous adventures against Assam, Manipur, and Siam and successfully defended Burma from four invasions by the armies of China. Burma's foreign adventures in the west brought the country into conflict with British power in India, and friction over Assam and Manipur and rebellious activity in Arakan finally precipitated the first Anglo-Burmese war (1824–1826). Superior British military technology helped the invaders score easy military victories; disease and poor communications caused the victors their major setbacks. The war ended with the signing of the Treaty of Yandabo.[3]

Following the war, Burma neither improved its military technology nor established friendly and realistic relations with the British. A trivial incident provided the Westerners with a pretext to renew the fighting in 1852.[4] As a result of the second Anglo-Burmese war all of lower Burma was annexed after the well-prepared British met only token resistance.

During the next two decades the Burman kings tried to reform the government and establish friendly relations with the British. The arrival of the French as a major power in Southeast Asia in the 1870s and 1880s alarmed the British and caused them to use an incident between a British commercial firm and the Burman king in 1885 as a basis for launching the third and final Anglo-Burmese war. British military operations began in November; by the end of the month the Burman king had been captured. Following their victory, the British, on January 1, 1886, proclaimed the annexation of the remainder of Burma.[5]

Two institutions of precolonial Burma—the monarchy and the bureaucracy—merit closer examination to understand some of the causes of this long record of instability and war. The king—in theory—exercised absolute power. He was assisted by a royal council—hlutdaw—whose members he appointed and who served at his pleasure. As a semidivine personage, he was isolated from the public; the power struggles, the intrigues, and the court life were shielded from the public view. The king had numerous wives and even more offspring. There was no prescribed pattern of succes-

---

3. William F. B. Laurie, *Our Burmese Wars and Relations with Burma* (2d ed.; London: W. H. Allen, 1885). The treaty provided that Burma would cede Arakan and Tenasserim to the British, renounce all claims to Assam, give up the right to interfere in the affairs of Manipur, and pay an indemnity.

4. See Richard Cobden, "How Wars Are Got up in India: The Origin of the Burmese War," in Louis Mallet, ed., *The Political Writings of Richard Cobden with an Introductory Essay* (London: W. Ridgway, 1878), pp. 223–257, for an example of liberal criticism in England of the policies of the East India Company.

5. For a good discussion of the background to the third Anglo-Burmese War, see Maung Maung, *Burma in the Family of Nations* (Amsterdam: Djambatan, 1956), p. 5.

sion, thus the murder or natural death of a monarch always produced a period of political instability while rival claimants fought for the office. Nearly as important a cause of instability was the failure of the Burmans to develop an enduring bureaucracy with some degree of independence and standing, such as existed in China. Instead, each member of the Burman bureaucracy depended on the monarch for the authority to function in his assigned office. When a king died or was displaced, all bureaucrats had to leave their posts to return to the capital to receive a new commission from his successor. The frequency of change in monarchs meant that the bureaucracy was unstable, insecure, and lacked independence.

Compared to the administrative instability, warfare, and short-lived dynasties, Burman society at the local level proved to be relatively stable. Organized under the leadership of hereditary chieftains called *myothugyis* in upper Burma and *thaikthugyis* in lower Burma, the people performed services and paid taxes. Each village had a headman who, under certain conditions, was inferior to the chieftains. Because authority was personal rather than territorial, the people owed allegiance to their chieftain regardless of where they lived. When disputes arose, both the chieftain and the headman served as arbitrators and based their recommendations on the moral teachings of the Buddha and on local custom. A Burman version of the Code of Manu called the *dhammathat* played a relatively minor role in the people's daily lives. No formal system of courts and no class of legalists emerged to serve society.

Most of the people either farmed royal or state lands operated under limited leases, or their own land which they or their ancestors had reclaimed from the jungle or swamps. These reclaimed lands were the property of the cultivator as a member of a village. Although the owner had the right to sell and dispose of his property, his family had first right to buy it back. The economy was stable because most of the population practiced subsistence agriculture with a small surplus for taxes and barter. The chieftain dealt in behalf of the people with the provincial and royal government, so village life remained relatively insulated from the struggles for power around the throne and among the contending ethnic groups.

Social stability in precolonial Burma drew its main strength from the fact that nearly all Burmans and most of the minorities under their direct rule shared a common faith—Buddhism.[6] The monkhood or *sangha* served the community by providing teachers and schools. Learning was available to all; even the meanest peasant learned to read and memorize the teachings of the faith. All male adherents entered the religious order during some period of their lives and became monks for a limited time. Education, participation in the religious hierarchy, and feeding the monks to earn merit for the next rebirth all fostered close relationships between the people and the religion and bound the community together.[7]

Religion was not rigidly institutionalized. At the village level there were monasteries or *pongyi khaungs* under a semi-independent abbot. Usually one or two *pongyis* were permanent and the rest local residents who entered and left at will. The monasteries were outside the administrative control of the village, subject only to the *thathanabaing*—the head of the *sangha*—who was appointed by and served at the pleasure of the king and the royal religious council. Only the *thathanabaing* had authority to discipline the monks who violated their vows. He could order them to be defrocked—remove their sacred yellow robes—and thereby become subject to civil authority.[8]

The Buddhist believed the universe was governed by fixed and orderly laws. Among these was the law of impermanence and change, to which everything was subject, such as passing from youth to old age, life to death, day to night. Man is part of the changing world of appearances, and according to the doctrine of *samsara*—the wheel of rebirth—he passes through an endless cycle

6. The term Buddhism in a formal sense encompasses the doctrine, the formal ritual, and the daily practices of the believers. As practiced by the people in Burma, Buddhism includes local beliefs and rituals that give it its local character and meaning. To appreciate the interaction of the great tradition with local practices, see John F. Brohm, "Buddhism and Animism in a Burmese Village," *Journal of Asian Studies*, 12, no. 2 (February 1963), 155–167; for a larger and more detailed treatment of the same subject see Melford E. Spiro, *Buddhism and Society: A Great Tradition and Its Burmese Vicissitudes* (London: Allen & Unwin, 1971).

7. John S. Furnivall, *Colonial Policy and Practice* (New York: New York University Press, 1956), pp. 12–13.

8. Donald Eugene Smith, *Religion and Politics in Burma* (Princeton: Princeton University Press, 1965), chap. 2.

of birth, death, and rebirth. Until he realizes the true nature of things, he cannot escape this cycle. The goal of all living things is to escape from rebirth. The Buddha expressed these ideas in his Four Noble Truths and offered a way of escape through the Eight Fold Path of right living, right thought, and right actions. Thus, for the Buddhist, desire for power, prestige, and material things is false; further, since man's present situation is based upon his previous existence, he can do little in this lifetime to change it, although he can affect the future by following the Buddha's teachings.

The teachings of the Buddha as accepted in Burma placed full responsibility upon the individual for his future. This idea of self-reliance draws its inspiration from a statement attributed to the Buddha—"in the end, each man must work out his own salvation." But the idea of individual responsibility did not carry over into the political realm. Government, the Buddhist was taught, was one of the five evils all men must endure. Man, therefore, lived in a political order he could not change, and his responsibilities did not extend to politics. The idea of individual responsibility did not transcend the religious realm and become a basis of popular government.

Authority was seen as having two major sources—place and heredity. Regardless of how he reached the throne, the king drew his authority from the office and from his control of the symbols of authority—the palace and the regalia. He was shielded from the eyes of his subjects, wrapped in ritual, and responsible for the faith; his authority was viewed as semidivine and unbridled. He could give and withdraw authority to subordinates; he could determine life and death of his subjects. Local chieftains, like the king and other members of the royal family, based their claims to authority on heredity. The values and beliefs of the people provided no basis for a doctrine of popular sovereignty. As a result, there was no tradition of holding elections, consulting the people, or involving them in the political process. The villager did not question this pattern of authority or those who justified their claim to it. In modern as in ancient times, authority from above has been accepted by the majority of people, and the leader who holds the palace or seat of government and controls the symbols of authority has the right to rule.

As a result of this pattern, the people were little concerned with the affairs of state. The average peasant did not expect the state to do anything to improve his life, believing that only an individual, through his own actions and thoughts, could affect his status and circumstances in the next existence. The state therefore was not a vehicle for social and economic change. If the state was venal—took an excessive amount of taxes or forced men to fight in needless wars—the individual could do little but accept the situation. The political culture of the Burman early was characterized by the people's stoic acceptance of misfortune and the government's excessive demands and victimization through theft, war, and plunder.

In theory, religion and the state were connected in many ways—through the king, the *thathanabaing*, and the general respect toward the wearer of the yellow robe. Even though the king controlled the *thathanabaing*, he did not interfere with the independence of the monasteries and took action against a rogue monk only after he was defrocked. At the same time, the importance of religion was transcendent, and, in theory, the meanest monk was above a layman, whether peasant or king. In practice, the state supported the faith and did not consider it a political rival. Close and harmonious relations between the people's religion and their government formed a major element in Burma's traditional culture.

In their social organization, the Burmans did not develop a rigid class structure. Society was divided in at least two ways—between royalty and commoners and within the population between those who performed military or some other personal service and those who paid taxes and were liable for miscellaneous duties. The lines were not rigid—the king could marry a commoner, and his children from that marriage would enjoy standing as members of the aristocracy. If that child married a commoner, he would slip down the social ladder. Movement up and down and across lines was relatively easy and of little importance. While hereditary leaders maintained their status vis-à-vis their followers, they did not become an identifiable class, for when they chose wives from the local community the children who did not inherit the father's authority returned to being followers. When it is remembered that everyone who entered the *sangha* theoretically was equal, the picture emerges of a loosely structured Burman society that possibly could have provided a basis for the introduction of democracy.

While relationships within Burman society were not rigid, those between Burmans and the minorities were somewhat different. Some of the minorities living among the Burmans, particularly the Karens, were treated with hostility and were not accepted as equals. Mons and Arakanese who were captured in war and forced to migrate to Burman population centers found it relatively easy to intermingle and intermarry with their captors. The Burmans did not exert pressure to assimilate or Burmanize the culture of minority groups living in the frontier areas, such as the Shans. As long as the conquered people sent a few sons as hostages and daughters as wives of the Burman monarch and accepted a Burman official at their court, few other demands were made. Thus, the Burman political culture treated non-Burmans who did not intermarry or assimilate as separate and different. Those who did intermarry and adopt Burman identity and culture were accepted into Burman society. No serious effort was made to Burmanize the minorities, and the ethnic and cultural diversity developed as part of the Burman tradition has carried over into the modern period.

The above brief survey indicates that many aspects of Burma's political culture have deep roots in the land and history of the people. The British conquest confronted it with the first really major challenge; the outlines of that history will show how the culture was modified.

Colonial Rule, 1826–1948

The British made several changes in Burma's social organization and political and economic institutions that thrust the country from the backwater into the mainstream of world events. The introduction of "law and order" throughout Burma altered the system of local government and destroyed the traditional pattern of authority. The conversion of the country into a commercial granary and the world's largest rice exporter brought tenancy, moneylending, and land alienation. The introduction of Western concepts of government and politics and the efforts to prepare the people for self-rule through the gradual introduction of new institutions of popular participation created a new indigenous political elite who were divided over the question of gradualism versus immediate self-government. British encouragement and protection of minorities at the expense of the dominant Burmans, plus large-scale immigration of Indians as laborers and financiers, gave rise to new social problems that exploded into violent communal riots during the 1930s. These changes, together with the direct effects of World War II, stimulated the popular demand for Burma's independence in the postwar period.

Prior to the third Anglo-Burmese war of 1885, the primary political interest of the British was to establish law and order in the territories under their control. A centralized and bureaucratic administration was established to accomplish this aim as inexpensively as possible. The relatively stable local government met with little interference from the Europeans.[9] After the third war, the British were faced with a series of rebellions and dacoity that cost them dearly in money, men, and material but did not seriously threaten their rule. The support and sympathy given by the local chieftains to the insurgents were major reasons for Chief Commissioner Charles Crosthwaite's decision to replace the traditional system of local government with a new one modeled on the Indian pattern. The changes included making authority territorial instead of personal, eliminating the local chieftains, and elevating the village headmen to positions as salaried officials responsible to the central government rather than to the local community.[10] The significance of these changes was to replace the authority of the chieftain, who had exercised real power over the people, with a class of functionaries who had no prestige and therefore lacked the means for persuading the people to obey the laws.

The elimination of the monarchy also meant the end of the royal religious council which, in the past, had authority to discipline the monks. As no new council or governing body to censure the hierarchy was established, discipline in the religious orders deteriorated.

9. Government of Burma, *Selected Correspondence of Letters Issued from and Received in the Office of the Commissioner, Tenasserim Division, for the Years 1825–26 to 1842–43* (Rangoon: Government Printing and Stationery Office, 1929); John S. Furnivall, "Fashioning of Leviathan," *Journal of the Burma Research Society,* 29 (1939), 11–137.

10. Furnivall, *Colonial Policy and Practice,* p. 74.

At the same time, the number of English and Anglo-vernacular schools that concentrated on training for government and commercial employment rather than on righteous behavior increased. The slackening in public demand for traditional education deprived the Buddhist monks of their chief social functions, and the bonds between them and society weakened. The removal of the local chieftains and the deterioration of the Buddhist order were two of the main causes for the breakdown of traditional society in Burma. During the twentieth century, social unrest and crimes of violence increased continually in spite of the growth of the colonial police force, the courts, and the administrative system.

The shift from subsistence to commercial agriculture began between the second and third Anglo-Burmese wars, stimulated by an increased demand for rice in India and Europe, the opening of the Suez Canal, and the improvement in sea transportation. The British encouraged the peoples in upper Burma to move south and cultivate the rich delta soils. At the same time, the colonial authorities opened Burma to immigration of Indian laborers, merchants, and moneylenders. Both Burmese and aliens moved into the delta and established new communities. Coming as individuals and isolated families with relatively few social bonds to unite them, they owed no allegiance to a traditional chieftain and were not subject to social pressure and surveillance of lifelong friends. Most came to depend upon Indian moneylenders for the annual capital they needed. Since land ownership was a legal right under the British, land could be sold, traded, or repossessed without consideration of the rights either of the village or of the owner's family, as had been customary under the Burman kings. Tenancy, rackrenting, and land alienation became commonplace, and people drifted from area to area with no ties to bind them. The system produced rice; it also allowed the land to fall into alien hands and created a landlord class that dealt in land speculation rather than in cultivation, which in turn contributed to social dislocation and unrest.

Before the twentieth century the British made no effort to introduce institutions of self-government into Burma. The first administrative reform came in 1897, when the chief commissioner was raised to lieutenant governor and given a council of nine members (English, Indian, and Burmese) with limited authority. The Morley-Minto Reforms of 1909 provided for expansion of the council to fifteen, with two members elected by a restricted electorate from the European business community; in 1915 the council was expanded to thirty members, but no provision was made for additional elected members. In 1917 the secretary of state for India announced that Britain promised India eventual self-government. The Burmese interpreted the announcement as applicable to their country because it was then a province of India. British indecision and refusal to include Burma in the original statement led to a storm of protest. Local agitation forced the British to reconsider their decision, and in 1923, as they had done earlier in India, the British introduced dyarchy. Under this system certain areas of administration were transferred to ministers responsible to the legislative council and others were reserved to the governor.

Political awakening among the Burmans can be traced to the agitation in 1917–1918 over the issue of eventual self-government. Previous organized demonstrations had been limited to demands to end the deterioration of discipline in the Buddhist hierarchy and the desecration of sacred shrines by non-Buddhists. The earlier protesters were organized in a nonpolitical Young Men's Buddhist Association (YMBA), which the events of 1917 transformed into a political organization. Under the title, General Council of Burmese Associations (GCBA), this group was broadly based and generally nonreligious and had branches throughout Burma. In 1920 the university students called a national strike to protest the education plans connected with a new university. The strike marked the entry of students into national politics.[11]

From 1923 to 1941 there was a steady movement toward granting self-government to the Burmese. In 1921, the India Act of 1919 was applied to Burma and after adaptation it was implemented two years later. It gave Burma its first elected assembly. Of the 103 seats, 79 were filled by popular election. Under the system of dyarchy, the ministries of forests and education were transferred to two members of the legislature who were nominated

11. Josef Silverstein, "Burmese Student Politics in a Changing Society," *Daedalus*, 97, no. 1 (Winter 1968), 275–277.

by the governor and responsible to the legislature. Since all other areas of administration were under the governor's control and had first call upon revenues, the transfer gave the Burmese ministers prestige but little power. During this period, the GCBA split into shifting factions mainly over the question of whether to participate in politics or to remain aloof to fight for a new political system. In 1928 the British government created the Simon Commission to investigate how well the newly established institutions were functioning. As a result of their inquiries and the Round Table Conference discussions in London with Burmese leaders, Burma was separated from India and given a new constitution.

The 1935 constitution established a legislature with a lower house of 132 elected members and a cabinet government wherein nearly all internal matters were transferred to ministers responsible to the parliament. The most important ministries, such as finance, defense, and foreign affairs, still were reserved to the Governor, and he administered the Frontier Areas without consulting parliament or his ministers and possessed extreme emergency powers. The new constitution came into effect in 1937. During its four years of operation, four Burmese prime ministers held office; they made a creditable start at tackling some of Burma's worst problems—land alienation, immigration, and credit. Such leaders as Dr. Ba Maw and U Saw made a real effort to work within the framework of the constitution. Much of their work, however, was overshadowed by their intraparliamentary struggles for power, and this widely known and reported activity played an important part in undermining their hold on the electorate. Although the experiment in near self-government, halted by World War II, was brief, the people could look back on almost two decades of political experience.

During this period, developments in another field tended to create tension and violence rather than peace and unity. From the beginning of their rule the British had sought to protect the minorities from the dominant Burmans. The indigenous minorities, most of whom lived in areas fringing the Burmese heartland—such as the Shans, Kachins, and Chins, who collectively occupied approximately 45 percent of the country's area—were administered under the direct authority of the governor separately from the rest of Burma. Minorities such as the Karens, who lived among the Burmans, were given reserved seats in the legislature to protect their interests. The Indians, too, were accorded special treatment and under the 1935 constitution were granted special seats in the elected assembly. Using the pretext that Karens, Kachins, and Chins made better soldiers than Burmans, the British recruited members of these indigenous minority groups into the British-Burma army and generally excluded Burmans from its ranks. As a rule, ethnic groups divided along occupational lines, with the indigenous peoples in agriculture and the Indians and Chinese in urban occupations. This division was partially destroyed during the 1930s when many farmers lost their lands and were forced to move to the cities to find employment. The resultant competition for urban occupations led to violent communal riots. These circumstances made the several peoples of Burma conscious of their ethnic and cultural differences and kept the society divided.

World War II and the Japanese invasion of Burma brought British rule to an abrupt end. Defeated by the invaders, the British together with thousands of Indians evacuated the country; many of the Burmese civil servants and political leaders accompanied the government into exile at Simla in India. The majority of the people who remained in Burma underwent new experiences that helped shape their ideas and demands after the war was over.

During the four years of occupation, the Japanese did not succeed either in bringing the whole of Burma under their control or in winning the universal support of the people. Faced with harassing tactics by the Allies and the threat of invasion, the Japanese tried to gain support from the Burmese by promises of freedom and the creation of an indigenous army commanded by Burmese. Led by Aung San—who had received secret training along with twenty-nine other "heroes"[12] in Japanese-occupied Hainan Island—the Burmese Independence Army followed the invading Japanese from Thailand to Burma, adding recruits as it advanced. Although this army changed its name from "Independence Army"

12. The "thirty heroes" were a group of young Burmese who were smuggled out of Burma prior to the war and trained under the Japanese in anticipation of a war against the British.

to "Defense Army" in late 1942 and to "National Army" in 1943—after the Japanese granted nominal independence to Burma—it remained essentially Burmese in membership and orientation and on March 27, 1945, revolted against the Japanese and joined forces with the Allies.

During the Japanese occupation many Burmese acquired administrative experience by filling important positions in the government. When Japan allowed Burma to proclaim independence on August 1, 1943, a government headed by Dr. Ba Maw, a former prime minister under the 1935 constitution, was permitted to take charge of most of the administrative apparatus under the watchful eyes of the colonial tutors.[13] Although this government had no real authority outside the urban areas, its members gained invaluable experience and confidence in their ability to govern themselves. In this period of nominal independence an anti-Japanese resistance movement arose under the direction of the Anti-Fascist People's Freedom League—AFPFL—whose leadership included a number of Burmese who had been cooperating with the Japanese. The AFPFL opened its ranks to all the peoples of Burma, regardless of ethnic group, religion, or political belief, and after the war it emerged as the most important voice in Burmese politics.

The war caused a radical change in the economy and in the society. Disruption of the internal system of communications isolated large areas and produced widespread economic dislocation.[14] Destruction of key military targets such as harbors, railway centers, and roads forced the people to leave the urban areas and return to rural communities, where many remained after the war.

In the spring of 1945 the Allies drove the Japanese out of the Irrawaddy valley and into the Shan hills and western Thailand[15] and with them went the nominally independent government of Burma. Most took refuge in southern Burma and Thailand while a

13. Thakin Nu, *Burma under the Japanese* (London: St. Martin's Press, 1954), pp. 39ff. Ba Maw, *Breakthrough in Burma: Memoirs of a Revolution, 1939–1946* (New Haven: Yale University Press, 1968), pp. 261–306.

14. James R. Andrus, "Burmese Economy during the Japanese Occupation," in *Burma during the Japanese Occupation*, 2 vols. (Simla: Manager, Government of India Press, 1944), II, 173–181.

15. William Slim, *Defeat into Victory* (London: Cassell, 1956); Louis Mountbatten, *Report to the Combined Chiefs of Staff by the Supreme Allied Commander, South-east Asia, 1943–45* (London: H.M. Stationery Office, 1951).

few, including Dr. Ba Maw, went to Japan. At war's end in August 1945, government in Burma was under the control of the British Military Administration. Its chief concern was to re-establish law and order and restore the normal conditions of living. To distribute needed supplies and collect and export rice, the British organized the economy with the assistance of former British commercial firms as their managers. The Burmese interpreted this move as calculated to re-establish the prewar economic order.

In October 1945, the British-sponsored Burma government in exile returned from Simla to take charge of the administration. Governor Reginald H. Dorman-Smith brought with him a parliamentary declaration that Britain's ultimate aim was to grant self-government to Burma. It also stated that because of the internal economic and political conditions, suspension of the 1935 constitution would be continued, leaving all power in the hands of the governor and his council; as soon as possible a small legislature nominated by the governor would be created, but at least three years might elapse before elected representative government was re-established.[16] The policy failed because the AFPFL refused to cooperate on the grounds that the British program was regressive and its goals too distant and uncertain. Strengthened by the solidarity of its popular support, its paramilitary forces, and its determined leadership, the AFPFL called for immediate elections, a constitutional convention, and self-government.[17] Governor Dorman-Smith's failure to win the backing of the AFPFL and his inability to find local leaders with popular support who would oppose it led to a breakdown in his efforts to implement official policy. He returned to England in June 1946 and in August was replaced as governor by Hubert Rance, the former director of civil affairs under the previous military administration.

Rance's arrival was greeted by a police strike that quickly became a general strike. In an effort to avoid confrontation he consulted London and was permitted to negotiate with Aung San and the AFPFL. On September 26, Rance announced the formation of a

16. Great Britain, *Burma: Statement of Policy by His Majesty's Government, May, 1945* (London: H.M. Stationery Office, 1945).

17. AFPFL, *From Fascist Bondage to New Democracy: The New Burma in the New World* (Rangoon: Nay Win Kyi Press [1945?]).

new Executive Council that included six members from the AFPFL and three independents, with Aung San, the AFPFL leader, serving as chief councillor. The change led to a quick settlement of the strike and marked the beginning of a period of cooperation in Burmese-British relations.

Although the AFPFL cooperated with Rance, the Burmese were not convinced of British sincerity until after Prime Minister Clement Attlee announced in Parliament on December 20, 1946, that the British government would invite Burmese representatives to England to discuss the transfer of power. The peoples of Burma were to be given a chance to decide whether they wished to remain in the Commonwealth. The London meeting in January 1947 resulted in agreement that elections would be held in April and a constituent assembly would be convened in May; that until the transfer of power the governor's Executive Council would act as the interim government in Burma; that the Frontier Areas would decide whether to join with ministerial Burma; and that a high commissioner for Burma would be appointed immediately.

Between the London meeting and the April elections, the frontier peoples met, as they had agreed to do a year earlier, at Panglong in the Shan states to decide whether to join with Burma. The Shans, Kachins, and Chins agreed to join, but the other minorities remained uncommitted. It was understood that a decision to join would in no way prejudice the future right of those minority peoples to remain autonomous—politically, financially, or socially. To measure the sentiment of the frontier peoples, the British Parliament created an Enquiry Committee, as agreed to in the Aung San-Attlee Agreement of January 1947, under David Rees-Williams, which heard testimony and made recommendations with regard to the unification of the Frontier Areas with ministerial Burma.[18]

The April elections confirmed the right of the AFPFL to lead the nation; the party captured 172 of the 182 noncommunal seats. Its

18. Burma, *Frontier Areas Committee of Enquiry* (Rangoon: Government Printing and Stationery Office, 1948), pt. 1, pp. 22–32. The committee recommended that the Frontier Areas be represented in the Constituent Assembly, that their delegates be chosen indirectly, and that they have a veto over all decisions relating to their areas and upon all questions of the future federal union.

affiliate, the Karen Youth Organization, took all 24 Karen-reserved seats because the older Karen organization, the Karen National Union, refused to participate in the election. The AFPFL's principal rival, the Communists, at first refused to contest seats but later entered candidates on an individual basis who won 7 out of 26 contests.

Aung San opened the historic Constituent Assembly by presenting a seven-point resolution drawn up by the AFPFL. Among its major points were that Burma should be an independent sovereign republic called the Union of Burma; that all power should emanate from the people; that the constitution should guarantee social, economic, and political justice to all; and that the minorities must be granted safeguards.[19] The next day the assembly elected a Constitutional Committee consisting of seventy-five members and several subcommittees charged with writing the constitution. The parent body then recessed. While the assembly committees were at work, Aung San convoked a Rehabilitation Conference to examine the problems of reconstruction and suggest future economic goals for the nation. The conference concluded its deliberations by producing a two-year plan for economic development.

On July 19, 1947, during these deliberations, Aung San and six members of the Executive Council were assassinated. Governor Rance immediately called upon Thakin Nu[20] to succeed the fallen Aung San as chief councillor and reorganize the government; the police quickly rounded up the assassins. Nu spoke to the nation by radio and pledged himself to follow the road marked out by Aung San.[21] The loss of Aung San at this critical juncture was immeasurable; as a prewar and wartime resistance leader and as the symbol

19. Ministry of Information, *Burma's Fight for Freedom* (Rangoon: Government Printing and Stationery Office, 1948), pp. 92–93.

20. The prefix Thakin or master was adopted by the nationalists in the 1930s as a symbol of their defiance of British rule. Since independence, Nu and many others have dropped the prefix because the Burmese are masters in their own country, and they have returned to using the traditional prefix Maung. At the same time, people use U or uncle, the traditional term of respect in addressing an elder, a leader, or an esteemed person.

21. Josef Silverstein, ed., *The Political Legacy of Aung San* (Ithaca: Southeast Asia Program, Cornell University, Data Paper no. 86, 1972). Thakin Nu was a longtime friend and co-worker of Aung San who had retired from politics after the war. He returned in 1947 after Aung San persuaded him to accept the office of vice-president of the AFPFL.

of the drive for political independence he held the confidence of the peoples of Burma and was acknowledged as the postwar architect of national unity and independence.

After the constitution was drawn up, a final settlement was negotiated with Britain and signed by Nu and Britain's Prime Minister Clement Attlee on October 17, 1947. This agreement provided that Burma would become a fully sovereign and independent state outside the Commonwealth; Britain was to cancel a debt of £15 million; and if British property was nationalized Burma would make equitable payment.[22] A supplementary defense agreement also was negotiated. The British Parliament ratified the agreements in December, and Burma became independent on January 4, 1948.

Under colonial rule Burma's political culture had been modified but never really changed. The country's isolation was breached by its linkage to India and the West, and the opening of Burma to immigration from Europe, India, and China exposed the local population to alien ideas and values, which in the past had been excluded. At the same time, British rule had continued the practice of the Burman kings of maintaining political and social separation between the hill and plains people.

Colonialism also altered the role of the city in Burma. Under the Burman kings, there was only one real city—the royal capital—which was the religious and political center of the society and was located in the heartland of the country, away from contact with the outside world. The specific location of the capital was determined both on the basis of religion and astrology. Under foreign rule it was moved to Rangoon in lower Burma—close to the sea—and was not only the center of administration, but the hub of trade and finance. Unlike previous Burman capitals, Rangoon was populated predominantly by aliens and its activities were secular. For Burman Buddhists, Mandalay—the last royal capital—remained the religious and spiritual center of their lives. Thus the unity of politics and religion, as symbolized by the precolonial capitals, was broken.

Urbanization, commerce, and foreign rule gave primacy to Western ideas and practices. The Burmans who gradually came to

---

22. Ministry of Information, *Burma's Fight for Freedom*, pp. 101–110.

settle in and around the new and enlarged urban areas adopted a Western veneer over their deeply held Burman-Buddhist values. From their ranks sprang the new indigenous elite. This Western-ized sector of Burmese society remained relatively small, but its exposure to Western education and its predominance in the new professions of law, medicine, administration, and commerce made it both the interpreter of the West to the rural section of the society and the opinion leader of the nation. The city became a new force in Burmese life where traditions were challenged and sometimes changed.

Chief among the modernizing institutions of British Burma were education, law, administration, and commerce. The need for Burmese to speak English and understand Western ways prompted the British to build government schools and to support pri-vate, usually missionary-connected, schools. The curriculum of the English-language schools was almost wholly Western, while that of the more numerous Anglo-vernacular schools was a mixture of the two traditions, with neither predominating. From them came the leaders and the clerks who filled the administration, the commer-cial houses, and eventually the political movements and parties.

Among the new ideas introduced through the schools were the liberal doctrines of individualism, liberty, freedom, and popular government. Liberalism, with its secular roots and its emphasis upon man in this existence, stood in opposition to the traditional values and ideas of the Burmese Buddhists. Both emphasized individualism; however, in Western liberal thought this was the basis for individual political responsibility—freedom to govern oneself and to pursue one's interests, and thus fundamental in the struggle to free the individual from restrictions of birth, class and place. Liberty in this Western sense had no meaning in traditional Burmese thought, and popular sovereignty and democracy had no counterpart in the political heritage of the Burmese. Such ideas led many Western-educated Burmese to question their own political heritage and seek to replace the old with the new or find an acceptable way to unite the two.

The rule of law and contract as developed in the West and imported into Burma was alien to Burmese political culture and thought. As noted earlier, the Buddhist believed that impersonal forces and laws governed man and the universe. Man sought to understand and harmonize himself with these laws. The Western concepts of law concerned only man's relations with other men. These laws were either natural or man-made, and all men, including the ruler, were subject to them. But the laws were changeable and subject to interpretation, so that introduction of the rule of law brought with it a system of courts, judges, and records. More important, this imported code did not directly relate to the traditions and needs of the local people. In place of mediation by men of standing in the local community, Western-trained lawyers and judges argued and decided questions that came before the court. Because the system used an alien language, based its arguments on alien precedents, and ruled on laws made by foreign legislators, it was little understood and generally feared, except by the few Burmese who had received Western legal training.

Contract, for example, is an important concept in Western law and plays a major role in the commercial life of a society; both parties to a contract are obligated to fulfill certain functions and, if either fails, a penalty is imposed. Such a concept was new and alien to the Burmese, and a peasant or trader often found himself the victim of a contract he did not understand. Under the laws of contract, land could be sold, money could be borrowed, and sales of crop surpluses could be made. Western law contributed to converting Burma from a subsistence to an exchange economy; contracts and law made it possible by 1936 for 25 percent of the best land in lower Burma to fall into the hands of noncultivating landholders.

The Westernizing and modernizing appearance assumed by Burma under the British was a thin covering over deeply held Burmese traditions, and colonial rule actually reinforced the traditional pattern of authority. By right of conquest, a new monarch—physically located outside Burma—was the source of authority; power was exercised by an alien administration, police, and military. Constitutional rule was granted from above and could be withdrawn in times of emergency. The Japanese, too, had imposed their will on the basis of conquest, and no one in Burma was deceived by the wording of the 1943 constitution that stated that authority was derived from the people.[23] Thus, under both the British and the Japanese, the precolonial pattern of authority from above was reinforced and remained deeply ingrained in the attitudes of the majority of Burmese.

More important was the effect of colonial rule on Buddhism, which lay at the heart of Burma's culture. With the displacement of the king and religious council, the Buddhist religion lost the patronage of the government and the discipline of the *sangha*. In and around the urban areas, secular schools displaced those run by the monks, and the monks thus lost one of their most important social functions. Having lost a central source of discipline and one of their principal occupations, many monks assumed a new role—that of political leaders—filling the void created by the colonial government's displacement of the traditional hereditary leaders. Political monks became a major force in the nationalist movement. This new activity for members of the *sangha* spread to the countryside and involved many monks who continued to function as educators to rural youth.

Although counter to the teachings of the Buddha and to local traditions, the role of leadership assumed by the monks was acceptable to most Burmese in the absence of other indigenous leaders. Their involvement in political matters gave legitimacy to political participation by the people. Despite a considerable amount of criticism, the politicization of the *sangha* went forward, and among the heroes of the early nationalist movement were monks who led strikes and political demonstrations.

Buddhism itself became a political vehicle and a major inspiration in the development of Burmese nationalism. Western-educated Burmese in the towns looked to the Buddhist faith as the source of their identity and traditions. Fearing the loss of their Burmese identity, they organized the Young Men's Buddhist Association to make themselves and the people aware of their heritage and to preserve their shrines from violations by non-Buddhists. Such an organization for the preservation and propagation of the faith was acceptable in a society that did not believe the

23. "The Constitution Act of Burma No. 1 of 1305," in *Burma during the Japanese Occupation*, II, 247–252.

ordinary man had a political function. Members of the association were made aware of the threats of the political situation to the faith, and they were trained for political action. It was only a short step from the religious orientation of the YMBA to that of the secular orientation of the General Council of Burmese Associations. The politicization of the *sangha* and Buddhism altered the attitude of the people to allow, support, and encourage political action. Only after this major change was achieved could the peoples of Burma accept the secular ideas of Western political thought propagated by the new elite.

All these changes affected the development of the nationalist movement. Defeated by the British in three wars, all residents of Burma were aware of their common status as subjects of the British monarch. More important, these defeats made them conscious of their common land and interests, despite their historic separation and loose association, and planted among them the hope of ending foreign rule. Religion, too, was an important element in Burmese nationalism. The YMBA movement, the political activity of the monks, and the need to protect the faith all contributed to transforming a divided, nonpolitical people into a unified society with a sense of nation and purpose. Western thought and institutions provided ideas, rationale, and organizational forms for uniting the peoples to press for independence. The university students and other segments of the Western-oriented elite gave leadership and formulated the issues for political action. Although their leaders argued in the rhetoric of democracy, the new organizations were run along authoritarian lines, thus becoming a blend of traditional and modern elements. World War II provided the opportunity for the Burmese to share power and to develop a miliary organization to support their political ends. The new leaders were able to create an all-embracing political movement, awakening the people to the failure of foreign rule and uniting them in the struggle for freedom.

In the discussion above, I have suggested that while foreign rule displaced the local system of government and foreign values and ideas were introduced, the root of Burmese political identity and activity was to be found in traditional values and ideas which, though modified, remained in their source. If the form of government, popular participation in politics and administration, and the new elite's adherence to Western ideas were evidence of change, the Buddhist root to Burmese ideas, the politicization of the monks, the persistence of authority at the top, and the limited contact between the majority of the rural Burmese and the urban elite were among the chief causes for the survival of their close ties to precolonial traditions. Nationalism, which embodied both the new and the old, became the catalyst for uniting the people and spurring them to political action.

The Constitutional Period, 1948–1962

Independence did not make a utopia of Burma. During the first decade (1948–1958) an enduring insurrection kept the country in a state of semiwar. Three important groups resorted to arms in an effort to gain their political objectives. The Communists initiated the revolt in March 1948. Shortly thereafter the People's Volunteer Organization (PVO)—created by Aung San as the miliary arm of the AFPFL—split and a dissident group joined the Communists in revolt. As the government attempted to rally public support to its side, a third and larger group, the Karen National Defense Organization (KNDO), rebelled and encouraged a large number of Karen soldiers in the Union Army to desert. Only disunity among the various rebel forces and the leadership displayed by Nu enabled the government to build a new army and save the nascent Union. By 1952, when the new army was about to take the offensive and end the rebellions, a further complication arose. Remnants of Chiang Kai-shek's Nationalist Chinese Army that had escaped from China and taken refuge in Burma joined forces with the indigenous rebels in the Shan State, and thereby posed a new threat to the Union. On March 24, 1953, the Burmese asked the United Nations to help remove the Chinese soldiers from their territory. The General Assembly passed a mild resolution noting the existence of "foreign forces" on Burma's soil, but left the problem to be settled through a private arrangement between the United States, Thailand, Burma, and the Nationalist Chinese regime on Taiwan. The effort succeeded in removing no more than 5,500 Chinese, and many more remained behind to plague the local population. Because Burmese leaders knew that the United

States had supported these illegal Chinese forces, this episode strongly influenced later relations between Burma and the United States.

In dealing with the indigenous rebels, the government used peaceful as well as warlike methods. Amnesties were offered on numerous occasions, and although they did not move the diehard rebels, they did obtain significant results. By 1958 the insurgents appeared to have become demoralized, and many responded to the government's offer to leave the jungle, lay down their weapons, and rejoin society. Some were welcomed as heroes by high officials of the government, while others drifted back to their villages and resumed their former occupations without formal demobilization. These measures, however, did not bring peace and security to the countryside. Beginning in 1959, new rebellious forces emerged to challenge the government. Shan youths, with the aid of dissident Shan chiefs, took up arms to fight for greater political autonomy; other chiefs who did not join the miliary revolt sought to mobilize political support for a secessionist movement. Despite the government's effort to minimize these movements, they continued to expand. Similar rebellious activity developed among the Kachins, increasing the dangers of the existing insurgencies and posing a serious threat to the nation's unity.

In the provisional Burmese parliament, which lasted until 1952, the dominant AFPFL had no real opposition. In 1950 a small pro-Soviet group in the AFPFL was expelled because of its criticism of Burma's foreign policy toward the war in Korea and its efforts to capture control of the party. It reformed as the Burma Worker's and Peasant's party (BWPP) and assumed the role of the opposition in parliament. In the first national election, held in 1951–1952, the AFPFL retained its overwhelming dominance in parliament, and the BWPP emerged again as the leading party in opposition. The second national election, held in 1956, resulted once more in an AFPFL victory, but the margin this time was smaller, and a formidable opposition emerged as the National Unity Front (NUF), wherein the BWPP was the largest constituent group. Following the election, Nu stepped down from office for nine months while U Ba Swe, Socialist and AFPFL leader, took over the reins of government. Nu's purpose in resigning was to purge the party of corruption and to re-establish harmony among rival leaders; his efforts ended in failure. The inner party rivalry continued despite a public display of unity among the leaders at the third All-Burma Congress of the AFPFL in January 1958. By April the power struggle within the party no longer could be hidden, and Nu gave up his efforts to hold the dissidents together. Joining forces with Thakin Tin and Kyaw Tun against Kyaw Nyein and Ba Swe, he forced the party to divide. After the month of accusations and revelations of corruption and crime, Nu sought to end the dispute by calling a special session of the parliament and letting it decide which faction would govern. He won a vote of confidence by seven votes; but in doing so he had to accept the support of the NUF and the representatives of the minorities. The resulting unstable political situation led to widespread unrest and confusion. Unwilling to face the regular session of parliament and recognizing that the budget and other matters had to be settled, Nu turned to General Ne Win—the head of the army—and agreed to resign in his favor. Parliament accepted this arrangement, and a so-called caretaker government was created. Its leaders promised to maintain law and order, establish conditions for free and fair elections, and continue Burma's unaligned foreign policy. The new government consisted of nonparty notables, and its key administrative posts were filled by senior military officers.

The caretaker government remained in office for eighteen months, during which time it sought to clean up the cities, modernize the administration, end the insurrections, and prepare the country for elections. It also amended the constitution to prevent the feudal chiefs in the Shan and Kayah states from holding their seats automatically in the parliament's Chamber of Nationalities, and it paid them large sums of money to surrender their hereditary political rights in their states.[24] The methods of the caretaker government were direct and sometimes severe; they produced results, but did not gain popularity. During the eighteen-month period, the two AFPFL factions competed for support in the promised election. The U Nu group (Clean AFPFL) disassociated itself

24. Ministry of Information, *Burma Weekly Bulletin*, 8, no. 4 (May 21, 1959), 26–37.

from the Ne Win government and its methods, while the Ba Swe-Kyaw Nyein group (Stable AFPFL) approved of and identified itself with the caretaker government. When the third national election was held in February 1960, the Clean AFPFL won an overwhelming victory.

The new parliament convened in April 1960; the Clean AFPFL, now renamed the Pyidaungsu or Union party, took its place as the majority party, and U Nu was elected prime minister. The new government was in a position to enact its program, for it had gained a large national mandate, and the army had retired from politics. Its program called for strengthening of democratic institutions, establishment of Buddhism as the state religion, creation of new states within the Union for the Mons and Arakanese (provided real support for this action could be demonstrated), and development of a plan for promoting economic and social growth. From the outset, the Pyidaungsu government encountered serious obstacles. The secessionist movement among the Shans and discontent among the other minorities came to dominate relations between the states and the Union government. The non-Buddhist minorities, alarmed by the implications of the creation of a state religion, mobilized in opposition to the government. The return of civilian government brought a relaxation of internal security measures and a resulting increase in crime and lawlessness. Even within the governing party, factionalism developed with each side emphasizing its rival's ambitions and shortcomings. Only the power and prestige of U Nu prevented an open split and a repetition of the events of 1958. On the positive side, the Pyidaungsu government made headway in formulating a realistic economic plan, in preparing to carry out a national census, and in studying ways to strengthen democracy. On the question of re-establishing harmony among the peoples of Burma, especially the Shans, Kachins, and Burmans, the government expressed its trust and confidence in the minority leaders by leaving them in their cabinet posts and other positions of authority, while discussing their complaints and seeking ways to solve the problems peacefully. The government hoped that a final solution could be worked out at a federal seminar held in February and March 1962 at which all leaders from Burma proper and the states were invited to air their views publicly and to

examine the various alternative solutions advocated by the participants. The seminar convened in Rangoon while parliament was
meeting in regular session. On the night of March 2, 1962, General
Ne Win and the army overthrew the constitutional government,
arresting the members of government and the leaders of the
minorities. They dismissed parliament, dissolved the federal seminar, and took over full control of the state.

After the coup all power was concentrated in a new seventeen-
member Revolutionary Council (RC). Speaking for this body,
Brigadier Aung Gyi stated that the coup had been necessary because "we had economic, religious and political crises with the issue
of federalism as the most important reason for the coup."[25] Prior
to the coup the military was most concerned with problems of the
secession of one or more of the states, which made the defense of
the nation nearly impossible, the fears created by the acts making
Buddhism the state religion among the non-Buddhist members of
the military, and the struggles for power within the Union party at
a time when the military thought all should be united and working
for the nation's progress. The federal seminar focused attention on
the demands of the minorities, and members of the military as well
as the society at large generally believed that U Nu would give in to
their secessionist pressures.

There are many reasons for the failure of democracy in Burma.
At the root was the inability of the party system to become a deep
and meaningful part of the society. Residents of rural Burma had
little understanding of, and practically no commitment to, party
ideals and institutions. The struggle among the members of the
ruling elite for power and prestige gave the people no basis for
confidence in their leadership. The government's failure to end
insurgency and to curb the predatory activity of rebels and bandits
left the people with no real protection against the constant threat of
victimization. As always the peasants had to cope with this reality as
best they could and look to their immediate leaders, the village
elders, the clergy, and a few national figures, such as U Nu, to guide
and instruct them. More than a decade of democracy had provided
no evidence that it was a system that could govern and harmonize

25. *Guardian* (daily), March 8, 1962.

the interests of the people. A second reason for its failure was the inability of the national leaders to solve the minority questions. While most of the people trusted U Nu, the peoples of the plains and those of the hills did not trust each other. Fears of Burmanization among the minorities, resulting in the loss of their culture and identity, and fears among the military that secession of the minority areas would leave the country nearly indefensible placed constant pressures on the men in power. None of the proposed solutions—the creation of more states, the relaxation of controls from the center, the physical integration of the minorities in a centralized state—appealed to a majority of the people. Fourteen years of experimentation with democracy gave way to authoritarian rule while the people looked on in stoic silence.

Military Rule in Burma

After arresting all the potential opposition leaders, the Revolutionary Council permitted the parties to continue and the press to publish without censorship—as long as no encouragement was given to opposition to the new government. Institutionally, the revolutionary government began its reforms by altering the character of the state governments, abolishing the Union Constabulary and absorbing it into the army, and recreating security councils composed of leaders from the army, civil service, and police to restore law and order in the countryside. It also moved quickly to abolish advisory councils and to regroup the ministries and departments. Its apparent aim was to create an atmosphere of confidence and to give an impression of the continuity of its actions. To underscore the revolutionary character of its regime, the coup leaders promulgated an ideological declaration entitled *The Burmese Way to Socialism* which set forth its goals and outlined its program.

The coup was so swift and effective that no countercoup developed. In the absence of competing leadership and with the weak popular commitment to the constitution and the institutions of democracy, with the harvest in and society in a state of tranquillity, the Revolutionary Council found no need to invoke martial law.

The military maintained absolute rule until 1974 when it implemented a constitution it authored and then permitted nominal sharing of power with civilians who were elected with the aid of the party it created and controlled, the Burma Socialist Program Party (BSPP). The military has sought to erase capitalism, parliamentary democracy, and social disunity, hasten the transformation of the society and economy to socialism, build a popularly supported authoritarian regime, and unite the peoples under its leadership. The attitude and policies as well as the style of the military rulers reflected elements of the precolonial past, the colonial past, and the nationalist movement. Their direct seizure of power, elimination of rivals, and separation of government from the people all were consistent with the precolonial style of government. From the colonial period came their emphasis upon law and order, centralism, and efficiency; from the nationalist movement came the elements of a socialist ideology, a small governing elite, and a single party. The military broke with the indigenous tradition by their separation from and antagonism toward Buddhism and the monks.

The efforts of the military rulers to convert the economy from mixed to socialist must be seen against the experience of the past quarter of a century. The economy has been subject to constant tinkering and change as Burmese civilian and military leaders sought to bring practice into line with ideology. Following the grant of independence, the AFPFL made an immediate attempt to create a socialist state. The government nationalized a few industries, passed a land nationalization act, and took other actions aimed at realizing this goal. Enthusiasm waned as the leaders were forced to retreat and rewrite their plans in the face of the lack of money and of trained technicians and administrators. The initial financing had come from the surplus revenues earned from the sale of rice in the world market, but following the end of the Korean War, demand dropped, and Burma was left with unsold surplus stocks. The government was forced to re-examine its methods and plans. In June 1957, U Nu proclaimed a new economic policy that promised less socialism and more free enterprise. He and the AFPFL leaders assured the people that socialism was still the ultimate goal, but that they must recognize that it would be preceded by the stage of mixed economy—state and private capitalism. The caretaker government continued along this line by abolishing all state projects that were deemed not absolutely necessary while at the same time encouraging the creation and growth of joint ventures between the Burmese government and foreign firms and the expansion of the business activity of the Defense Services Institute (DSI).[26] The civil government that returned in 1960 made no effort to alter this policy. The coup government completed the circle when it once again proclaimed socialism as its goal and guide for reorganizing society, the economy, and the polity. In 1963 it began by nationalizing the banks, and shortly thereafter it took over all importing and exporting, production, and distribution. Without adequate preparations, trained personnel, and specific goals, it made a shambles of the economy; by 1967 there were widespread shortages of rice, cooking oil, and other basic items in the urban areas; as a consequence, black markets and other illegal operations came into being. By 1968 the government began to relax its economic control and to open small areas for the return of private activity, but this temporary measure reflected no departure from the goals previously outlined by the government. By 1972 black-market trading was taking place alongside government stores, with the government making no move to halt the practice. Despite more than a decade of economic failure, socialism remains the goal of the military.

The social revolution has many aspects. In their first moves to regiment society, the military leaders denounced the faculties and student bodies of the universities, causing resignations among the former and a riot by the latter. The civil servants and the school-teachers also were singled out for public attack, while urban workers were exhorted to do their jobs with efficiency and without strikes and delays. Mass social and political organizations, which before the coup were allied to the political parties, were disbanded or quietly forced out of existence. Failing to secure backing from the old political parties for creation of a single political party supporting the military government, the coup leaders organized their own party, the Burma Socialist Program Party. The government sought to unite the people behind its programs through active social organizations under its control. All members of society

26. Government of the Union of Burma, Ministry of Information, *Is Trust Vindicated?* (Rangoon: Director of Information, 1960), pp. 223–250.

were classified as either workers or peasants and urged to join a local unit of the People's Workers or Peasants Councils. The councils were united into two vertical pyramids and, at the top, a joint People's Workers and Peasants Council was created. To manage and control the councils, the military placed members of its political party in positions of authority both in the separate councils and in the national organization.

If the above structure suggests a tightly organized society, in reality this was not the case. While the military leaders moved directly against the urban population by taking over businesses and professions and by currency and other controls, it moved only slowly and cautiously against the peasants. Title to land and ownership of produce remained with the farmer. He was encouraged to farm and market cooperatively; he was given incentives such as cheap loans and freedom from land rent to encourage him to follow the new government leadership and produce more for the good of society and, ultimately, to give up his private ways for a socialist system. Throughout the military period the farmer remained free to follow his own rather than the state's interest in the planting, harvesting, and marketing of his crops. Despite the military's efforts to change the society by giving the people new and larger identifications, local, ethnic, and religious affiliations are still supreme; village elders and monks continue to have strong influence upon the rural population, and the new social and political institutions have yet to strike deep roots among the people.

During this period, the military rulers made a real effort to strengthen the bonds between the dominant Burmans and the minority peoples. In 1963 the government invited all insurgents to Rangoon to discuss their differences and seek an end to warfare. The discussion failed, and the several insurrections continued but became less of a threat after 1967 as a result of the government's military offensive in that year and of internal conflict within the Burma Communist party (BCP). A major victory over the Communists in 1975 eliminated them temporarily as a threat to the state. The capture of Thakin Soe, leader of the Communist party of Burma (CPB), virtually ended the threat from his dissident movement. Despite these successes, secessionist movements among some of the hill peoples continue. In addition, U Nu in 1969 proclaimed open revolt against the government and launched an attack by his followers from Thailand. Although Nu abandoned the revolt and left Thailand in 1973, the groups who joined him continue their struggle. Despite the successes in battle and the positive measures by the government to win the support of the minorities, both ethnic disunity and insurrections continue, and Burma still faces this major challenge to its existence.

The military has maintained the foreign policy followed by Burma since independence. It has avoided both war with its neighbors and becoming the battleground for the warfare of them and others; and, despite sharp differences has remained at peace with China. Throughout the period, Burma refused to join the various political, economic or social organizations created by other states in the region to unite the nations and peoples of Southeast Asia. If its policies "leaned" a little to the left and in support of the socialist world, it managed to maintain a correct posture in dealing with the United States and other non-Communist nations.

In 1971 the military rulers ordered the BSPP to begin planning for a constitutional form of government. Under the leadership of General San Yu, the second most powerful man in the country, three drafts of a constitution were written before one was adopted by the party and submitted to the public for ratification. Early in 1974, elections were held to fill the new councils, and on March 2, 1974, military rule entered its second phase: constitutional dictatorship in which Ne Win and his senior military officers continued to rule under a constitution that legally concentrated power in their hands and in the political party of their creation.

Conclusions

Many of the traditional values and attitudes that characterized precolonial Burma persisted through the period of foreign rule and into that of independence. Burma remains isolated both from its near neighbors and from the outside world. As a society it is still divided between the Burman majority and the ethnic minorities of the plains and the hills. The Burmese continue to accept authority from above and have never widely accepted the idea of authority stemming from the people. Buddhist values and attitudes toward government, personal responsibility, and improvements in their existence are still the major influences on the thought of rural and the less Westernized urban Burmese. While Western liberal and socialist ideas have made an important impression upon segments of the nation's leadership after World War II, the failure to develop an educational system to replace old ideas has meant that Western thought remains a veneer upon a basically traditional people. Although many traditional precolonial leaders were displaced, the rural population found acceptable substitutes in the monks, and some of the national figures, in most cases the village elders and educated young people who returned to their homes, still serve as the natural leaders. Nationalism, which had provided a unifying force against foreign rule, receded in importance after independence as older and deeper loyalties re-emerged to divide the people.

2 | The Contemporary Setting

Burma is the second largest state in Southeast Asia, with an area of approximately 261,100 square miles. Most of the country lies in the latitudes of the tropics and is richly endowed with fertile land, plentiful rainfall, and a variety of natural resources. But wide areas are blighted by wind erosion and denuded of topcover because of poor agricultural practices, and some areas are barely inhabited because of extreme malarial conditions. Despite its many favorable natural resources, Burma is an economically underdeveloped nation. A profile of its underdevelopment, together with an examination of its society, political forces, and leadership will provide a background for understanding important aspects of its politics and policies.

The Economy

Burma's natural resources include an abundance of teak and other woods. Underground are a variety of minerals, such as petroleum, lead, zinc, tin, tungsten, and precious stones. All except petroleum are located in isolated regions and are difficult and costly to extract. The military rulers have given special attention to the search for and production of petroleum, both to satisfy domestic needs and to produce revenue from sales abroad. In 1975 the government announced that it had achieved self-sufficiency from domestic sources by raising production to 7.7 million barrels annually; it estimated that production in 1976 would increase to 8.5 million barrels. Although Burma's daily production of 21.1 thousand barrels is only a fraction of Indonesia's daily output of nearly 2 million barrels, Burma is the largest mainland oil producer in Southeast Asia. The military government nationalized the oil industry shortly after seizing power and has given high priority to the search for new sources. Beginning in 1964, four important fields were opened at Myanaung, Prome, Mann, and Shwepyitha. A decade later Burma asked for Western help in searching for and developing its offshore oil resources; eight foreign firms entered into production-sharing contracts, and drilling started in late 1975. The first year saw little success.

The significant progress in development of oil is not matched for other extractive resources. During the period of military rule, the government reported slight increases in extracting teak, coal, and lead sulphide ore, but announced decreases in the extraction of other hardwoods, jade, silver, zinc concentrates, copper, nickel, lead, tin, and tungsten.[1] Because these items were intended for export and considered an important source of foreign exchange, their declining production contributes to Burma's stagnation.

The surface of the land always has been the mainstay of the economy. Among the key crops are paddy (the major crop), sugar cane, groundnut, pulses, and sesamum. Before World War II, Burma was the world's largest exporter of rice,[2] but invasion, warfare, and liberation caused loss of this position. Since independence the various governments have sought to increase rice production, both to earn foreign exchange and to provide more food for the growing population. At the time of the military coup Burma's production of paddy reached 6.726 million tons, of which 1.746 million tons were exported. In 1970–1971, 8.033 million tons were produced, but exports fell to 527 thousand tons. In the next three years, production continued to increase while exports declined. Whether the decline was caused by an increasing population consuming more, as suggested by F. S. V. Donnison,[3] or by withholding by the farmer and disposal through the black market,

1. Revolutionary Council of the Union of Burma, *Report to the People by the Government of the Union of Burma on the Financial, Economic and Social Conditions for 1973–74* (Rangoon: Ministry of Planning and Finance, 1973), Book 1: *Report Relating to the Nation*, Tables 60 and 66. Hereafter this and earlier annual reports will be cited as *Report to the People*.

2. In the prewar period the export of rice reached a high of 3.5 million tons. See James R. Andrus, *Burmese Economic Life* (Stanford: Stanford University Press, 1948), pp. 18–19.

3. Frank S. V. Donnison, *Burma* (New York: Praeger, 1970), p. 193.

as suggested in 1974 by Ne Win, is not clear. Other crops have not increased appreciably despite government efforts to stimulate agricultural production for both domestic consumption and export. Government figures indicate that despite increased production, earnings from agricultural exports have fallen markedly since 1961–1962 in every commodity except jute. The same reasons are given to explain smaller exports as for rice. As long as rice exports remain low and other crops and minerals fail to increase substantially, Burma will have little foreign exchange to purchase the machinery and technology necessary to modernize the economy.

An examination of transportation demonstrates further the problems of Burma's underdevelopment. Prior to World War II a good rail system had been developed with its main lines paralleling the rivers, but with relatively few east-west spur lines. Destruction of tracks, deterioration of rolling stock, and the loss of many railway workers during the war crippled this vital means of transportation in the postwar and independence periods. Both civilian and military governments have given high priority to its reconstruction and expansion. In the 1970s the railway is the major carrier of goods and the second largest carrier of people.[4]

Slower progress was made with other modes of transportation. The national airline organized after independence played a vital political role when insurgency was at its height (1949–1953) by linking the isolated cities and towns with the capital. Equipped in the main with World War II surplus aircraft and routed to serve outlying areas difficult to reach by other means, it never developed into a major element of the nation's transportation system. During the period of military rule, efforts were made to replace the old and outworn equipment and to update the service. The number of passengers carried has tripled, but is only 1.2 percent of total passengers carried by all means of transport. Via its services to neighboring states of Thailand, Singapore, India, and Bangladesh the airline is the major means for passengers entering and leaving Burma.

The Burmese began and the British improved a highway system

4. *Report to the People, 1973–74*, Table 89. In June 1973 the International Development Association granted Burma a loan of U.S. $16.7 million to complete its four-year railway rehabilitation and modernization program.

ranging from jungle paths to modern paved highways that provides the major lateral transport system for the nation. Since independence road transportation, too, has made slow progress. After the military seized power, 1,352 miles of main road were built and a number of older roads were resurfaced. Relatively few vehicles exist outside the military and government. Private individuals can purchase the few vehicles left behind by departing foreign diplomats at government auctions. The government reported in 1972 that most of the buses and taxis were still in private hands and together carried 76.6 percent of passengers transported throughout the nation, making them the most important means of passenger travel in the country.

The river system provides the people with a natural north-south transport network. It has received the least improvement of all. After a decade of military rule, the government operated 262 power craft, an increase of 56 over the ten-year span. Because many of the river vessels were worn out, spare parts were nonexistent, and port facilities were in disrepair, the government borrowed funds from abroad in 1973 to undertake major repairs and modernize the entire system.[5] But there is so much to do that it is unlikely that the project will be completed in less than a decade.

The limited and poor state of transportation in Burma clearly has proved a serious handicap in developing the national economy.

Other factors in the modernization of Burma's economy are power capacity, electrification, domestic manufacturing, and the character of imports. During the period of military rule, power capacity increased by 5 percent. In 1961 the nation's power output was 241.22 million kilowatts; in 1972–1973 it was 253.17. During that period, the unit cost declined, and the nation increased its use of electrical power from 231.16 million kilowatt hours to 539.[6]

During this period industrial growth was very slow. According to the 1953 urban census, 88 percent of the nation's industrial capacity was absorbed by six major industries: food and beverages, tobacco, textiles, footwear, wood products, and chemicals. The 1973–1974 *Report to the People* listed the six major industries as food

5. Burma received the loan from the International Development Association in June 1973.
6. *Report to the People, 1971–72*; pp. 70–72; *Report to the People, 1973–74*, p. 90.

and beverages, wearing apparel, construction materials, minerals, industrial raw materials, and personal goods, which, together, absorb 91.7 percent of the nation's industrial capacity. Despite the extensive government takeovers of private factories, the private sector continues to produce most of the nation's manufactures.[7] Factories remain small; 88 percent of them employ 50 workers or less.

Under the military, the government has reordered its import priorities; in 1961–1962, 26 percent went into capital goods, 43 percent for interindustry goods, and 31 percent for consumer goods; in 1973, the figures for the three categories were 35 percent, 50 percent, and 15 percent. The redistribution between capital and consumer goods has been reflected in the general short supply of necessary items from safety pins to automobiles and the emergence of a black market the government no longer tries to stamp out. The increase in capital goods has improved Burma's capacity in such areas as manufacture of fertilizer, industrial tools, and electrical goods, but has not reached the point where its utilization can sustain production to maintain the 1961–1962 standard of living. Because of worker discontent and riots in June 1974 over high prices and the shortage of consumer goods, the government increased sharply its imports of consumer goods in the winter and spring of 1974–1975.

The Society

Probably the most useful system for classifying the peoples of Burma is by their origin—as either indigenous or alien. Within the indigenous group, the major subgroups, identified along ethnic lines, are the Burmans, Arakanese, Karens, Shans, Mons, Kachins, and Chins. Anthropologists find it meaningful to identify the indigenous peoples according to whether their culture can be classified as a hill or a plains type. By "hill culture" they usually mean one in which the people live in small units on the slopes or tops of hills, with relatively autonomous and uncomplicated political organizations; they usually are animistic in their religious beliefs and practice a shifting, slash-and-burn type of agriculture called *taungya*,

7. *Report to the People, 1971–72,* p. 63.

hunting and raising nearly everything they eat.[8] The Kachins, Chins, and hill Karens fit roughly into this pattern. "Plains culture" is that of people who live in the valley or on the plains and have a relatively complex social and political organization extending beyond the village or family group; their centers of population are permanent, and their religion, language, arts, and crafts are influenced by Indian culture; their main agricultural occupation is wet rice farming.[9] The Burmans, Mons, Shans, Arakanese, and delta Karens generally fit into this category.

The dominant religion throughout Burma is Theravada Buddhism, the same varient practiced in Ceylon, Thailand, Cambodia, and Laos. Buddhists in Burma have resisted almost all efforts to convert them to Christianity; only the non-Buddhist delta Karens among the plains people have accepted conversion to Christianity.

Indians and Chinese are the major alien minorities. Both trace their presence to the earliest times. Although the government has published no population data on the racial composition of the society since the sample 1953 urban census survey, it was estimated in 1970 that there were approximately 450,000 Indians and about the same number of Chinese in the country.[10] Since independence new immigration has been banned; however, over the years, a steady illegal trickle of Chinese crossed the land frontier into Burma. Many of the Chinese intermarry with Burmese, adopt their dress and language, and assimilate into the society. Most observers believe the Chinese are the largest alien minority in Burma, and their absolute number is growing. Until the military coup, both Indians and Chinese played major roles in the commercial and financial life of the nation. While the 1964 exodus of

8. John K. Musgrave, "An Introduction to the Anthropology of Burma," in Frank N. Trager et al., *Burma*, 3 vols. (New Haven: Human Relations File, 1956), II, 598–620; Edmund R. Leach, "The Frontiers of Burma," *Comparative Studies of Society and History* 3 (October 1960), 49–68.

9. Musgrave, "Introduction," pp. 600–620.

10. Based upon actual counts in 252 cities and towns, the 1953 urban census reported 287,000 Chinese and 175,000 Indians. Since this was a partial census, the reported population must be taken as a low figure. Most recent publications on population in Burma, such as Charles A. Fisher, "Burma: Physical and Social Geography," in *The Far East and Australasia 1975–76* (London: Europa Publications, 1975), p. 416, suggest that the Chinese population exceeds the Indian and the gap between the two is growing.

Indians reduced their role in the economic life of the nation, their place in finance and commerce, both legal and illegal, has been taken over by the Chinese. Outside of the diplomatic community, very few Europeans live in Burma today.

According to the census of 1973, Burma's population was 28,885,867; an analysis of population growth rate made two years earlier indicated an increase at a rate of 2.23 percent per year.[11] Since the military coup in 1962 the population increased by 19 percent.[12] Despite this rapid population growth, Burma had a density ratio of 110.6 per square mile, well below the average of 155 for Southeast Asia. In terms of the ratio of people to land under cultivation, Burma had the second lowest nutritional density in the area.[13] According to the population analysis made by the government in 1973, nearly half of the people (46 percent) were either below the age of fifteen or above the age of fifty-nine and therefore outside the national work force. During the decade between 1961 and 1971, the number of those under fifteen and above fifty-nine increased by 1 percent and, therefore, a shrinking work force needed to produce more to maintain the 1961 level of living.[14]

Estimates in 1972–1973 indicated that the work force consisted of 11.415 million persons. Of these, 2.853 million were engaged in some work of urban occupation or government employment, while 8.562 million were engaged in rural labor.[15] Twenty years earlier, the 1953 urban census reported 1.074 million of a total urban population of 2.13 million in the work force. Thus, Burma's urban labor force more than doubled in a generation. This is not a very rapid rise despite the instability in the countryside and the attractions of the city.[16]

11. *Report to the People, 1973–74*, p. 7.
12. All population data are based on estimates with the last published census (1931) serving as the baseline. In 1973 the government began a new census that was intended to cover the nation; at the time of the constitution referendum, the new total population figure was published, but no specific population data were released.
13. Keith Buchanan, "Southeast Asia: An Introduction to the Physical, Social and Economic Geography," in *The Far East and Australasia, 1973*, p. 379.
14. *Report to the People, 1973–74*, p. 10.
15. *Ibid.*, p. 11.
16. Central Statistical and Economics Department, *First Stage Census, 1953, Population and Housing*, 4 vols. (Rangoon: Superintendent, Government Printing and

Political Forces and Leadership

Since 1962 two major political forces have provided leadership in the nation: the military and the insurgents. Of the two, the military is cohesive and in control of the state while the insurgents are divided and control only the border areas in the north and east of Burma.

During the past thirty years, the military's role and authority have changed dramatically. Prior to independence, it participated in the nationalist movement, but after reorganization following the end of World War II, its leaders sought to create a purely professional army devoted to the defense of the state and protection of the people against insurgency. The insurrections of 1948 and the defection of Karen units exposed the nascent national army to the political threat of forces trying to secede and others attempting to overthrow the government. The military remained outside of politics until called upon in 1958 to establish a temporary caretaker government. During the eighteen months of this government's existence, the military leaders gained experience in politics and management of the economy while carrying out their traditional professional functions. After a brief return to the barracks from 1960 to 1962 military leaders seized power and displaced the civilian leaders and the constitutional processes under which they had operated. At the time of the coup, the Defense Services were believed to be incorrupt, and its leaders enjoyed the respect of the people in most of the areas where they were stationed.[17]

The military was recruited from all ethnic and religious groups and was a truly national force; however, it was organized on an ethnic basis, and its ranks were never fully integrated. It enjoyed special privileges and status that tended to set it apart from the rest of society.

Stationery, 1957), I, 136. In this census the beginning work age was placed at eleven, not fifteen, as used in the later reports. For an interesting discussion of factors influencing change in a village located near Rangoon, see U Khin Maung Kyi et al., *Process of Communication in Modernization of Rural Society: A Survey Report on Two Burmese Villages* (Rangoon: Department of Research, Institute of Economics, 1972), Rural Socio-Economic Series (2).

17. For an example of its activity in the Shan State during a period of emergency, see Josef Silverstein, "Politics in the Shan State: The Question of Secession from the Union of Burma," *Journal of Asian Studies*, 28 (November 1958), 51–53.

Leadership of the military is limited to a few men. Its leader and dominant figure in Burmese politics since independence is General, now U, Ne Win.[18] Despite his dominance of politics since the coup, little has been written about him either in Burma or abroad.[19] Born on May 24, 1911, at Paungdale in Prome district and named Shu Maung, he attended National High School in Prome and spent two years at the university in Rangoon. After failing his examinations in 1931 he left the university and took a series of jobs before settling on one at the post office. During his spare time he worked with the Thakins in the Dobama Asiayone.[20] In July 1941 he and twenty-nine others left the country secretly to receive military training under the Japanese. While in training on Hainan Island he adopted the name Ne Win. Along with Aung San, he and a few others were selected for officer training, and when World War II broke out he returned to Burma as an officer in the new Burma Independence Army. When it was reorganized and its name changed to Defense Army, Ne Win was commissioned as a major and given command of the First Battalion. Following the army's second reorganization in 1943, he was promoted to colonel and given command of Zone 2, the delta region of Burma. As one of Aung San's most trusted officers, he was given the honor of broadcasting to the nation in May 1945 following the fall of Rangoon. In that speech he said, "The Burmese Army is not only the hope of the country but its very life and soul."[21] After the war the British created a new Burma Army, and Ne Win was recommissioned as a major and given command of the Fourth Burma Rifles. He rose rapidly during the next three years and in February 1949, following the outbreak of insurrections and defections from the

18. Ne Win dropped his military title in 1971 when he retired from the military. The U, as noted earlier, is an honorific used in addressing someone of age or standing or as a way of showing respect.

19. Dr. Maung Maung, *Burma and General Ne Win* (New York: Asia Publishing House, 1969); Willard A. Hanna, "From Thakin to Bo to Chairman," in *Eight Nation Makers* (New York: St. Martin's Press, 1964), pp. 239–264.

20. The Thakin movement was launched by young Burmese in the early 1930s as a way to recapture pride and to enlist Burmese in a truly nationalist movement. The word Thakin meant master. The Dobama Asiayone (We Burman Society) was their political organization.

21. AFPFL, *From Fascist Bondage to New Democracy: The New Burma in the New World* (Rangoon: Nay Win Kyi Press [1945?]), p. 30.

army, he was appointed chief of staff and supreme commander of the armed forces. He continued in those roles until he chose his successors after he became the unchallenged leader of Burma.

During both the caretaker and the coup governments, Ne Win relied upon a relatively small circle of senior officers, most of whom had served with him in the Fourth Burma Rifles. Throughout the period of miliary rule, Ne Win has been able to dismiss senior officers without provoking a split in the army or threatening his own leadership. Ne Win clearly has been the commanding political figure in Burma since 1962 regardless of his formal position in or out of the army.

The military coup leaders initially sought to use their own personnel to perform civilian tasks. Finding it necessary to co-opt civilians to carry out various duties, they created and controlled such organizations as the Burma Socialist Program Party, the hierarchy of People's Peasants and People's Workers Councils, and the Security and Administration Councils (SAC). The civilians who were admitted were carefully screened to ascertain whether they retained their loyalty to former parties, leaders, or institutions. While a few civilians, such as Ba Nyein, enjoyed the confidence of the general, they never were given independent power under military rule.

The only viable alternative leadership to the military and its political organizations is provided by the insurgent groups still active throughout the nation. Insurgency and rebellion began shortly after independence and continue to the present. The insurgents include a variety of individuals and groups who differ in origin, aims, and tactics. Their common denominator is their use of force and violence to solve grievances. Insurgency waxed and waned in direct proportion to the strength of the military and the stability of the government. Between 1949 and 1951, it was at its height and nearly brought an end to the constitutional government. After a period of decline, it surged forward as new dissident groups formed in 1959 among the minorities and for short periods joined with some of the older ones still active in revolt. A year after seizing power, in 1963 the military government launched a major effort to end insurgency through face-to-face discussions with the rebels. Despite the efforts of the coup leaders to meet many of the insurgents' demands, only one faction of Karens accepted the government's offer, and the rest returned to the jungle to resume fighting. The military government has been challenged constantly by ethnic and political dissidents, but the inability of the rebels to unite in common organizations and under unified leadership has prevented their achieving any real success. Internal dissension within such groups as the Burma Communist party is a second factor underlying their failure and a third is their military failure in the field. While dissident groups pose a threat to the state, in nearly thirty years they have never realized their ambitions because the group in power, whether civilian or military, has been able to maintain the loyalty of a majority of the people while the rebels dissipate themselves, either in factional or intergroup disputes.

The return to a form of government wherein a political party leads the nation no doubt revived memories of the precoup period when leadership was truly exercised by the political parties and individuals of national standing. As noted earlier, most of the precoup party leaders were arrested at the time the military seized power, and they languished in jail for at least five years without trial or formal charges being brought against them. The break in their connection with their former followers ended their role as leaders; most volunteered to retire to a quiet civilian life after being released from jail. A few, such as U Nu, went abroad and organized an insurgent force with the hope of toppling the military through their own armed strength and the hoped-for support of their former followers. But their goal was not realized. Their former party organizations had been outlawed in 1964, and the membership and many of their subordinate leaders who were not imprisoned in 1962 had defected to the military's BSPP; therefore any hope of reviving and reorganizing their following was almost impossible in the face of the military's hold on the populace.

Before the coup, the Burmese press was vigorous and while it did not seek leadership directly, it strongly influenced those both in and out of power. During the constitutional period the government was extremely sensitive to the press. As inquirer, critic, and reporter, and especially in its frequent interviews with the prime minister, the press acted as the unofficial opposition during the period between 1951 and 1956, helping to compensate for the absence of any significant parliamentary opposition. Occasionally, the government used its legal powers to silence a critical newspaper, but until 1962 its policy generally was not to restrict but to encourage free and responsible reporting.

Following the coup, the government at first watched the papers carefully and reprimanded those that were critical and inaccurate in their reporting. Gradually, it either shut down or took over established papers. In 1963 it created its own newspaper, the *Working People's Daily*, which, with the official fortnightly, *Forward*—started a year earlier—became the voice of Burma from which all remaining papers took their cues. Although several papers from the precoup period were permitted to continue to publish, they no longer represented an independent and different point of view. As they were supplied by the government-controlled news service, their messages and reports were identical. They offered a means of communication between the government and the people through their letters to the editor columns. People were encouraged to write their praise for and complaints against the government or its officials. The letters give the papers a veneer of open communications between the state and the people and serve a useful purpose for those in power by allowing popular grievances to be aired directly and not smothered as they would be if channeled through the hierarchy of the party, the SAC, or some other institution of the government. Except for this one aspect of freedom of the press, it, like the state-controlled radio, is an instrument of government for communication and not an independent source of ideas and leadership as it once was.

From 1920 onward, the students of Burma, especially those from the universities, played an important leadership role in the nation. Before World War II, they were in the forefront of the nationalist struggle and provided the present civilian and military leaders. Both in the last days of colonial rule and in the constitutional period of independence, the students were well organized and active in a variety of political and social movements. Generally, the students were nationalistic, opposed to authority and government, and sympathetic to the forces in revolt. Most came from urban areas and planned to remain there when their education was completed. Their influence extended beyond the campus because they were courted and used by the political parties and the insurgents for purposes of organization, propaganda, and direct political action. In their home areas, in both urban and rural Burma, they enjoyed respect and deference from their elders as well as from their younger siblings because they were educated and aware of the ways of the world. During the constitutional period, the government gave the students great freedom to express themselves and to participate in the political life of the nation.

The change in government in 1962 sharply curtailed student political activity. When, in that year, the students protested new university regulations, the Revolutionary Council took direct and violent action against them; students were killed, the university student union building was destroyed, and the universities were closed temporarily. A year later the military rulers reversed themselves and approved the reconstruction of the student union and the recreation of student organizations. In November 1963, following a demonstration by the students against government policy toward the rebels and insurgents, the Revolutionary Council again closed the universities and jailed hundreds of students and their leaders. When the universities were reopened the next year, the government was in firm control and, with the exception of an occasional outburst, such as in the anti-Chinese riots of 1967 and a 1970 riot against officials for not providing enough tickets to a regional sports meeting, the students were politically inactive and lacked organization and leadership.

Since the spring of 1974, in the second phase of military rule, the students once again have shown signs of returning to political action. Although they did not initiate or lead the protests and riots over food shortages and high prices in June 1974, they did participate and, as usual, the government responded by closing the universities and sending them home for a period of time. In December of the same year, the university students took the lead in challenging the government's insensitiveness and unwillingness to give U Thant, the former secretary general of the United Nations, a fitting tribute and burial when his body was returned to Burma. This provoked a riot that lasted for several days; martial law was proclaimed, and the universities once again were closed. In June 1975 there were student protests against the high cost of living and the continued incarceration of students arrested in earlier demonstrations. Despite strong government reaction to these demonstrations, the students continued their antigovernment activity; in March 1976 a new demonstration took place on the Rangoon campus that again provoked the closing of the universities and the arrest of some demonstrators. The incidents suggest that the students are still a potential source of leadership and that the tradition of students in opposition has not been obliterated despite more than fourteen years of authoritarian rule.

Buddhism and the *sangha* are yet another political force and source of leadership in the nation. During the constitutional period, U Nu and the AFPFL used Buddhism to build cohesion among their adherents by staging a revival of building and restoring pagodas, holding examinations, and giving prizes for monks who showed exceptional ability in learning and reciting the scripture. In addition, they strengthened the authority of the religious leaders in the maintenance of discipline in the Buddhist orders.

The revival and propagation of Buddhism antagonized the religious minorities. Despite constitutional protection, the adherents of other faiths felt threatened and insecure. When in 1960, U Nu promised to make Buddhism the state religion, the Muslims, Christians, and some animists began to organize to bring pressure on the government to alter its course. In spite of their efforts, parliament made Buddhism the state religion in 1961 by amending the constitution. Political pressure from religious minorities, however, forced it to pass another amendment that restated and reinforced the protection of religious freedom and toleration for all faiths. These amendments, however, did little to satisfy all sides; the religious issue inflamed the nation and lost the government widespread support.

The military made a concerted effort to separate religion and politics. The monks challenged the military by refusing in 1964 to register in new government-sponsored organizations. The conflict between the government and the monks led finally in April 1965 to the arrest of ninety-two monks and an open effort to suppress their political activity.[22] For nearly ten years the monks did not take any public stands or offer open resistance to the government; they remained close to the people in the villages and the cities and reverted to their more historic role as religious leaders and teachers. The U Thant incident brought the monks back to political action. In the riots of December 1974 the monks, with the students, led the popular response to the brutality of the police and soldiers. The event demonstrated that the monks are still a potential source of leadership if the military's hold on power weakens or if the people are pushed too far by the soldiers and civilians who exercise authority.

Among the hill peoples, leadership has been exercised by the traditional hereditary chiefs and students who achieved some amount of university education. Despite efforts of the civilian and military governments alike to displace the hereditary leaders with new ones drawn from the people and to exercise leadership on the basis of election or some other means of popular choice, the traditional leaders continue to exercise authority among revolters as well as those willing to live under government rule. The government, through the Security and Administration Councils, sought to establish a form of bureaucratic control and leadership to displace that of the traditional leaders. Since most of the council members are alien to the local communities in the hill areas, the councils never developed the personal links necessary for their acceptance as the natural leaders of the people in their charge. Under the new constitution, the councils have been dissolved and replaced by local elected councils. The government hopes that democratic leadership in the hill areas can be created and thus break forever the authority and power of the traditional leaders.

The peasantry, unlike the city workers, are not a cohesive, politically conscious, well-organized force with a common set of values and goals. As the largest identifiable group in Burmese society, the peasantry was and still is conservative in nature and local in outlook. During the constitutional period, the political leaders sought

22. Josef Silverstein, "Burma: Ne Win's Revolution Considered," *Asian Survey*, 6, no. 2 (February 1966), 101.

to arouse the peasantry through party-created organizations, but most peasants continued to look to the traditional and local leadership provided by the village headmen, elders, and Buddhist monks.[23]

Since World War II both the Socialists and Communists have sought to associate the labor movement with their leadership. The Socialists were more successful and brought the majority of the urban workers under control of their Trade Union Congress and the political leadership of the AFPFL. During the first decade of independence, urban labor supported the government; after the AFPFL split, the rival political factions fought to capture control of this force but succeeded only in dividing it into rival factions. Political rivalry had a dual effect upon labor; it made the workers politically aware but disappointed and alienated a large segment who felt they had been used in ways that had not given them direct benefits.

Following their seizure of power, the military rulers sought to unite the people by mobilizing the peasants and workers. Through its program of socialism, the government passed laws that freed the peasants from rent, provided new loans, and directed the peasants to create local land committees to reallocate land held by absentee landlords or in excess of what one family could farm. In the cities and towns it seized factories, businesses, and shops and sought to associate the workers with their management. It fostered the development of People's Peasants and People's Workers Councils which it hoped would become the means for mobilizing these two classes and providing them with a forum and mechanism for the expression of their ideas. At the same time, the councils acted as a vehicle for supporting the military government. Despite its emphasis upon socialism and cooperatives, the military did not socialize the land or seize its produce. Thus, farmers remain the largest bloc of private owners and producers in the country. As noted earlier, they have not become completely pliable and accommodating to the government. Both workers and peasants have demonstrated an ability to pursue their self-interest, and with the

23. For an excellent discussion of politics in the villages and the problem of leadership, see Manning Nash, "Party Building in Upper Burma," *Asian Survey*, 3, no. 4 (April 1963), 197–202.

1974 military-civilian government showing more interest in their grievances, the workers and peasants are beginning to use their potential power in the political arena.

Burma, unlike India, had an administrative bureaucracy during British rule that was composed mainly of alien personnel. When the war came, most of the Indian and British personnel evacuated the country. The Burmese in the lower ranks filled the vacated higher posts. After the grant of independence, the old AFPFL discouraged some of the best-trained administrators from continuing in office, fearing that they were too closely allied to colonial thinking and therefore hostile to the new government. As a result, the few trained older personnel who stayed on absorbed the bulk of the work, and the lower ranks were filled with partially trained, inexperienced men and women. For these reasons, the bureaucracy did not provide a stable administrative organization around which the new state could develop. Burma's leaders, whether civil or military, have not enjoyed the support of a well-trained and efficient administration; the civil leaders tried to build a new bureaucracy with workers who were politically loyal but were technically only partially skilled. What creativity these bureaucrats might have shown was discouraged by the policy of the ministers to make all decisions, no matter how trivial, and by the existence of an overly zealous special police force charged with finding corruption and establishing responsibility for faulty administrative decisions.

The Revolutionary Council inherited this bureaucracy and has attempted to strengthen it with an infusion of miliary officers in key roles. After more than a decade of military rule, the government shows no signs of developing a new and creative bureaucracy. Indeed, policy seems directed toward replacing the professional with the amateur. Emphasis is upon the people doing things for themselves and upon transferring as many functions as possible from the bureaucracy to the people. The reorganization of the administration in 1972, which eliminated the district officer from the hierarchy, is an example of the effort to alter the former colonial system but not to reconstruct it. The bureaucracy never developed into a viable political force or a leadership group.

3 | Constitutional Government, 1948–1962

Prior to the coup d'etat of 1962, the people of independent Burma lived under a constitution of their own making, under leaders of their own choice, and within a framework of law that recognized legislative supremacy, judicial independence, and personal freedoms. The system was far from perfect, and a close examination of it reveals both its weaknesses and its failure to meet some of the basic problems of the young republic. Study of the politics of this period sheds light upon and provides a basis for comparison with the military period that followed.

The Constitution and the Formal Structure of Government

A primary goal of the founders of independent Burma was to create a government blending the values and ideas of liberal democracy inherited from the British with the socialist values and goals expressed in revolutionary and evolutionary Western socialism.[1] The constitution also sought to solve the major problem facing the Burmese—how to construct a union in which formerly separate peoples could join together so as to benefit from unity while retaining a nominal degree of autonomy.[2]

1. AFPFL, *From Fascist Bondage to New Democracy: The New Burma in the New World* (Rangoon: Nay Win Kyi Press [1945?]), pp. 13–16; Josef Silverstein, *The Political Legacy of Aung San* (Ithaca: Southeast Asia Program, Cornell University, Data Paper no. 86, 1972), pp. 91–100.

2. Two analyses of the Burmese constitution that merit consideration are Maung Maung, *Burma's Constitution* (The Hague: Martinus Nijhoff, 1959), and Alan Gledhill, "The Burmese Constitution," *Indian Yearbook of International Affairs, 1953,* II (Madras: Indian Study Group of International Affairs, University of Madras, 1954), 214–224.

The liberal tradition provided the basic idea underlying the constitution, that power emanated from the people. It also supported the idea that the rights of citizenship were conferred automatically on all indigenous people of Burma and on the offspring of all naturalized citizens. Other ideas that drew their inspiration from the liberal tradition were equality of all before the law; freedom of speech and assembly; the right to hold property, to maintain the inviolability of the home, and to form associations; the right to vote and hold office, to move freely, to enter any trade and profession, and, under certain circumstances, to operate a public utility. Under normal conditions, citizens were protected under due process of law. Women were entitled to equal pay for equal work. All were guaranteed religious freedom, and no minority could be denied an education at state schools or forced to accept religious instruction.

The socialist basis was reflected by the imposition of certain limitations. Private property was subject to expropriation and could be limited, but only in accordance with law. The state was declared the ultimate owner of all the land, and it could regulate, alter, or abolish land tenure and "resume possession of any land and distribute [it] ... for collective or cooperative farming." Monopolistic practices were forbidden. The state declared itself to be the protector of the workers' right to organize, to obtain safe employment and holidays, and to be the promoter of "schemes for housing and social insurance." Despite the occasional use of class terms, the main focus of the constitution was upon the individual.

A unique aspect of the constitution was the inclusion of directive principles intended to guide the state that were enforceable in law only upon passage of specific legislation. These included the right of all people to work, maintenance in old age, rest, leisure, and education. The directive principles were goals of the founding fathers toward which future generations should aim.

The structure of government followed the British parliamentary model. The head of state was the president, who was elected indirectly by parliament for a five-year term. The two-house parliament was directly elected by the people; the Chamber of Deputies consisted of 250 members, while the Chamber of Nationalities was allotted 125 seats. The life of parliament was four years, but could be less if the prime minister asked for its dissolution.

The dominant branch of parliament was the Chamber of Deputies, which nominated the prime minister and to which he was responsible. The Chamber of Nationalities represented the states. Its seats were divided according to a fixed ratio that could be altered by amendment.[3] Anyone in a particular electoral district could run for election to the Chamber of Deputies. The seats in the Chamber of Nationalities were allotted to ethnic and social groups so as to reflect the class structure of society and the ethnic composition of the several states. The two houses met in joint session to approve appointments to the High and Supreme courts, to elect the president, to approve constitutional amendments, and to pass legislation each chamber had passed previously in different form. Parliament could declare war and make peace, approve treaties, and ratify any treaties whose implementation required the passing of domestic legislation.

The real power of the government was concentrated in the hands of the prime minister and his cabinet. Together they formed the Union government. All were members of parliament although nonmembers could serve in the cabinet for a limit of six months.[4] The executive authority of the Union extended to all matters in which the parliament constitutionally had power to make laws. The prime minister was required to inform the president on all domestic and international matters of policy.

The constitution created an independent judiciary, with a Supreme Court, a High Court, and a system of inferior courts located throughout the nation. The High Court had both original and appellate jurisdiction. The Supreme Court was the court of final

3. Originally the seats were allotted as follows: Shan State, 25; Karens, 24; Kachin State, 12; Chin Special Division, 8; Kayah State, 3. The Constitution Amendment Act of 1951, created a Karen State with 15 seats in the Chamber of Nationalities, and transferred the remaining 9 seats to Burma proper, where Karens competed with other Burmese for general seats.

4. Constitution of the Union of Burma, Article 116. The Constitutional Amendment Act of 1959 provided that during the period of the caretaker government members of the Union government did not have to be members of parliament. The act provided for its own repeal when a general election was held and the president appointed the prime minister in the new parliament.

appeal. The justices in both courts were nominated by the president and approved by parliament.

Because they venerated the legacy of the rule of law from the British period, the justices of the Supreme and High courts established an enviable record for independence of action and created respect for their jurisdiction. During the first decade of independent government, when the Union and the constitution stood in danger of being overthrown, and afterward, the Supreme Court worked unremittingly to establish a tradition of due process of law in Burma.[5] Despite the grave conditions at the time, the courts worked to protect the individual against arbitrary action by the government. They challenged the government's use of preventive detention as an easy means to curb the actions of the opposition, legal and otherwise, who might commit crimes against the state.[6] The courts refused to be intimidated by outside influences, and the justices were determined to establish beyond doubt that the courts were independent and responsible.

Unfortunately, a dearth of qualified persons prevented the court system as a whole from maintaining the high standards of the Supreme and High courts. As a result, incompletely trained and, in many cases, politically motivated magistrates and judicial officials filled the lower courts; their handiwork often had to be corrected by an overcrowded, overworked review tribunal system.

Probably the most distinctive and interesting feature of the constitution was the concept of the federal union. The constitution contained no definition of federalism, but it conformed with the federal idea by providing for a separate system of government in each of the several states. In all except Burma proper—which will be considered separately—executive authority was granted to in-

5. For a discussion of the court's principles as expressed by the first chief justice, see Ba U, *My Burma: The Autobiography of a President* (New York: Taplinger, 1958), p. 203.

6. For a complete discussion of this question see Hla Aung, "The Law of Preventive Detention in Burma," *Journal of the International Commission of Jourists*, 3, no. 1 (1961), 47–68. See also, N. A. Subramanian, "Some Aspects of Burmese Constitutional Law," *Indian Yearbook of International Affairs, 1956* VI, (Madras: Indian Study Group of International Affairs, University of Madras, 1957), 123–155; Winslow Christian, "Burma's New Constitution and Supreme Court," *Tulane Law Review*, 26 (December 1951), 47–59.

directly chosen heads of state while legislative power was vested in the state councils. The federal idea was reinforced in Schedule III of the constitution that enumerated in separate lists the legislative powers of the Union parliament and the state councils.

Offsetting these apparent grants of power to the states were a number of restrictions. All legislation from the state councils had to be promulgated by the president. He could suspend promulgation and call upon the Supreme Court for advice on questions of the constitutionality of any piece of legislation, returning it if the court advised him it was faulty. The constitution permitted the states to surrender their rights, territory, and powers to the Union but did not permit the Union to reciprocate. In a proclaimed state of emergency, the Union parliament could legislate for any state on any matter regardless of the legislative lists.

The line of federal separation was less pronounced with regard to the structures of the state governments. Unlike the other states, Burma proper, incorporating almost half the territory of the Union and including more than three-quarters of the population, was governed by the Union government and parliament. Representatives from all the states participated in considering matters that pertained only to Burma proper, whose residents were denied full and exclusive authority in their own area. Nor did the people in the other states have exclusive power over the institutions and the decisions concerning their territories. The constitution provided that all state offices were to be filled indirectly, that is, members of the state councils were also members of the bicameral Union parliament. A state legislator sat in two houses; part of the time he legislated in the national interest and part of the time in the interest of his own state. When the Union parliament was dissolved, the legislator automatically lost his state as well as his Union seat.

The Union government entered state politics in yet another way. With only one exception,[7] the minister chosen by the prime minister for any particular state automatically became the head of that

7. The one exception was the Chin Special Division, which was an appendage of Burma proper with special privileges. The parliamentary members sat in a Chin Affairs Council. There was no head of state. The minister for Chin affairs was in charge of Chin general administration, education, and culture; the council had no legislative power.

state. The combined head of state-minister owed his position solely to the Union prime minister. The state council had no authority to remove him, nor could it participate in his selection beyond offering advice to the prime minister.[8]

In terms of privileges, the states did not enjoy equal rights. The constitution provided that every state had the right of secession unless otherwise expressly stated. The Kachin and Karen states were expressly denied the right; the Shan and Kayah states were required to wait until January 4, 1958, before the right could be exercised. The right did not apply to the Chin Special Division because it was not considered as a state equal to the others.

All states were empowered to tax their citizens, but, since the economic base in each state differed and none was self-supporting, all looked to the Union treasury to augment their revenues for financing their expenditures. State budgets were scrutinized by the Union president and included in the Union budget when it was presented to parliament.

The federal structure was more nominal than real; effective power remained with the central government, and only incidental powers passed to the states. The desires of the minorities were not satisfied which provided a major cause for the institutional changes in 1962.

Local government technically was under state authority. The states, other than Burma proper, were empowered to legislate and tax according to the lists incorporated in Schedules III and IV. They were free to write their own laws and create their own institutions as long as there was no conflict with the Union laws. In reality, the institutions and practices in the several states were almost identical with those in existence prior to independence. In

8. The power of the prime minister was not absolute; following the 1958 split in the AFPFL, the prime minister was faced with selecting, as his head of state-ministers, leaders who were opposed to him but who, in their own states, held a majority. Initially, Nu refused to accept them and chose the leaders of the minority party who were personally loyal to him. The Supreme Court upheld him in this action. Following the 1961 election, he reversed himself and chose, as head of state-ministers, men with a majority in their state councils. He then developed a two-tier cabinet. Under this scheme, only members of his party and its affiliates were in the inner cabinet, while leaders of the opposition who came from the states were in the outer cabinet and excluded from most of the important discussions of policy matters.

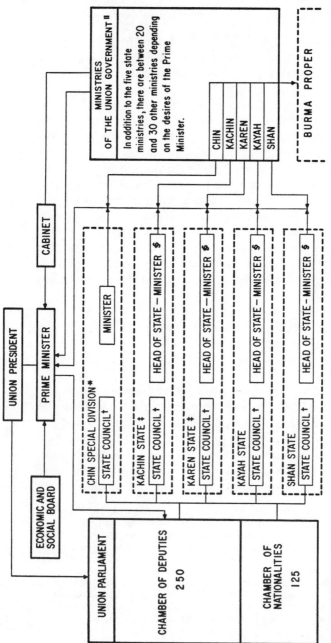

Chart 1. Federalism in Burma

* The Chin Special Division is an appendage of Burma proper with only a few of the rights accorded to other states.
† Members of the Union parliament from the states other than Burma proper automatically hold all seats in the state councils.
‡ Although the constitution recognizes the right of secession, it denies this right to the Kachin and Karen states.
§ A member of parliament appointed as minister for his state becomes thereby the head of his state.
|| The Union government is also the government of Burma proper.
Source: George McT. Kahin, ed., *Governments and Politics of Southeast Asia*, 1st ed., Cornell University Press, 1959, p. 108.

Burma proper, parliament established the local institutions and prescribed the methods for manning and operating them. In 1949 it passed a Democratization of Local Administration Act intended to create a new and less bureaucratic system. The act was tested in ten districts; after it was found defective and subject to manipulation by politicians, it was repealed in 1961, and a new act was under consideration by parliament when the coup occurred.

The constitution was amendable by a relatively easy process. In all, seven amendments were added.[9] None of the amendments made a radical change in the fundamental law; all were minor alterations to meet specific problems. Their passage demonstrated that the constitution was flexible and adjustable to changing times and conditions.

Political Parties

The constitution, like that of the United States, did not mention political parties. If a legal mandate for parties was sought, it probably could have been found in the right of individuals to assemble peacefully, to express their opinions and convictions, and to form associations.

Prior to 1958, although Burma had a multiparty system, the AFPFL dominated the political scene. In many ways it was the only modern party in the country; it had a national organization, a meaningful program, and an ideology to guide its future action. Following the 1956 election, its chief rival for power was the Na-

9. Two amendments pertained to Union-state relations: the 1951 amendment that converted the Kawthulay territory into the Karen State and reduced the number of Karen State representatives in the Chamber of Nationalities; and the 1959 amendment that revoked the privileges of the Sawbwas in Shan and Kayah to exclusive right to represent their states in the Chamber of Nationalities. Two dealing with religion were passed in 1961. The first made Buddhism the state religion, while the second allowed the free profession, practice, and teaching of any religion. One amendment changing the nation's boundaries was passed in 1961 to approve the transfer of territory from the Shan and Kachin states to the People's Republic of China, thus making it possible to implement the 1960 Sino-Burmese Treaty. A third amendment passed in 1961 established an independent election commission and drew up clearer and more specific guidelines for future parliamentary elections. A temporary amendment was passed in 1959 that allowed General Ne Win to remain in the office of prime minister beyond the six-month limitations for nonmembers of parliament. When the new parliament was elected and seated in 1960, the temporary amendment became null and void.

tional Unity Front (NUF). Unlike the AFPFL, the NUF was a loose confederation of minor opposition groups. It had no ideology, and its program was limited to unseating the party in power; its strength lay in its leaders and their desire for power and the fact that it was the only alternative offered to a people grown a little weary and disenchanted with the AFPFL.

Technically, the AFPFL was a coalition party, a combination of ethnic groups, mass organizations, independent members, and at least one political party—the Socialist party. Between 1945 and 1958, the Socialists were the most influential group in the coalition and provided it with leadership and ideas. The Socialists' power came from two sources: the importance of their leaders in the AFPFL's elite and their control of the mass organizations. In 1949, during a critical phase of the insurrection against the nascent independent government of Burma, the Socialist party disagreed with U Nu and other non-Socialist leaders in the AFPFL and withdrew as a constituent group. Individual Socialists remained in the AFPFL and retained their control of the mass organizations. Since the question of dual loyalties never was raised, no problem arose over this curious arrangement. Although some observers considered the Socialists as the real leaders of the party, independents and ethnic group leaders representing the minorities also provided some AFPFL leadership. The strength and influence of the independents and the minority group leaders in the AFPFL caused conflicts between the Socialists and non-Socialists over policies and programs. To compound the problem, the Socialists never presented a completely united front, and after the 1958 split in the AFPFL, they were to be found on both sides.

The NUF differed in that it was a coalition of near equals. The constituent groups ranged from the liberal-democratic Justice party to the Marxist Burma Worker's and Peasant's party. Within parliament from 1956 to 1958 the NUF cooperated with the Arakanese National United Organization (ANUO), a conservative, right-wing party, whereas outside parliament the constituent groups retained their original identities and their hold over their own organizations. NUF parliamentary unity was unbroken until the AFPFL split forced its members to decide which faction to support. After the emergency parliamentary meeting in June

1958, when the power struggle between the two AFPFL rival wings was settled temporarily, the Kyaw Nyein-Ba Swe faction of the AFPFL replaced the NUF as the official opposition party.

Power in the AFPFL was concentrated in the Executive Committee of the Supreme Council. The Supreme Council was elected by the National Congress, which, according to the constitution of the AFPFL, was supposed to meet annually.[10] The Executive Committee was empowered to co-opt members as it saw fit without referring its action to the parent body or the congress.

Within the AFPFL there were two types of members—direct and indirect. Direct or independent members joined a branch of the AFPFL. Indirect members entered the party through membership in an affiliated organization—All-Burma Peasant's Organization; Trade Union Congress, Burma; Women's Freedom League; Federation of Trade Organizations; Karen Youth League. Because leaders depended upon personal followings to elevate them into the ruling circle, the heads of affiliate organizations held tight control over their own organizations. It was possible, but not usual, for an independent or direct member to rise to the top. U Nu, as an independent, did not rise through the ranks but entered the party at the top, as vice-president to Aung San. He was able to maintain his control of the party from 1947 until the split in 1958 through his position as president of the party and his personal standing with the people.

In January 1958, the party held the third All-Burma AFPFL Congress. The party's membership stood at 1,368,014 and included 488,014 direct members. The congress chose a new Supreme Council and elected U Nu president; he chose an Executive Committee of fifteen and accepted five additional co-opted members.[11] Behind the scenes a struggle occurred over the naming of the secretary general. Socialist leaders Kyaw Nyein and Ba Swe supported Thakin Tha Khin, whereas U Nu demanded Thakin Kyaw Tun for the office. Compromise was effected by naming both, with Thakin Tha Khin becoming the assistant secretary general

10. The Constitution of the AFPFL (Rangoon [1949] in Burmese) provided for the holding of an annual national congress. Because of the internal situation after independence, however, none was held between December 1947 and January 1958.

11. *Nation*, January 12, 31, 1958.

to Thakin Kyaw Tun. The congress is noteworthy because U Nu declared that, henceforth, the AFPFL no longer was a coalition but a united party, wherein all affiliates must recognize the party ideology while accepting subordinate status within its organization. He rejected Marxism "as a guiding political philosophy or as the ideology of the AFPFL." He also stated that Burma's goal must be to become a socialist state that "can fully guarantee fundamental rights, economic security, a high standard of living, firm morality, opportunity to practice religion in a positive way . . . maintenance and preservation of our traditions, culture and heritage."[12]

In neither the AFPFL nor the NUF was there a clear line by which new leaders could rise to the top. Most of the contemporary leaders were the men who had founded the organizations. In theory, the AFPFL—with its widespread organization and affiliates—was best equipped to select, train, and elevate leaders from the ranks. Few, however, actually rose to high office. The NUF did not have a similar apparatus, but it had strong support from the university students, and their organizations and parties provided a ready-made recruiting ground and willing adherents.

The breakup of the AFPFL in 1958 came as a result of long personal antagonisms, structural defects, and the changing political climate in Burma.[13] Personal rivalries and jealousies among the leaders had existed since independence; because of the nation's difficulties and the political responsibility of the AFPFL, the leaders had sought to keep their private quarrels and differences from public view. During the third Burma AFPFL Congress these problems flared up over the choice of the secretary general and a second issue, Kyaw Nyein's desire to build a power base in the form of a mass youth organization. Following the congress, Kyaw Nyein's lieutenants began to raid other AFPFL mass organizations for recruits, and this provoked a fight between rivals that could not be settled peacefully. At this point U Nu decided he no longer could keep the factions together and would join one against the other and split the party. A second and deeper cause of the split in the AFPFL

12. Ministry of Information, *Burma Weekly Bulletin*, n.s. 6, no. 41 (February 6, 1958), 376.
13. See Sein Win, *The Split Story* (Rangoon: Guardian, 1959), for an informed Burmese journalist's account of the breakup of the AFPFL.

lay in the structure of the organization. Despite the theoretical and constitutional basis for impersonal party and mass organizations, the AFPFL in fact was overburdened with private followings attached to particular leaders. These, in many cases, were territorially based, and, in the internal struggle for power, a leader was measured by his following. This system encouraged rivalries between the opposing factions and led to the growth of a spoils system whereby jobs, organizations, and territories were distributed among the rival leaders. The potential of the AFPFL as an efficient and impersonal structure was never realized. Finally, time contributed to the decline and split of the party. Having weathered multiple threats to the survival of the Union from 1948 to 1950 and having maintained a wide majority in two national elections, the party's leaders felt a decreasing need for cohesion. Further, the continuing petty rivalries that always had existed among the followers of the various national leaders gradually alienated many past supporters of the party. These petty disputes were never eliminated or totally hidden from the public. Despite the vituperations of the rival national leaders at the height of the split, they were never far apart on matters of ideology, policy, and program, and therefore, the possibility of their eventual reunification was always very real.

The two rivals chose to retain the AFPFL name. The U Nu faction called itself the Clean AFPFL, and the Kyaw Nyein-Ba Swe group called itself the Stable AFPFL. During the life of the caretaker government the Stable AFPFL approved the army-led government's actions, while the Clean AFPFL denounced its policies and tactics. From mid-1959 onward, both factions campaigned vigorously for the elections that were held in February and March 1960, and U Nu's AFPFL won an overwhelming victory over both the rival AFPFL and the NUF. The results of the elections reduced the Stable AFPFL to a minor party, as most of its national leaders suffered defeats in their separate constituencies. The NUF was all but wiped out.

When U Nu's party assumed power in April 1960, it changed its name to the Pyidaungsu or Union party and permitted its rival faction to keep the AFPFL as its own. Among the first projects undertaken by the Pyidaungsu party was to seek to eliminate some of the problems that were undermining democracy in Burma. A neutral all-parties committee was formed under the leadership of a former Union president, Dr. Ba U, to work out an agreement whereby all could survive and have a relatively equal chance to win power in future elections.[14] But while the committee was working, a power struggle was developing among the leaders of the Pyidaungsu over which faction would lead the party after U Nu retired. One group calling itself the Thakins was composed of old AFPFL party members who had supported U Nu in 1958 and who were leftist in their ideology. Its rival, called the U-Bos, was composed of relative newcomers to party politics who were more conservative in their ideological beliefs. In addition to the issue of political succession to U Nu, the two factions divided on the issue of the future development of socialism in Burma. U Nu sought to halt the rivalry and threatened to resign. When this failed to solve the problem, he elevated himself above the struggle, promising to surrender power to the victorious side in 1964, if, prior to that date, the rivals competed within the party framework and closed ranks after a vote was taken. Once again, the contest between rivals brought forth personal attacks, accusations, and vituperations. As in 1958, the public lost confidence in all the governing party's elected leaders, except U Nu, who remained in the public's mind as an honest and moral man standing above the squabbles of his supporters. At the Pyidaungsu party conference in January 1962, the Thakins won control; U Nu sought to close the breach in the party by calling on all members to unite and declaring that the open rivalry had only demonstrated the freedom and democracy of the party. His optimism, however, was not reflected in the press or among the people in business and the civil service. During the final two months of constitutional government, the quarrels continued between the leaders of the party, and it declined in strength and popularity.

The new AFPFL did not suffer a similar fate to that of the Pyidaungsu. Lacking a truly national popular figure such as U Nu, its leaders depended upon their own cohesion and organizing

14. *Burma Weekly Bulletin*, 9, nos. 46 and 47 (March 15, 22, 1961), 421, 434. The participants were the Pyidaungsu, AFPFL, NUF, and ANUO.

ability to win public support. As the party out of power, devoted to the parliamentary system, the AFPFL cooperated with the government party when possible and gave constructive criticism when opposed to its policies. The public perceived the AFPFL as growing in strength and organization and presenting a determined alternative to the Pyidaungsu. During the last four months before the coup (December through March 1962), the breach between the two parties narrowed. On the question of separate states for the Arakanese and Mons—a promise made by U Nu in the 1960 election—the AFPFL cautioned U Nu not to act until the differences between the hill minorities—especially the Shans—and the government were settled and the federal relations were worked out to the mutual satisfaction of all concerned. Nu took this advice, delayed the statehood bills, and thereby alienated the representatives of the Arakanese and Mons from his leadership. Thus, while Nu and the leaders of the Pyidaungsu quarreled more openly among themselves during this period, he and the leaders of the AFPFL found more common ground and basis for unity as they sought to preserve the constitutional democratic system.

The NUF all but lost its parliamentary voice in the 1960 elections. Faced with the resignations of some of its independent leaders and the defections of some of its coalition members, the NUF in 1959 came under the open control of the leftist Burma Worker's party (formerly called the Burma Worker's and Peasant's party) and the People's Comrade party. It sought to rally popular backing by presenting itself as a truly nationalist organization with strong leftist ideas about internal development and outright support for the Sino-Soviet position on world affairs. It failed to develop as a clear alternative to the two AFPFL parties because it did not convert its loose confederation into a strong, disciplined organization with a broad popular base. After its defeat in the 1960 election, the NUF continued to operate on the fringe as a critic of both the Pyidaungsu's policies and the AFPFL's opposition.

Elections

During the constitutional period, Burma held three national elections. The first was conducted in 1951–1952 in three stages— one part of the country after another—so that available troops could be moved into each area to provide security for the candidates and voters. The chief contestants for seats were the AFPFL, the BWPP, the Independent Arakanese Parliamentary Group (IAPG), and some minor parties that eventually gravitated to the BWPP. Out of 239 seats contested, the AFPFL won 147 in its own name (about 200 if its affiliates were included), the opposition won only 30 seats, and the remainder went to independents.[15] The opposition might have been somewhat larger had the BWPP not withdrawn candidates to emphasize its charge that the election was unfair.[16]

The election revealed two interesting aspects of Burmese politics. The use of the single-member constituency ensured that there was no splitting of the vote. Like the British model, the Burmese electoral system did not demand that a candidate be a resident of his constituency. The parties were able to select the candidates and provide financial backing. Thus, the candidate was obligated to the party rather than to the voter, and party solidarity was maintained. But these two factors, combined with the use of the aforementioned three-stage election, gave an unusual result. Candidates who were unsuccessful in one constituency stood a second time in another, thus alienating many voters by forcing second-rate candidates on some of the constituencies. In such cases the people frequently responded by giving an unenthusiastic vote to the opposition candidate.

The second national election, held in 1956, duplicated the earlier overwhelming victory of the AFPFL. It also produced a new factor in Burmese politics—the emergence of an opposition large

15. *Asian Annual* (London, 1954), p. 15. No two public accounts agree on the distribution of seats because some local elections were disputed, some elected members of parliament shifted alliances, and some died before taking office. According to the parliamentary secretary of the Chamber of Deputies, U Nan Nwe, the true composition of the parliament between 1954 and 1956 was as follows. *Pro-AFPFL*: AFPFL, 143; United Hill People's League, 39; United Karen League, 13; Arakanese Muslims, 3: total, 198. *Anti-AFPFL*: BWPP, 9; Arakan Parliamentary Group, 9; Parliamentary Independent Group, 8; People's United Party, 2; Karen National Congress, 2; Pa-O Organization, 3; total, 33. *Independents*: 5. Grand total, 236.

16. Foreign observers reported that the election was as fair as possible under existing circumstances. See *Economist*, February 9, 1952, pp. 349–351, for an example of such reports.

enough to make its voice heard in parliament. The opposition NUF fought the election on the issues of ending the insurrection by peaceful means, stopping corruption in government, and correcting the faulty administration of state enterprises. The AFPFL countered with a campaign based on recounting its past achievements and promising more in the future. At the time of the election, the country was undergoing a mild inflation, while a restriction on imported goods and internal insecurity continued to plague the people. The army was able to provide sufficient security for elections to be held on a single day in all but nine constituencies. In view of existing conditions, local observers who usually were critical of the government agreed that the election was conducted fairly.[17]

An examination of the 1956 election demonstrates a number of characteristics of the elections and politics of Burma at that time (see Table 1). The AFPFL vote in Burma proper of 147, together with its support in the states, gave it 173 seats. Its 55 percent of the vote in Burma proper and just under 56 percent of the total vote—including its affiliates—was a national victory and indicated that the strength of the AFPFL was sufficient to carry out its programs during its term of office. While the NUF won 48 seats in Burma proper and had the backing of minority candidates from Arakan (ANUO) and the Shan State United National Pa-O (UNPO), its total percentage of the vote of 36.9 indicated that a basis for a two-party system had been established. The surprising showing of the Burma Democratic party (BDP) suggested that a strong minority of voters favored a freer economy and a foreign policy oriented to the West, instead of a continuation of nonalignment.[18]

The 1960 election (see Table 1) provided new party identities for the same group of candidates. The campaign started almost from the day U Nu stepped out of office in 1958, and by February 1959, when Ne Win asked for a new mandate to govern because he

17. *Nation*, May 15, 1956.
18. For a discussion of the election and some of the issues see Josef Silverstein, "Politics, Parties and the National Election in Burma," *Far Eastern Survey*, 25 (December 1956), 177–184; Geoffrey Fairbairn, "Some Minority Problems in Burmese Politics," *Pacific Affairs*, 30 (December 1957), 287–313.

had failed to achieve his original tasks in the six months the constitution permitted a nonmember of parliament to hold office, U Nu's faction was accused openly of being antagonistic to the caretaker government. On May Day 1959, U Nu made his most outspoken attack on Ne Win's caretaker government, charging it with partisanship in favor of the Stable AFPFL. Nu added positive issues to his campaign; he called for the establishment of Buddhism as the state religion, and he promised to create new states for ethnic minorities if such a move received sufficient popular backing. The Stable AFPFL countered both issues by also promising to raise the status of Buddhism and make it a compulsory subject in the public schools for all students born of Buddhist parents,[19] but it rejected the idea of adding new ethnically based states. It introduced a new issue, the continuation of the caretaker government's policy of Burmanization of industry and commerce. Nu's supporters played down this last issue because many of his closest advisers were naturalized Burmese citizens or still held citizenship in a foreign country.

The elections were conducted cleanly and fairly. In Burma proper, insurgency was at its lowest point, and its increase in the states did not appear to obstruct the election. Almost twice as many voted as in the previous election. U Nu's party won overwhelmingly; all the leaders of the rival AFPFL went down to defeat; and the NUF did the poorest of all. In addition to its lack of voter support, it lost two important constituent groups to the Clean AFPFL, the Justice party, and the ANUO. The leader of the Justice

Table 1. Elections in Burma (Chamber of Deputies)

1956	Votes cast	Percentage of total vote cast	Seats won
Burma proper			
AFPEL	1,844,614	47.7	147
NUF	1,170,073	30.4	48
BDP	113,091	2.9	0
BNB	77,364	2.0	1
ANUO	38,939	1.0	5
Independents	119,148	3.1	4
Minor parties	35,943	0.8	0

19. *Nation*, December 15, 1959.

Other states			
UHPC	163,283	4.2	14
PECDO	49,203	1.3	4
ASSO	41,940	1.1	4
SSPO	31,112	0.8	2
KNC	30,837	0.8	2
UNPO	22,185	0.6	1
Independents	120,018	3.2	9
Minor parties	4,462	0.1	0
Contests not held			9
Totals	3,868,242	100.0	250

1960	Votes cast	Percentage of total vote cast	Seats won
Burma Proper			
Clean AFPFL	3,480,588	52.7	157
Stable AFPFL	1,974,469	29.8	42
NUF	362,495	5.4	4
BDP	7,788	0.1	0
ANUO	51,611	0.7	9
Independents	281,127	4.2	6
Minor parties	59,214	0.8	0
Other states			
PECDO	51,060	0.7	2
ASSO	17,904	0.3	0
KNC	46,950	0.7	3
UNPO	49,131	0.7	3
SSHPUO	78,090	1.1	9
SSUP	30,781	0.4	2
IPUO	13,583	0.2	1
Independents	172,189	2.5	12
Minor parties	33,425	0.5	0
Totals	6,633,802	100.0	250

Shan State Parties
   UHPC—United Hill Peoples Congress
   ASSO—All Shan State Organization
   SSPO—Shan State Peasant Organization
   UNPO—United National Pa-O
   SSHPUO—Shan State Hill Peoples Organization
   SSUP—Shan State Unity Party
   IPUO—Independent Party Unity Organization
Kachin State Parties
   PECDO—Peoples Economic Cultural Development Organization
   KNC—Kachin National Congress

party became a key official in U Nu's party while the leaders of the ANUO joined the same AFPFL faction on the basis of a promise of statehood for Arakan. The victory of U Nu's party was nationwide. In addition to winning heavily in the urban areas of Rangoon and Mandalay, it made strong showings in nearly all the districts of Burma proper. Affiliates of the Clean AFPFL won majorities in the Shan State and Chin Special Division. The rival Stable AFPFL had no areas of concentrated strength; the seats it won were scattered throughout Burma proper and in the Karen and Shan states, while the voters in the Kayah State voted for two independents. The lopsided victory of the Clean AFPFL meant that Burma was still a one-party state. An opposition existed, but it was fragmented and without leadership and strength to challenge the governing party. Although the actual election appeared to draw the nation closer together through voter participation, the issues that were raised, especially the state religion question and the statehood promises to the minorities, were potentially divisive.

As a result of the experience in three national elections, the Clean AFPFL—now called Pyidaungsu—led a move in 1961 to amend the constitution to create an independent election commission with power and responsibility for holding impartial and honest elections. The new commission was never tested as it was abolished by the military leaders shortly after the coup.

Politics under the AFPFL

The prime minister held basic responsibility for all formal or informal decisions, whether he acted on his own or in association with the party's executive committee or the formal organs of government. There were three levels of decision making. At the government level, the cabinet was the formal body that made the decisions. The cabinet ministers met weekly and worked on the basis of a formal agenda prepared in advance by the cabinet secretary. The prime minister presided, and minutes were taken and kept secret. Decisions by common agreement and discussion continued until a consensus was reached. At this highest level, the prime minister clearly dominated. When be was abroad, as in 1955, the government was forced to delay the presentation of the budget, and no one else could take responsibility for the final version to be presented to the parliament.

On key questions of economics and financial matters, the issues after 1952 were considered first by a special board under the chairmanship of the prime minister. This Economic and Social Board was created first as a planning branch under the control of the Ministry of National Planning and Religious Affairs. In 1953 it was moved to the office of the prime minister and reconstituted, and thereafter became, in effect, a supercabinet composed of the prime minister, several key ministers, the chairman of the Union Bank of Burma, a representative of the Economic and Social Advisory Council, and its own executive secretary. It, too, decided issues on the basis of consensus, and all questions were "under consideration" until the prime minister made up his mind. Once the Economic and Social Board disposed of a matter, it was sent to the cabinet where the decision was confirmed and acted upon.

Decisions affecting other aspects of national life were taken outside of government by the AFPFL's Executive Committee of fifteen, which included the prime minister, several cabinet officials, and members who held no elected office and had no responsibility except to the party. The importance of the Executive Committee to the decision-making process was exposed in a public exchange of letters between Kyaw Nyein and U Nu, wherein the prime minister wrote that he worked constantly to abide by the policy decisions of the party on internal and external matters. When Kyaw Nyein accused him of placing so many fetters upon the ministers that they were nothing more than head clerks, Nu replied, "Was it I who placed the controls upon the Ministers? It was the Executive Committee which ordered these checks."[20] The same letter revealed that when Nu returned from his trip to the USSR in 1955, he made his first report to a joint meeting of the party Executive Committee and the cabinet. While it may not be surprising that in a country with a relatively small elite, the elected officials and the party leaders are interchangeable, the prime minister and his cabinet felt an obligation to discuss with and seek approval from the party's

20. "Kyaw Nyein-U Nu Exchange of Letters, July 3–6, 1956," *Nation*, May 10, 1958.

leadership before deciding an issue in their responsible capacity as the government of Burma.

The third level was the independent, personal, and sometimes impetuous decisions of the prime minister. Although he was sometimes called the "serene statesman," on several occasions he demonstrated anger in reaching decisions in the heat of the moment. At the time of the 1956 school examinations, just prior to the elections, a student was shot and killed in a riot. To mollify the enraged students and their families, U Nu decided, without consulting others, to pass all of the pupils who took the examinations. His action had the long-term effect of overburdening an insufficiently staffed school system with a large percentage of unqualified students. Nu's personal decision making occasionally was influenced by an apparent reliance on the revelations of a favorite astrologer. This practice was in consonance with Burmese tradition as well as with his own beliefs. Examples of his reaching decisions in this manner were determining the exact moment for Burma to become independent in 1948 and the most auspicious hour for him to move out of the prime minister's residence in 1956.

Burma's problem was not making decisions but implementing them. An examination of attempts to implement the Land Nationalization Act will demonstrate some of the difficulties encountered even with a measure supported by the party, the government, the parliament, and a large portion of the people.

One of the rallying cries of the prewar nationalists had been for aid to the farmers; land alienation and exploitation were regarded as two of the worst abuses the peasant faced. As if to honor a pledge, one of the first pieces of legislation passed in parliament in 1948 was the Land Nationalization Act. The act's purposes were to take over all land held by nonagriculturalists and to distribute it among tenant farmers; to confirm the land rights of owner-cultivators; to survey and record landholdings; and to bring waste lands into production by distributing them to landless peasants. The ultimate goal, as stated by the minister of agriculture and forests, was to establish "collective farming and mechanization."[21]

21. *The Land Nationalization Act, 1948* (Rangoon: Ministry of Information, 1958), p. 8.

In reality, the act was hastily drawn up and contained numerous defects; it made no provision for nonfarming landowners to take up cultivation rather than have the land confiscated, and it made no clear provisions for eventual compensation for confiscated land. The government's haste was prompted by its desire to seize the issue from the Communists, who in 1948 were active among the peasants. Its implementation was delayed because land records were missing and maps had been destroyed during the war, and because the insurrection in the countryside limited the government's freedom of access to many of the rural areas and there were no trained personnel to administer the law.

A pilot project was launched in 1950 in Syriam to test the possibilities for implementing the law's provisions. It failed for many reasons; poor administration, the unworkability of some of the law's provisions, the political activity of the All-Burma Peasant's Organization, and its interference with the various land committees charged with deciding which lands were to be taken by the government and which were to be exempt. A second Land Nationalization Act was passed in 1953. This new act corrected many of the defects in the earlier one; a new ministry was created for the explicit purpose of implementing its provisions. By this time, internal security had improved, and the government was able to mount pilot projects in eight townships involving 142,737 acres of land.[22] A corps of trained administrators worked directly with village and township committees composed, in the main, of local farmers. Gradually, the government expanded the program. By the end of 1958, a total of 3.35 million acres of the approximately 19 million under cultivation had been reviewed. Between 1953 and 1958, 1.48 million acres were redistributed to 178,540 agricultural households, while the remaining 1.86 million acres were confirmed to the 305,490 households that originally held the land. The history of the law suggests many of the difficulties faced by the government in carrying out legislation, even with widespread support. Through methods of trial and error, the government gradually made the necessary corrections, but the long process, following

22. *Burma: The Seventh Anniversary* (Rangoon: Ministry of Information, 1955), p. 18; *Burma: The Eleventh Anniversary* (Rangoon: Ministry of Information, 1959), pp. 51–52.

initial failure, obscured the causes of the difficulties, the government's efforts to correct them, and the ultimate results.

The Caretaker Government

For eighteen months, Burma experimented with constitutional authoritarian government under the leadership of General Ne Win. This caretaker government was intended to last for only six months while preparations were made for holding new national elections and installing a new government with a popular mandate and was created because the political leaders could find no other way to solve the parliamentary problems they had wrought.

U Nu's triumph over his former AFPFL colleagues in the parliamentary vote of June 9, 1958, proved to be a Pyrrhic victory. Because his majority consisted of support from the NUF and the minorities, he could not pursue any legislative goals without their approval. Anticipating the forthcoming budget session in August, Nu feared a vote of no confidence if he did not present a budget his new allies would support. Rather than face a floor fight with both his allies and his opposition, Nu asked the Union president to cancel the session and promulgate the budget without debate. There was no constitutional basis for this action, and it revived an atmosphere of political tension and uncertainty in which no national elections could be held and Nu could not continue to govern. Rumors of a possible coup heightened tensions. Nu asked General Ne Win to form a caretaker government to restore order in the nation and to create the proper atmosphere to hold elections by April 1959. In an exchange of letters, the general accepted the conditions outlined by Nu and insisted that the Chamber of Deputies must elect him in accordance with the constitution and that his government would include no members of the active political parties. Parliament accepted his conditions and elected him to office.

The military leaders who joined Ne Win in governing assumed power with a well-thought-out set of ideas and goals for the present and future of the nation. In 1956 they had begun to study and discuss an ideology for the Defense Services. Two years later the armed forces adopted a national ideology based on three documents: the Declaration of Independence, the first address of the first president, and the constitution of the Union of Burma. When the split in the AFPFL developed, Ne Win cautioned those officers who were closely associated with political leaders in both factions of the divided governing party that their first duty was loyalty to the constitution and they should not take sides. He also called upon the political leaders to settle their differences within the framework of the constitution and not to involve military personnel in political quarrels.

Under the caretaker government the ideological development of the military advanced a step further with the publication of a statement on national ideology and the role of the armed services. The document set forth three objectives: restoration of peace and the rule of law, consolidation of democracy, and establishment of a socialist economy. "To establish a socialist economy, democracy is prerequisite. For democracy to flourish, law and order is essential."[23]

The keynote of the caretaker government was legality and constitutionalism. The general proved his devotion to the letter of the constitution by resigning his office when he found he could not complete his task within the six months a nonmember of parliament was allowed to serve in the government. Only after the constitution was amended did he consent to resume office.

The caretaker government was composed of distinguished civilians, drawn mainly from the civil service. The cabinet was small, with a few members holding several portfolios. In each ministry, military officers held important posts, and they often were the real decision makers in the government.

Ne Win sought to unify the administration and tighten the links in its hierarchy. At the center he placed the Ministry of National Planning. With himself as its head and Brigadier Aung Gyi as chairman of its key committee, Budget Allocation Supervision (BAS), he was able to gain better control over the economic life of the nation and plan and coordinate the policies of his government. The BAS played a similar role to that of the Economic and Social

23. "The National Ideology and the Role of the Defense Services," in Government of the Union of Burma, Ministry of Information, *Is Trust Vindicated?* (Rangoon: Director of Information, 1960), p. 536.

Board in the previous government, but had greater power to enforce decisions through budgetary control.

In its effort to deal more effectively with insurgency and lawlessness in the countryside, the caretaker government formed security and administrative committees composed of representatives from the army, police, and administration to coordinate and cooperate in establishing or restoring law and order. In the states located on the nation's frontiers, the government recreated a form of administration used originally by the British. The Frontier Areas Administration assumed direct jurisdiction over remote border areas and took responsibility for security and improvement in services to the peoples in those areas. As a result of these changes a more centralized administration was developed throughout the nation, and internal security was improved. At the same time, control by the states over their own territories was weakened, and their peoples were tied more closely to Rangoon.

One of the most radical acts pursued by the caretaker government was the democratization of the states. The Panglong Agreement of 1947 had allowed the frontier peoples to govern themselves along traditional lines, with little or no interference from Rangoon. The local chiefs and princes retained their privileges and positions and held all the seats allotted to their states in the Chamber of Nationalities. The caretaker regime brought pressure on the chiefs in the Shan and Kayah states to surrender these historic rights and transfer administration to elected leaders. The chiefs agreed to surrender their privileges and rights in exchange for a cash settlement and the retention of some minor titles and rights. A constitutional amendment, passed in 1959, confirmed these changes and was hailed as an important step in the democratization of the frontier areas. But the change did not bring peace to these troubled states. Some of the deposed chiefs became insurgents, and the newly emerging popular leaders who were dependent upon the caretaker government for financial and other support did not become a real alternative to the traditional leaders. Thus, a move to foster popular rule had the immediate effect of broadening and increasing national disunity.

The caretaker government sought to bring down prices and to stimulate production and export. In place of licensing imports by private traders, as had been the practice in the past, the government entered into joint ventures with local Burmese businessmen and private firms that became the major importers and exporters of the nation. Through the Defense Services Institute—created in 1951 to provide the armed forces with consumer goods at reasonable prices—the military leaders enlarged the government's role in various aspects of commerce and economic development. During the period of the caretaker government, the DSI became the major commercial institution of the nation, involved in shipping, banking, construction, transport, hotel keeping, and a variety of other businesses and services.[24] Finally, a portion of the export trade in rice, rubber, cotton, and teak was opened to private traders, thus reversing the socialist trend encouraged by previous governments.

The caretaker government's program of national cleanliness and order received a great deal of attention. Citizens and soldiers alike joined in campaigns to clean up Rangoon and the other cities and towns. Squatters were removed and relocated in new towns erected on the edges of the cities. Heavy fines and jail sentences were imposed on those who littered and obstructed the government in the execution of the law.

The caretaker government lacked compassion, its leaders were direct and legalistic rather than indirect and moralistic, and its administration was firm and centralized. This was a new experience for the Burmese; they reacted by returning U Nu as prime minister and by casting an overwhelming vote against his rivals who promised to continue the work and style of the caretaker government.

24. Government of Burma, *Is Trust Vindicated?*, pp. 223–250.

4 | Military Rule in Burma: First Phase, 1962–1974

The military rule effected by the coup of March 2, 1962, was expected to last for a short time only; the people were told that its purpose was solely to preserve the Union, restore order and harmony in the society, and solve some of the economic problems that had developed and multiplied over the previous two years. The assumption that military rule would be temporary began to erode, however, as the new rulers—the Revolutionary Council—initiated and pursued policies with long-term goals. A month after the coup, Brigadier Sein Win characterized the military's seizure of power as the second half of a revolution that began with the fight for independence; now the army's task was to transform the society to socialism.[1] The coup leaders said of themselves, "We are just Burmese revolutionaries and socialists who are keeping pace with history."[2]

The Ideology of the Revolution

From the outset the coup leaders never seemed to doubt the legitimacy of their actions. Their publications and speeches demonstrated their belief in the right of the military to intervene and alter the government in the time of national crisis. From as far back as World War II, the army viewed itself as the driving force in the popular struggle for independence; the commanders had made

---

1. *Burma Weekly Bulletin*, 10, no. 49 (April 5, 1962), 417.
2. Government of Burma, Burma Socialist Program Party, *The System of Correlation of Man and His Environment* (Rangoon: Burma Socialist Program Party, 1963), p. 35 (hereafter cited as *SCME*).

the decision on the eve of the end of the war that Aung San should leave the military and assume the leadership of the political struggle for independence.[3] From that period, the army felt it had a continuous stake in the survival of the Union and the realization of the goals of the nationalist movement. In order to unite with the people and inform them where and how the military intended to lead the revolution, the coup leaders wrote a new ideology that would become their blueprint. This ideology is contained in two documents—*The Burmese Way to Socialism (BWS)* and *The System of Correlation of Man and His Environment (SCME)*; both were published during the first year of military rule.[4] They represented a new stage in the development and formulation of the military's concept of a national ideology. The armed services had promulgated a statement in 1959 on national ideology and the armed forces (see Chapter 3). At that time their priorities were to restore peace and the rule of law, to implant democracy, and to establish a socialist economy. In the *BSW*, the military's social theorists altered these priorities by declaring that both the economic and political systems must be altered before the nation's other problems could be tackled.

According to the *SCME*, the ideology of the Revolutionary Council rests on three basic principles: change, revolution, and socialism. It draws its ideas from a variety of contradictory sources: the Burmese Buddhist tradition, Marxism, socialism, humanism, and pragmatism. The *SCME* blends moral pronouncements, abstract generalizations, and utopian goals. Like Buddhism, it is based on the assumption that all things are subject to the law of impermanence and change. Change, it argues, takes many forms and is neither incremental nor dialectic. It varies in quantity and quality. As long as the changes alter things in only a limited way they may be considered as evolutionary; however, as the tempo quickens and the degree of change increases, they become revolu-

---

3. Ba Than, *The Roots of the Revolution* (Rangoon: Guardian, 1962), p. 59.
4. Government of Burma, Revolutionary Council, *The Burmese Way to Socialism: The Policy Declaration of the Revolutionary Council* (Rangoon: Ministry of Information, 1962) (hereafter cited as *BWS*), appeared on April 30, 1962, and *SCME* on January 18, 1963.

tionary. Social revolution is "an effect and not a cause; whereas the evolutionary process is the cause of that revolutionary change."[5]

While change, most frequently, is involuntary, it can be induced and directed by human action. Man is the mover; he also is the center of all things. "When the system of economic relations for a given age no longer serves the interests of his society, man thinks of, searches for and endeavors to establish new systems which can better serve his interests."[6]

According to the *SCME*, man's nature is dual—egocentric and altruistic. Man strives for freedom in order to fulfill himself; at the same time, his empathy and concern for others leads him to identify and work with his fellow men to achieve their common objectives. The military leaders seized power, according to the *SCME*, to transform society and improve the condition of the working people. They believed they were accelerating the rate and quality of change to a revolutionary level.

Man's nature, the military social theorists argued, has a propensity for evil as well as for good. "*Aware as we are of such human frailties* we must make our way of life a living reality, i.e., a *socialist way of democratic life* that can constantly check and control this evil tendency to lapse. Only then can every one have the right of using his own creative labor and initiative."[7] Socialism, according to the Burmese, is a necessary form of social control to restrict the unbridled freedom of individual man and channel his energy and effort along socially useful and constructive paths.

The socialist democracy envisaged by the military thinkers "includes the unity of the *will and initiative* of the individual man and group on the one hand and the *centralized guidance* of society on the other."[8] Democratic centralism and individual freedom, therefore, are compatible and when combined produce a progressive and prosperous society. Only when the stomach is full, these theorists argue, will there be wholesome morality.

5. According to *SCME*, "when an evolutionary process reaches a certain condition, point or stage, it passes into *revolution*—a form of fundamental and entire change of dynamic momentum; historians call such changes *social revolutions*" (see p. 17).
6. *Ibid.*, pp. 10–11.
7. *Ibid.*, pp. 28–29.
8. *Ibid.*, p. 31.

Society is defined as more than a collection of individuals—it is the interaction of people in a particular way. That way is determined by the productive forces—the interaction between the "spiritual life" (man's imagination and creativity), the "material life" (the instruments of production created by man), and the productive relationship. The latter, according to the *SCME*, means the mutual relationship between men as defined by their legal codes, traditions, and customs. Man inherited the social system of the previous generation and "by his own creative effort changes it as he deems to be good." History is the record of man's movement from one epoch to the next. The socialist thinkers of the armed forces did not see this as an inevitable development or a continuous process; nor did they see social change as the result of a dialectical process; they used such terms and concepts as "ruling class," "exploitation," "social antagonism between classes," and "violence" as possible characteristics of society as it passed from one epoch to another. They talked about class struggle and saw the march of social history in the West as evidence marking social movement from one epoch to another. They neither took note of Marx's concept of an Asiatic mode of production nor developed a theory of class struggle and changing social systems based on Asian or Burmese experience.[9]

Socialism, as espoused by Burma's military thinkers, is utopian in its goals. A socialist system, they argue, is based on justice; it "is a prosperous and affluent society free from exploitation or oppression of man by man, where there is no profiteering, . . . no class antagonism that threatens human welfare and where man's physical well-being and happiness are assured."[10] The published documents are vague about how these goals are to be realized. All that is certain is that there is a Burmese way to socialism, a guide to action that is flexible and tentative. Awareness of the goals allows the measurement of progress along the Burmese way and, if necessary, alteration of the course. In economic terms, Burma's socialist future will see production and ownership in the people's hands,

9. For a discussion and application of Marx's Asiatic mode of production to Burmese history, see Khin Maung Kyi and Daw Tin Tin, *Administrative Patterns in Historical Burma* (Singapore: Institute of Southeast Asian Studies, 1973).

10. *SCME*, p. 21.

rather than in those of a few individuals or a narrow social class. The state, either directly or through cooperative societies or collective unions, will manage the economy for the people. How exactly this will be done and in what proportion each will act is not stated in the two documents.

The military theorists employ a dialectical method, but do not define it in conventional Marxist terms. They employ it to mean "a middleway of practice which is free from both the left and the right deviation."[11] It is also defined as the "art of scientific approach to the phenomena of nature and society. It is an art and science of making a systematic and comprehensive study of the contradictions in nature and society . . . and putting them to good use."[12] Finally, it permits the systematic uniting of the "positive potentialities of each opposite by a method which ensures progress; to study the features and forms of such unity and put them to positive use."[13] Implicit in these definitions is a concept of progress— movement from a lesser to a greater complexity resulting in social improvement.

The *SCME* indicates that the theories and concepts of the Burmese military thinkers follow no particular school of socialist thought. Rather, they have sought to blend traditional Burmese ideas with popular Western concepts that are attractive to those who, like the leaders themselves, grew up under capitalism and colonialism and rejected both because of their negative impact upon Burma. The ideology provides them with a theoretical justification for changing the economy and polity of Burma in a direction they feel is more in keeping with Burmese traditions. By advocating socialism, they could unite with the anticapitalist sentiments of most of the newly independent nations of Asia and Africa.

The Burmese Way to Socialism is less theoretical than the *SCME*, focusing on the approach to be taken in transforming Burma. Its immediate economic goal is to expand production so that the general standard of living can rise, unemployment can disappear, and everyone will be assured of a means of livelihood. To gain these objectives, agriculture, industrial production, distribution, com-

11. *Ibid.*, p. 29.
12. *Ibid.*
13. *Ibid.*, p. 30.

munications, and external trade will be nationalized in various ways. During the transitional period, state ownership will form the main basis of the economy. During this period, however, there will also be a place and a need for private capital and enterprise; but these will be in Burmese hands and reasonably restricted. After socialism is attained, private capitalists will be assigned new tasks. All individuals will contribute according to their ability and will receive according to the quality and quantity of their work. Neither the transitional nor the new society will be egalitarian because men differ both physically and mentally; the aim of the government will be to narrow the gap between the rich and the poor.

To realize these socioeconomic goals the political system must be altered during the transitional period. A socialist democracy will replace parliamentary democracy because the latter failed to produce a truly socialist society. Under the new system, democratic centralism must be introduced and must respond to existing conditions and ever-changing circumstances by being flexible and nondogmatic.

During the phase of military rule, the people must begin to change—they must be re-educated. The guiding moral principles of this new education will be the following: human dignity is derived from one's own labor, and every religion and culture teaches the moral truth; the educational curriculum must be reorganized to emphasize science and moral training; basic education is open to all; higher education is open only to those with promise and potential.

The immediate objectives outlined in the *BWS* included the rebuilding of the administrative structure and the reordering of economic priorities. Because the existent bureaucratic machine is effete and a stumbling block in the path of change, the *BWS* stated that it must be reformed so it can contribute to the conversion of society. The modernization of agriculture and the building or expansion of industries—which are geared to the nation's resources and capabilities—will be given first priority in the allocation of new resources.

The new Burma, like the old, will incorporate all the indigenous peoples in its territory. In the new Burma, unity and fraternity between ethnic and religious groups and progress for all of them are the fundamental goals. As everyone has a place in the new society, the right of everyone freely to profess and practice his religion is recognized.

From the outset, Burmese as well as foreign commentators misunderstood or confused the ideology with various schools of socialism and communism found in the leftist tradition. In order to differentiate themselves from any other existing school of thought and to emphasize their unique approach, the leaders of the new Burma Socialist Program Party issued a pamphlet in 1964 that set forth the specific differences between their ideology and that of any other found in or outside of Burma.[14] The document emphasized five specific characteristics that had been explicit in the Burmese ideological statements. First, their ideas came from several sources, both Marxist and non-Marxist; second, the *BWS* recognized freedom of conscience and religion; third, the party was not the leader of a single class, but rather the vanguard of all the people except those who exploited others; fourth, the leadership of the party and society belonged to the working people regardless of race or religion; fifth, the Burmese beliefs were not based on a theory of inevitable progress—either unilinear or dialectic—but on the idea of change as a constant in all material and nonmaterial things, and men and society could progress or regress depending on their own ideas and endeavors. Although the Burmese leaders were satisfied that they had clarified the basic tenets of their doctrine, foreign commentators of both the left and right could link ideas and phrases in the Burmese ideological statements with almost any school in the socialist tradition.

Many of the socialist ideas expounded by the military ideologues were not new to Burma. Socialism, as noted earlier, was one of the goals of the first Burmese constitution and of the coalition of parties and groups in the original AFPFL. U Ba Swe, the secretary general of the Burma Socialist party, argued, as early as 1951, that Burma was in "an era of revolution," which he defined "as building up a Burmese socialist structure as a haven for workers and peasants." If Marxism was to be Burma's guide to action, then Ba Swe

14. Government of Burma, *The Specific Characteristics of the Burma Socialist Program Party* (Rangoon: Burma Socialist Program Party, 1964).

declared that "it must be adapted to suit our own surroundings." And in his effort to harmonzie Marxism and Buddhism, he went well beyond the subtle association found in the *SCME* and *BWS* when he proclaimed, "Marxist theory is not antagonistic to Buddhist philosophy. The two are . . . not merely similar. In fact they are the same in concept."[15] Ba Swe differed from the military theorists in this belief that socialism could be attained under democracy without an intervening period of dictatorship by pursuing five parallel aims: democratization of the administration; socialization of the economy in stages consistent with the nation's human talent and natural resources; mass free education from kindergarten through university; national health programs; and social security for all. "We must devise a way of life which will combine full political rights, economic security and a high standard of living with spiritual uplift and morality. . . . Socialism in Burma must be fully harmonized with the religious beliefs and cultural background and heritage of the people."[16]

Though vague and incomplete, the military theorists' ideas were part of a continuum in the growth of a Burmese socialist tradition. They provide a frame of reference for analyzing Burma's development under military rule and a rationale for the decisions and priorities of the men in power since 1962.

Political Institutions under the Military

The coup government neither replaced nor suspended the constitution, which technically remained operative in those areas where the government took no specific action.[17] Following the coup, all power was assumed by the Revolutionary Council. The council, in turn, conferred all legislative, executive, and judicial power on its chairman, General Ne Win. In addition, it decreed that in all existing laws, "Chairman of the Revolutionary Council" should be substituted for "President of the Union" and "Prime

15. Ba Swe, *The Burmese Revolution* (Rangoon: Information Department, 1952), pp. 10, 14, 17.
16. Economic and Social Board, *Our Goal and Our Interim Program* (Rangoon: Superintendent, Government Printing and Stationery, 1953), p. 1.
17. *Burma Weekly Bulletin*, 10, no. 46 (March 15, 1962), 396.

Minister"; and "Revolutionary Council" for the word "Minister."[18]
The RC dissolved parliament on March 3. The Supreme and High
courts were replaced by a new single Chief Court of Burma which,
a decade later—March 16, 1972—was renamed the Supreme
Court. These new institutions, together with others that will be
discussed below, conformed to no predetermined pattern, but
were created on an ad hoc basis. Once established, they remained
relatively unchanged throughout the period 1962 to 1974. If one
organizing principle underlay the political institutions created by
the military, it was that authority would be centralized at the top
and would extend to all the people.

The Revolutionary Council and the Government of Burma

The RC originated with the coup and was composed of seven-
teen senior military officers. During this first phase of military rule,
ten of the original members were replaced because of death, dis-
missal, or resignation. In 1971, following the first congress of the
Burma Socialist Program Party (Lanzin), which will be discussed
below, the council was formally reconstituted and its membership
reduced to fifteen including, for the first time, four civilians.

Under General Ne Win, the RC was essentially a small military
oligarchy, most of whose members had served together in the
armed forces since World War II and also in the caretaker government of 1958–1960. All had been close associates of General Ne
Win and were well known to one another (see Table 2). The public
record indicates that the general relied upon only two or three of
his associates to advise him on major policy decisions; when he went
abroad—which he did frequently from the beginning—he left the
affairs of state in the hands of his trusted lieutenants with no
apparent fear of being displaced. Initially, Brigadiers Aung Gyi
and Tin Pe were his closest confidants. But, by the end of the first
year of military rule, a crisis had arisen over the pace and direction
of socialism in Burma. As a result of this crisis, Aung Gyi resigned
from the RC and retired from the military, and Tin Pe became the
major influence upon the general for the next five years. In 1968

18. *Ibid.*, p. 396; *Nation*, March 13, 31, 1962.

Table 2. Revolutionary Council

Members	Original posting in Burma army, 1945	Participants in caretaker government, 1958–1962	Members of original RC, 1962	Members of revised RC, 7/9/71	Other information
Gen. Ne Win	4th Burifs	Prime Minister	Chairman	Chairman	Retired army Apr. 1972
Brig. Aung Gyi	4th Burifs	Ministry Natl. Plan.	Member		Resigned 1963, arrested, released
Comm. Than Pe		Ministry Natl. Plan.	Member		Died in office 1962
Brig. T. Clift		UBA/Ministry Transport	Member		Resigned 1964, went to Thailand
Brig. Tin Pe	4th Burifs	Min. Pub. Works & Mines	Member		Resigned 1968
Brig. San Yu			Member	Member	Prom. to gen. 1972
Brig. Sein Win	3d Burifs	Natl. Housing Board	Member	Member	Retired army 1972
Col. Thaung Kyi	3d Burifs		Member	Member	
Col. Kyi Maung	5th Burifs	Min. Agri./Forest & STB	Member		Resigned 1963
Col. Maung Shwe			Member	Member	Retired army 1972, arrested 1972
Col. Than Sein			Member	Member	Retired army
Col. Kyaw Soe	4th Burifs	Min. Transport & IWTB	Member	Member	Retired army
Col. Saw Myint	5th Burifs	Off. of P.M. & Frontier Area Adm.	Member		Arrested 1964, life sentence
Col. Chit Myaing	3d Burifs	Dir. Min. Immigration Trade Dev. Corp. & Min. Trade	Member		Dismissed 1964, arrested, released
Col. Khin Myo			Member		Dismissed 1965
Col. Hla Han			Member	Member	Retired army 1972
Col. Tan Yu Saing			Member		Resigned 1968
Brig. Thaung Dan				Member	Appt. 9/12/64
Col. Maung Lwin				Member	Appt. 9/12/64
Col. Tin U	5th Burifs			Member	Appt. 9/12/64, prom. to brig.
U Ba Nyein				Member	Civilian, formerly of BCS
Dr. Maung Maung				Member	Civilian, former chief justice
Mahn Tha Myaing				Member	Civilian
U Ba Nyein				Member	Civilian

Abbreviations are as follows: Union of Burma Airways (UBA); State Timber Board (STB); Inland Water Transport Board (IWTB); Prime Minister (PM); Burmese Civil Service (BCS).

Persons with military titles for whom a posting is not given in the first column were commissioned after 1945.

the many economic failures resulting from the socialist policies of Tin Pe led to his resignation and that of his brother-in-law, Colonel Tan Yu Saing. From then until the second phase of military rule in 1974, Brigadier San Yu, who was promoted to the rank of general in 1972, became Ne Win's most trusted subordinate. While San Yu concentrated upon political, administrative, and military matters, General Ne Win relied upon a civilian, U Ba Nyein—a former adviser to Tin Pe—for economic advice. Ba Nyein became a member of the RC in 1971 and a year later was appointed minister for cooperatives. In 1973 his influence declined when Ne Win decided to shift the direction of the economy toward a more moderate course.

Although the RC permitted very little information to be published about its methods of operations and decision making, the civilian elite assumed that Ne Win was the key figure in the council; that no decision was taken against his will; and that once he had made up his mind, debate was ended and implementation began. There are no indications of any serious challenges to his leadership within the council.

Unrestricted by the challenges that could have been posed by a constitution, a legislature, or an electorate, the RC governed by decree and proclamation. All its pronouncements had the force of law and remained in effect until withdrawn or replaced.

The line between the RC and the government was undefined. That the words "Member of the RC" was substituted for the word "minister," suggested that the power to be exercised by the member of the RC was actual rather than symbolic. Initially, the RC designated no prime minister; the government consisted of eight members, six drawn from the RC, one civilian—responsible for four ministries—and a military officer from outside the circle of leaders in the RC (see Table 3). The key Ministry of Defense was in the hands of General Ne Win. All members of government were responsible for more than one ministry and, therefore, depended upon the Secretariat and bureaucracy to do most of the administrative work. This pattern persisted through most of this phase of military rule. In 1971, following the first congress of the Burma Socialist Program Party, the formal government assumed a more traditional facade. But, although its name was changed to the

Name	Ministries held March 3, 1962	Ministries held July 15, 1971	Ministries held April 20, 1972
Gen. Ne Win	Defense, Finance & Revenue, Judicial	Prime Minister, Defense	Prime Minister
Brig. Aung Gyi	Trade Develop., Industries		
Brig. Tin Pe	Agri. & Forests, Commodities, Distribution & Cooperatives		
Comm. Than Pe	Education, Health		
U Thi Han	Foreign Aff., Housing, Mines, Labor		Foreign Aff.
Col. Kyaw Soe	Home Aff., Immigration	Home Aff., Judicial, Democratization of Local Bodies, Religious Aff., Immigration, Nationalities, Registration & Census	
Col. Saw Myint	Information, Culture		
Lt. Col. Ba Ni	Transport & Communications		
Brig. San Yu		Dep. P.M., Finance & Revenue, Natl. Planning	Dep. P.M., Defense
Brig. Sein Win		Pub. Works & Housing	Construction
Col. Thaung Kyi		Agri. & Forests, Land Natl.	Agri. & Forests
Col. Maung Shwe*		Industries, Labor	Indust., Labor
Col. Than Sein		Transportation, Communications	Transp., Comm.
Col. Hla Han		Foreign Aff., Education, Health	Education, Health
Brig. Thaung Dan		Information, Culture, Relief Rehabilitation, Natl. Solidarity, Social Welfare	Information, Culture, Social Welfare
Col. Maung Lwin		Trade, Cooperatives	Trade
Comm. Thaung Tin		Mines	Mines
Dr. Maung Maung			Judicial Aff.
U Ba Nyein			Cooperatives
U Sein Mya*			Home, Religion
U Lwin			Planning, Finance

* Arrested in 1972 and dismissed; both convicted of corruption.

Military command change announced on April 20, 1972

Brig. San Yu			Prom. to gen., chief of staff
Col. Tin U			Prom. to brig., vice chief of staff

Note: The three dates are those on which the Revolutionary Council officially organized or reorganized the government.

Government of the Union of Burma and its leader, Ne Win, was designated prime minister, there were few personnel changes. General Ne Win was still in charge of defense and all the ministries were under military officers, including one senior officer from outside the RC. In September 1971, Brigadier San Yu's rise within the RC and the government was confirmed by his appointment as deputy prime minister.

In April 1972, the retirement of twenty senior officers from the armed forces—including Ne Win—gave the government the appearance of being in civilian hands, as military titles were dropped in favor of traditional civilian prefixes. The government now consisted of U Ne Win and nine retired officers, together with three senior officers still in uniform and two genuine civilians, U Ba Nyein, discussed above, and Dr. Maung Maung, who became minister of justice. In one other important change, San Yu was promoted to general and given control of the Ministry of Defense while still retaining his post as deputy prime minister. This move clarified Ne Win's plans for succession and suggested the degree of trust he had in the man he had designated as his successor. It also indicated that a continuing close linkage between the armed forces and the government was anticipated, whether the members wore *gaungbaungs* (traditional headwear for Burmese male civilians) or military braid.

Accountable to no legislature or electorate, the small circle of men who exercised executive power were responsible only to themselves or, more precisely, to Ne Win. Despite the long personal friendship between the members of the ruling oligarchy, Ne Win did not hesitate to drop an individual from either the governing group or the military when disputes arose, as was evident in the removal of Aung Gyi in 1963 and of Saw Myint a year later. In these and other instances, little or no information was given on why the men were dismissed.

Informed sources in Rangoon suggested that ministries were not active sources of policy input, but were merely administrative units responsible for carrying out RC directives. The Secretariat, a symbol from the colonial past, continued to function as the real administrative body until it was decreed out of existence on March 15, 1972. According to Proclamation 97, which brought about the change, the powers and duties formerly exercised by the Secretariat passed to the ministers concerned. One object of the reform was to clarify the lines of responsibility between the minister and his office and to put him in direct contact with departments, boards, and corporations under his authority. Although the reform, on paper, looked like a major step forward, evidence as to positive results is difficult to discern.

The Security and Administrative Councils and the Administrative Process

Under the military, the Security and Administration Councils were the key organizations for unifying the national administration.[19] Each council was composed of representatives of the civil administration, the local police, and the military commander in the area. The RC created a hierarchy of the SACs both in Burma proper, through the Security and Administration Central Committee in Rangoon down to the division, district, township, and village, and in the states where they descended through the state supreme council down a parallel line to the village level. At the divisional and state levels, the divisional army commander served as chairman. Elsewhere in the hierarchy a civilian could and occasionally did serve as chairman. Thus the country was tightly linked through the monolithic structure of committees and the participation of the military at all levels of government between the RC and the village. In 1972, when the Secretariat was abolished, membership of the SACs was broadened by adding representatives from the Burma Socialist Program Party and the People's Peasants and People's Workers councils. Following the announcement of this change the daily *Guardian* editorialized that with the enlarged membership, "the SACs are bound to become more dynamic . . . they will be able to do better in paving the way to socialist democracy."[20]

The initial purpose of the councils was to improve law and order

19. The SACs came into effect on May 9, 1962; originated by the caretaker government in 1958–1960. When U Nu and the Pyidaungsu party assumed power following the 1960 election, the councils were abandoned. In April 1961, Dr. E Maung, the acting home minister, created law and order committees with roughly the same composition as the earlier councils, but with less power and facilities. The law and order committees helped arrest the growing insecurity in the countryside. See *Burma Weekly Bulletin*, 9, no. 52 (April 27, 1961), 463.

20. March 17, 1972.

throughout the land. According to Colonel Kyaw Soe, speaking at a SAC training course, the councils were to regard themselves as responsible to the people; they should listen to the people and help to pave the way for creation of a socialist society. They were transitional bodies for translating government policy into reality until such time as elected public administrative bodies come into existence.[21] The addition of popular representatives could be seen as an advance toward that goal.

When the SACs were inaugurated an administrative system already existed with its center at the Secretariat in Rangoon and its hierarchy descending through the division to the village. The key official in this system was the subdivisional or district officer who had executive, legislative, and judicial power. During the colonial period, he had been the most powerful official with whom the peasant was likely to come into contact. The introduction of the SACs by the military government severely curbed the powers of the district officer; the reforms of 1972 eliminated the position. This action was designed to bring local government into closer contact with the administration at the divisional and the national levels.

Elimination of the Secretariat at the top and the district officer near the bottom tied the state administrative hierarchy directly to the RC; the military rulers achieved both greater centralization and control of the national government and the introduction of a degree of popular participation in local administration.

The Judicial System

The military leaders of Burma described their reorganization of the judicial system as a humanizing process. They abolished the Supreme and High courts on March 31, 1962, replacing them by a single new Chief Court of Burma. This change reflected their conviction that the old courts served the interests of the wealthy

21. *Guardian* (daily), October 22, 1971; in 1965, Colonel Tin U said that the purpose of the SACs was to protect the interests of the working people; to improve the lot of the workers and peasants in the shortest time; to protect the productive forces, equipment, machinery, workers, and peasants; and to bring harmony and unity under the Burma Socialist Program Party. See *Guardian* (daily), August 17, 1965.

and the privileged.[22] The new court consisted of six judges; as the court of final appeal, it was authorized to exercise the powers and the functions of its two predecessors.[23] Over the years nearly all the original members were replaced. Dr. Maung Maung, journalist, writer, and scholar-lawyer, became a member in 1962 and shortly thereafter replaced U Bo Gyi as chief justice. In 1971 the RC changed the court's name to the Supreme Court and increased its membership to seven.

In an attempt to deal more quickly and effectively with acts of insurrection, crimes against public safety, and those endangering life, property, culture, and national economy, the RC created a new set of Special Crimes courts. Each of these new courts consisted of three members, one of whom "must have some legal training." These courts had power to impose the death penalty, exile, and ordinary imprisonment, but all sentences were subject to review by a new confirming authority and, in the case of extreme penalty, by the Chief Court.[24]

An objective of the RC in altering the court system was to achieve uniformity in the administration of justice throughout the Union. Achievement of this goal was hindered because standards differed in Burma proper and in the states. The military rulers argued that "where justice is dispensed with according to local usage and custom," the government's goal should be "to get these areas . . . eventually to adopt the same set of laws and courts as are functioning in Burma proper."[25] The government worked with officials in the states to try to create a uniform pattern of justice.

22. For a critique of the Supreme and High courts under the 1947 constitution, see Government of Burma, Burma Socialist Program Party, *Address Delivered by General Ne Win, Chairman of the Burma Socialist Program Party at the Opening of the Fourth Party Seminar on 6th November, 1969* (Rangoon: Burma Socialist Program Party, Central Press, 1969), pp. 14ff.

23. *Guardian* (daily), March 31, 1962. The amalgamation of the two courts created some technical problems. Formerly, one could appeal a High Court ruling in the Supreme Court. With the creation of the new Chief Court, the court's decisions were appealable to itself, if the decisions were made by one or two of the judges sitting as the court. See "Union Judiciary Act Amending Law, 1962," in *Forward*, 1, no. 9 (December 7, 1962), 22.

24. *Guardian* (daily), July 11, 1962.

25. Government of Burma, Director of Information, *Burma: Administrative and Social Affairs, 1962–1963* (Rangoon: Director of Information, 1965), p. 37.

One of the many problems facing the military rulers was the contradiction between the emphasis upon the rights and duties of the individual under common law as inherited from the British and the responsibilities and objectives of a socialist system. Despite the government's effort to create local people's courts, appeals courts, and other administrative judicial bodies with nonlegalists as members, the basic legal structure remained professional and bureaucratic. The reforms of March 16, 1972, established a new hierarchy of courts and jurisdictions closer in form to those of the colonial past than to the ideals of the socialist future.[26]

Union-State Relations

Brigadier Aung Gyi, speaking for the RC shortly after the coup, said that one of the main reasons for the military's seizure of power was to prevent the breakup of the Union. Leaders among the indigenous minorities, he said, sought greater autonomy or even secession, some threatening open revolt if their demands were not met. In addition, some of the feudal lords wanted a return to feudal rule, and he claimed there was evidence of misuse of state money by these leaders. The military feared that U Nu might accede to some or all of the minorities' demands at the federal seminar in progress at the time. To avert this possibility the military seized and imprisoned all suspected minority leaders especially from the Shans.[27]

After removing the hereditary leaders, the military moved quickly to bring the Shan and other states under more direct control by Rangoon. They abolished the elected state councils and the appointed head-ministers of state, replacing them with centrally appointed state supreme councils composed of local civilian leaders and military commanders. Among the civilian appointees were several politically independent leaders as well as a few, such as Dr. Saw Hla Tun in the Karen State, who had strong party connections in the old regime. Each new supreme council established its

26. U Hla Aung, "The Common Law in Burma," *Guardian* (daily), April 10, 1971; for a discussion of the reforms, see *Guardian* (daily), March 25. 1972.

27. *Guardian* (daily), March 10, 1962. Among those arrested on the night of the coup was Sao Shwe Taike, the first president of the Union of Burma. In the course of his arrest, his son resisted and was killed, the only known casualty of the coup.

headquarters within the state and was allowed to develop its own administrative structure. A States Liaison Committee in Rangoon was to act as an intermediary between the central and the state governments; however, on occasion the chairman of the state supreme councils dealt directly with the RC. Creation of the Security and Administration Councils in Burma proper and in the states allowed the coup leaders to tighten their hold over administration in the several states more directly under the authority of Rangoon than ever in the past.

During this period, the central government drew up a single national budget, including the requests from the states. Monies were allocated for programs that fit the needs of the nation and were not given as grants to the states on the basis of their size and importance.[28]

Liberty under the Military

Although the coup leaders were determined to concentrate power in their own hands, initially they were equally concerned that the individual appear to retain a limited area of privacy. With regard to religious freedom, they did not repeal laws that furthered Buddhist interests, but moved more indirectly, such as by ending observance of the Buddhist sabbath days and lifting the ban on slaughter of cattle in order to increase the food supply and to lower prices. The government also de-emphasized religious observances that were a drain on the national treasury and for one year banned all foreign religious pilgrimages.[29]

Although some measures were directed against non-Buddhist religious groups, the military rulers were most intent on restraining the Buddhists. In 1962, for example, they ordered the monks to register; and when a large portion of the *sangha* refused and tried to take their case to the people, the government responded by repealing the three basic laws pertaining to religion passed in the

28. The budget process under the 1947 constitution was not systematic. Each state drew up its own and adjusted its expenditures according to the lump sum allotted to it. State budgets were appended to the budget of the Union of Burma and together they were considered the national budget.

29. *Nation*, March 23, 1962. The ruling affected Muslims and Hindus more than Buddhists and Christians.

early 1950s. In March 1965 a government-supported All Sangha Conference drew up a constitution for an All Buddha Sasana Sangha Organization with an identification card and a program for reforming religious education. Several Buddhist monasteries and many individual monks rejected the conference and denounced its results, particularly registration of individual monks. After a month of violent protest the government moved forcefully, arresting ninety-two monks and closing several monasteries. Defending his government's action, General Ne Win used his Worker's Day speech to argue that he and his fellow leaders were not antireligious and that he personally was a good Buddhist. The actions of the government, he said, were necessary to combat the misuse of religion.[30] Outright opposition from the Buddhist clergy ceased after these incidents. In the years that followed, the government organized class, mass, and political organizations, excluded the clergy from direct participation either as voters or as officeholders, and re-established the Ministry of Religious Affairs. Religious freedom was maintained but restricted. Buddhism was treated the same as other religions, and the clergymen of all religious organizations were barred from political participation.

Having imprisoned its potential rivals and persuaded their followers against further interference, the RC permitted the press a limited degree of freedom and retained the rights of public assembly and freedom of speech. None of these rights, however, was to be used against the new regime. When the government viewed reporting as inaccurate or obscene, swift and direct action was taken against the offenders. Despite efforts of the press to police itself, in September 1962 the government promulgated a new law requiring all publishers to register annually. The next year saw the arrest and imprisonment of the editor of the *Nation* and ten political leaders for "hindering the implementation of internal peace."[31] A year later the government created its own news service to which all local papers were required to subscribe and began to publish its own newspapers in Burmese and English. From 1964 to 1969 it gradually absorbed nearly all other Burmese papers or made cer-

---

30. *Forward*, 3, no. 12 (February 1, 1965), 2; *ibid*, 3, no. 19 (May 15, 1965), 14.
31. *Guardian* (daily), April 5, 1962; *New York Times*, August 10, 1963.

tain that those that nominally were independent published only what the government allowed.

The government's control over information was not limited to newspapers. It replaced private and foreign-owned libraries and reading rooms with its own, continued the policy of state-controlled radio, and expanded into the production and distribution of films and written materials. The government thus controlled all media so that only those with shortwave radio could hear news and opinions that differed from the official Burma line.

The RC initially was relatively lenient toward the existing political parties, which were permitted to hold meetings, print newspapers, and propagate their views. Party leaders who were not under arrest were allowed to travel freely and, upon occasion, were consulted by the coup government. Criticism was tolerated provided it was polite, carefully presented, and not intended to cause an uprising. This tolerance was reversed during the second year of military rule. In August 1963 top leaders of the AFPFL and the Pyidaungsu were arrested for their public criticism of a number of government policies, especially the military rulers' effort to make peace with the insurgents and dissidents. From September, the government grew more oppressive, rounding up numerous secondary leaders of the AFPFL, leaders and followers of the NUF, and many prominent figures in leftist organizations. On March 28, 1964, the RC took its final step by banning all political parties except its own Burma Socialist Program Party.

After the coup, freedom of movement in Burma and personal contact with foreigners was seriously curtailed. Visits by foreign tourists and journalists were restricted, and by 1965 their stay in Burma was limited to twenty-four hours in transit between flights. For several years after the coup, Western journalists were barred from residing in Burma and reporting directly on Burmese affairs. These restrictions were relaxed briefly in 1966 before Ne Win's visit to the United States and gradually, after 1969, tourist visas were granted for up to seven days to be spent in limited and specific areas of Burma. Burmese who met with foreign travelers or diplomats had to report immediately to the government on the content of their conversations.

Travel outside the country by Burmese citizens was restricted.

Both to conserve foreign exchange and to control their people, the government made it almost impossible for Burmese to take jobs outside the country or to travel for personal reasons. During the mid-1960s citizens who insisted on leaving Burma had to surrender their passports for letters of identity which made them almost stateless. They had to leave nearly all their personal possessions behind and take with them only a meager amount of money. To go abroad for personal reasons was seen as turning one's back on his country. Internal travel to areas of insurgency or where military rule was under direct challenge was forbidden, and even in government-controlled areas the traveler had to report to local officials.

The elimination of political parties and the severe restriction on civil liberties and freedoms marked the expansion of authoritarian rule and contrasted sharply with political life under constitutional rule.

The Burma Socialist Program Party

Although the Revolutionary Council had a monopoly of power, it needed to win and hold public support. As the representatives of the military—a class that historically was not popular—the council recognized from the beginning that it had to establish contact with the people and win their loyalty if it was to convert its authoritarian rule into a more democratic form.[32] The history of the caretaker government was fresh in the minds of the men who made the 1962 coup. Despite the caretaker government's achievements, in the election that preceded its departure from office in 1960 the party that promised to continue its reforms and techniques was overwhelmingly defeated by the party that disassociated itself from the military and pledged a more humane and less harsh government. The lesson from that experience was not missed by the coup leaders, and in their search for links with the

32. In the section of the *Constitution of the Burma Socialist Program Party* entitled "Origins and Purposes," the authors wrote, "The Revolutionary Council, forged by peculiar and powerful historical forces is revolutionary in essence, but wears the outward garb of a military council. This the RC deems undesirable. The RC believes that the natural leader of the revolution is a revolutionary political party."

people, they saw two existing alternatives, the National Solidarity Association (NSA) and the old political parties.

The NSA was a quasi-political organization established during the caretaker regime as an attempt by the military and nonpolitical leaders in the government to create a national alternative to political parties. As an adjunct to the interim government and under authoritarian military leadership, it failed to attract strong popular support. The NSA continued to exist under the Pyidaungsu government, but did not play a creative and positive role in the nation's political life. The Revolutionary Council leaders made no effort to use the NSA as their political vehicle for fear that to do so would continue their estrangement from the people.

The coup leaders initially chose the alternative provided by the existing political parties. They asked the party leaders voluntarily to amalgamate the existing parties into a new national party under RC leadership. Most NUF leaders quickly agreed, hoping this would give them some power. The Pyidaungsu leaders not under arrest were divided; the AFPFL leaders refused. Faced with this alignment, the RC announced in July 1962 that it was creating a new party to be known as the Burma Socialist Program Party (BSPP), known in Burmese as Lanzin. In making the announcement the council expressed the hope that members of the old parties would be able "to discard their partisan feelings and come closer for unity and understanding through intimate exchange of views."

The BSPP was to be a transitional party under the leadership of the RC, and its purpose was to start the country toward the ideological goals expressed in *The Burmese Way to Socialism*. At this early stage of development it was to be a cadre party with emphasis upon identifying, training, and indoctrinating members who would assist the military rulers in carrying out their programs. The BSPP remained a cadre party until 1971, when it was transformed into a mass national party and given the responsibility of drawing up the new constitution and the opportunity to assume leadership of the nation.

The party was open to all citizens who were eighteen years or older; applicants had to accept the ideology "out of conviction," to be prepared to carry out "unswervingly" all tasks assigned, and to be willing to accept the authority of the party. Each applicant had to be supported by two party members. Since the only founder members were the Revolutionary Council, the coup leaders had picked its members from its most loyal supporters. All candidates were required to serve for at least two years before becoming eligible for full membership. During the initial period, candidates were permitted to resign; after obtaining full membership, they forfeited that right. Although the constitution of the party was silent on the issue, persons who offered themselves for membership were graded initially as candidates—men likely to earn full membership—and sympathizers—men of questionable social and political background and therefore required to prove loyalty to ideas and party discipline.

To transform the idea of a party into a reality, the RC appointed two committees drawn exclusively from its own ranks to create the party units, recruit, screen, and train the candidates and to plan the mass organizations that would be subordinate to the party. The membership of the two committees remained fairly constant throughout the cadre period of the party (see Table 4).

Table 4. Committees of the Burma Socialist Program party

Members	Discipline Committee	Central Organizing Committee
Gen. Ne Win	Chairman	Chairman
Brig. San Yu	Member	Member after Jan. 1965
Brig. Sein Win	Member	
Col. Hla Han	Member	Member after Jan. 1965
Col. Chit Myaing	Member (dropped in 1964)	
Col. Kyaw Soe	Member (added in 1964)	Original member
Brig. Aung Gyi		Original member (dropped Feb. 1963)
Brig. Tin Pe		Original member (dropped in 1968)
Col. Than Sein		Original member
Col. Saw Myint		Original member (dropped in 1964)
Col. Thaung Kyi		Member after Jan. 1965
Col. Maung Shwe		Member after Jan. 1965
Col. Maung Lwin		Member after Jan. 1965

After several months of preparation, applications for party membership were accepted between March 2 and June 30, 1963. In November the party leaders began to announce the names of the successful candidates and the party, technically, sprang to life.

The party's success depended upon the quality and commitment of its cadres. Despite the screening procedure and probationary period, the problem of finding and recruiting good and reliable cadres persisted. The reports of the secretary general and the speeches of General Ne Win at party meetings and conferences gave particular attention to this problem, stating that many recruits were actually party saboteurs, self-seekers, or nonconformists.[33] Despite the military leaders' efforts to rid the party of any whose loyalty was in doubt, its ranks were never fully purified. With recruiting under military control, the bulk of the recruits were drawn from the armed forces and the police. Three years after the party was founded, it had only 20 full members though there were 99,638 candidates and 167,447 sympathizers. The *Report of the Secretary General of 1966* published the first occupational breakdown of cadres, showing that 31 percent of the candidates were drawn from the military and police. Six years later the same two occupational groups provided 33 percent of the candidates and full members combined. More important, however, they provided 58 percent of the full members—more than twice the number of full members drawn from the peasantry and workers combined (see Table 5).

Table 5. Occupations of BSPP members

Occupational background	1966 candidates	Members	1972 candidates	Members
Armed forces	54,028	20	63,537	42,359
Workers	91,999	—	123,098	20,316
Peasants	15,383	—	43,553	8,207
Police	2,875	—	4,644	308
Others	21,662	—	26,025	2,179
Totals	185,947	20	260,857	73,369

33. Government of Burma, Burma Socialist Program Party, *Party Seminar 1965* (Rangoon: Burma Socialist Program Party, 1966), pp. 10ff, 128–141.

Failure to recruit peasants was a particularly vexing problem for the party leaders. In 1966 the secretary general said that this was because recruiting was limited to the towns; the peasants were politically backward and indifferent.[34] During the first phase of military rule this problem was never solved, despite the efforts of the leaders to draw the peasants into their political web via mass organizations or other means.

In 1972, the national population numbered slightly more than 28 million; of that total, the party represented a very narrow elite of 1.2 percent. As nearly one-third of its members and candidates were drawn from the military and police, the remaining members and candidates represented no more than 0.8 percent of the population. Clearly, the military and police were the new political elite, and through the party and its subordinate organizations they are likely to continue dominating the government.

To train the cadre, on July 1, 1963, the party organized a Central School of Political Science at Chawdwingon outside Rangoon. Here the candidates received instruction in basic policy, political thought, economics, politics, organization, and management. The Defense Services also created a political leadership school—Command Inservice Training Courses. Together these schools gave instruction to 44,173 civilians and servicemen. To support the program the party published a variety of papers, journals, and special studies. Despite all this attention to education, the party leaders complained about the poor quality of recruits and their failure to become successful cadres. In 1966 *Report of the Secretary General* it stated that once cadres finished their courses at the Central School, they "puffed up with arrogance thinking they alone were the most learned." They failed to realize, he said, that real learning could come from working with the people.

The structure of the party during its cadre phase—lasting until 1971—was based upon tight central control. At the base was the local unit, which drew its members from the community where it was located. Recruits were selected because of occupation or social background and were organized in functional units, factories, mili-

34. In mid-1969 there were 22,677 peasants among the 257,463 party candidates, as reported in an editorial in the *Guardian*, March 6, 1971. The reasons for the low numbers were the same as those given in 1966.

tary units, administrative organizations, and the like. Above the local and functional units were the township, divisional, and national organizations. All were under the supervision and control of the Central Organizing and Disciplinary committees. At the national level, the party was divided into six divisions, corresponding exactly to the six military commands, which together were divided into fifteen party subdivisions, also corresponding to military commands.[35] Both in structure and composition, the party and the Defense Services were interlocked.

A basic organizational problem arose because all who sought candidate status applied to the party headquarters rather than to a local unit. If accepted they were supposed to be assigned to a local unit, but this did not happen in all cases. As the secretary general noticed in 1966, three years after recruitment began, "Some party members still do not belong to any of the party organs and are detached from the party, alone and isolated, outside the pale of party influence."[36] This problem persisted throughout the cadre period. In July 1971, 102,320 members were still unaffiliated with any local unit.

Among the most important party functions during the cadre stage was to mobilize the nation behind the party's leadership. Mass and class organizations were formed under the control of the Central Organizing Committee. In 1966 departments of this committee were set up to organize Peasants' Affairs, Workers' Affairs, and Mass Affairs councils. During that year work went forward in recruiting peasants and workers for separate organizations, and planning began for the creation of mass organizations, the first being a youth organization. Through either the party or its mass and class organizations, every citizen had a place in the new political order.

Despite the structure of the party, its monopoly of power, and

35. The six commands and fifteen subdivisions were as follows: Eastern Division comprised of Northern Shan, Eastern Shan, Southern Shan, and Kayah; Southeast Division comprised of Kawthoolei; Southwest Division comprised of Tenasserim and Irrawaddy; Central Division comprised of Arakan and Pegu; Rangoon Division comprised of Rangoon; and Northwest Division comprised of Mandalay, Magwe, Chin Special Division, Sagaing, and Kachin.

36. *The Political Report, Submitted by the Secretary General of the Central Organizing Committee of the Lanzin Party, to the 1966 Party Seminar* (mimeo), p. 12.

the absence of open opposition, it failed to attract widespread support. Part of the reason was the government's economic failures; in spite of the government's efforts to re-educate the people to new values and a socialist system, hoarding, black marketing, and other illegal activity developed and thrived. When, in 1971, the government finally stopped trying to halt the black market, it was an open admission of the failure of the RC and the party to transform ideals into social realities.

In 1971, the party transformed itself from a cadre to a mass organization. From June 28 to July 11, 825 delegates and 302 alternates met in Rangoon to carry out the planned changes. The delegates represented a total of 334,226 full and candidate members and 763,133 sympathizers. The party had grown to include 17,559 cells, organized into 2,595 sections in 313 party units. In attendance at this meeting were 532 delegates representing area and functional civilian units and 125 delegates representing military units. The remainder were designated as central delegates. Although the civilian delegates outnumbered the military, they did not take over the control of the new structure elected by the congress.

The congress elected a Central Committee of 150 members and 50 alternates to reorganize the party. Of the total number of full members elected, 118 were drawn from the armed forces while 32 represented the civilians; the alternates were almost evenly divided with the military having a slight edge, 26 to 24.

The Central Committee elected Ne Win as chairman, Brigadier San Yu as secretary general, and Colonel Thaung Kyi as joint secretary general. These men formed the nucleus of the Executive Committee; twelve additional members were elected—eight were granted the status of full members and the remaining four were designated as alternates. Of the eight, only U Ba Nyein was a civilian; the four alternates were all military persons.[37]

The congress also set up several subordinate committees: a Party

37. The elected members of the Executive Committee were: Gen. Ne Win, chairman; Brig. San Yu, secretary general; Col. Thaung Kyi, joint secretary general; Col. Maung Lwin; Col. Maung Shwe; Col. Hla Han; Col. Kyaw Soe; U Ba Nyein; Brig. Thaung Dan; Col. Sein Mya; Col. Maung Lwin; Comm. Thaung Tin; Col. Tin U; Col. Aung Pe; Col. Maung Maung Kya.

Inspection Committee of fifteen full members (four civilians) and five alternates (three civilians) with Brigadier Sein Win as chairman; a new Discipline Committee of eleven full members (one civilian) and four alternates (two civilians) with Dr. Maung Maung as chairman; and a Central Affairs Committee to assist the Executive Committee in formulating policies, with eighty-one members, though only seventy-four were elected.

The day-to-day affairs of the Central and Executive committees were concentrated in the hands of a small Secretariat that included the secretary general, San Yu, the joint secretary general, Colonel Thaung Kyi, and three senior military officers, Lieutenant Colonel Tun Lin, Lieutenant Colonel Kyaw Zaw, and Colonel Than Sein.

One of the most important actions of the Central Committee was its reconstitution of the Revolutionary Council. Although this appeared to place the party above the government, there was in fact no change in power, for the leaders of the Revolutionary Council were merely seeking to give legitimacy to their creation, the BSPP, by placing themselves technically under the party.

The only change made at the lower levels of the party was the declaration that centralism had been replaced by democratic centralism, thus signifying that the members were to participate a bit more fully in the affairs of the party than they had while it was a cadre party.

The highlights of the congress were the opening and closing addresses of the chairman, Ne Win, and the report of the secretary general, San Yu. General Ne Win set the tone of the meeting by indicating three goals for the party—party unity, national unity, and the writing of a new constitution for the nation. This was the first formal mention of a new constitution, and it signaled the nearing of the end of the first phase of military rule. The report of the secretary general concluded by outlining the new tasks of the party; first priority would be given to the drafting of a new constitution. During this final transitional period, the RC would acknowledge the leadership of the party, the Council of Ministers would act like a cabinet and acknowledge the principle of collective responsibility, the administration would be streamlined and the Secretariat abolished, and the policies of the state toward the minorities would be guided by the RC declaration of 1964. The report also called for the formation of mass organizations under the leadership of the party and set as the immediate goal the creation of a youth organization. It also said that there would be no changes in Burma's foreign policy.

For the next two years, the party devoted itself to fulfilling its tasks.

Mass Organizations

The RC sought to create mass and class organizations with the party as their core in order to mobilize the nation behind the military leadership and, in a limited and controlled manner, to involve the people in politics. Dividing the population roughly into peasants and other workers, the government sought to create a separate organization for each group. The larger and more difficult to unite was the peasantry. Beginning within nine months of the coup, the military organized the first of several peasant seminars at Ohndaw. Here the leaders discussed both the technical and particular problems of the participants and the broad ideological goals of the government. In their effort to link the peasants with government, in 1964 the military changed the date of Peasant's Day from January 1 to March 2 to tie the peasant celebration to the anniversary of the military's seizure of power. At a regional seminar in Toungoo, in March 1964, the delegates decided to form peasant councils. The government entrusted this task to the BSPP; a Peasant's Affairs Division of the Central Organizing Committee was created under the leadership of Colonel Thaung Kyi. In 1967 a constitution for the new organization was approved and recruitment began at the village, or basic unit, level. By 1969, two-thirds of the required township councils had been formed, thus permitting the Central People's Peasant Council (CPPC) to be created. By Peasant's Day 1972, there were 263 township councils and organizing committees, 10,116 village PPCs, and over six million members. Because the People's Peasant councils were designed to unite the peasant with the new political order, the leadership at all levels included both elected peasants and government appointees drawn from the party and the bureaucracy. The structure was such that the councils were closely supervised and coordinated by the military leaders at the top and by party members and government appointees throughout the hierarchy.

There were several reasons for establishing this kind of a controlled mass organization. According to Colonel Thaung Kyi, the peasants needed an organization "with a common outlook, common convictions, common aim and a common way of effort"[38] because they were vulnerable to insurgent pressure and coercion. In addition, they lacked education, held many incorrect values, and had been divided in the previous constitutional period by rival political parties and leaders.

Membership in the organization was not compulsory. Members were sought who believed in its goals and in the need for peasant unity. The duties of the councils were to build solidarity among the peasants and to help build such rural organizations as SACs, land committees, agricultural and multipurpose cooperatives, and village bank committees. They also included promoting production and enhancing agriculture, husbandry, and social services.

From the outset, the government encountered difficulties in building PPCs in the outlying areas because of the peasants' insecurity and basic conservatism; many resisted being brought into new organizations whose values and purposes were not self-evident.

The government created a parallel organization for the workers. On Worker's Day, May 1, 1963, the RC called for the workers to form associations; a year later, it promulgated the Draft Law on the Basic Rights and Responsibilities of People's Workers Councils, and this was followed by active recruiting and organization.[39] Under the leadership of Colonel Maung Shwe, by 1968 the organization had grown to a membership of 1.3 million; there were 225 township people's workers councils and 2,196 primary units. This permitted the creation of a Central People's Workers Council. Four years later, the colonel reported that these numbers had increased to 1.5 million members in 261 township people's workers councils and 2,662 primary units.

As with the peasants, the RC leaders argued that a single national workers' organization could reverse the trend toward competitive-

38. *Forward*, 7, no. 15 (March 15, 1969), 6.
39. Government of Burma, *Party Seminar 1965*, pp. 57–58.

ness in the labor movement that had obtained during the party-dominated years between 1948 and 1962.

The workers councils, like the peasants councils, were composed both of workers and party and state appointees. Leadership, while in theory shared between the two, in fact was tightly held by party loyalists. Official policy called for the workers to be free to criticize and make suggestions while supporting the programs of the party and the government. During the period of drafting a new constitution for Burma—1971–1973—the workers councils were encouraged to criticize the drafts and suggest improvements. They also shared responsibility for achieving the economic goals set by the state, maintaining labor discipline, and watching the workers so that waste, pilfering, and shoddy work might be eliminated.

The apparent key role of the two organizations in the political system was to draw the workers and peasants into controlled political activity and to create a popular base for the military in power.

Although several more specialized mass organizations had been projected, the only other one to emerge during this period was the Youth Organization that began to take shape after the party converted from a cadre to a mass organization. Founded in August 1971, this new organization was open to all youths between the ages of fifteen and twenty-five. In time it enlarged its goal to include children from the age of five. The organization was divided into three groups; Teza Youth, five to ten years; Shaysaung Youth, ten to fifteen years; Lanzin Youth, fifteen to twenty-five years. The goal of the Youth Organization was to turn the youth of the nation into an auxiliary force of the party and to make them into "good socialist workers who will build and defend the socialist system."[40]

These three mass organizations give a clear indication of how the military rulers intended to mobilize, socialize, and weld the people to the new order.

The Opposition

Throughout this first phase of military rule, the government faced opposition from several quarters—the indigenous minorities, political parties, religious groups, and particular individu-

40. *Forward*, 9, no. 22 (July 1, 1971), 2.

als. Because of their differing goals and tactics, these groups never coalesced into a unified opposition, though occasionally they were drawn together for brief periods and limited objectives. The basis of their unity—when it occurred—was opposition to the Ne Win government, but that was never strong enough to transcend the issues and personalities that divided them.

When the military seized power it silenced the legal political opposition by imprisoning some leaders while allowing others their freedom as long as they remained silent and uncritical and supported the new regime. At the time of the coup, the military captured and imprisoned many of the minority leaders who were in Rangoon for the federal seminar. Underground insurgent minority and political opposition leaders continued to maintain their freedom and sought ways to enlarge their authority.

During the first years of military rule, the most vocal and active aboveground opposition came from university students and Buddhist monks. The students were the first to protest, but following the reopening of the universities in May 1962, they were placed under new and more restrictive regulations. Following tradition, the students protested in July 1962 and, contrary to tradition, the military responded with gunfire, killing at least sixteen, closing the universities, and blowing up the student union building at the University of Rangoon.[41] Those students who were not arrested were sent home. When the universities were reopened later that year, the students were required to present suitability certificates and agree to abide by regulations; in turn, the government appeared to ease its harsh policies. During 1963, however, the students were emboldened to make fresh demands and to support some of the opposition during the negotiations between the military and insurgents that took place during the summer and fall of that year. When the negotiations were broken off in November 1963, the soldiers in power moved against the students once again, closing the universities and sending the students home. Although

41. The government claimed that the students were prompted by the Communists, and General Ne Win declared, "I had no alternative but to meet *dah* with *dah* and spear with spear." See Josef Silverstein and Julian Wohl, "University Students and Politics in Burma," *Pacific Affairs* 37, no. 1 (Spring 1964), 50–65. Also see Government of Burma, *Party Seminar 1965*, pp. 60–61.

the universities were reopened the next year, they were reorganized, and the students who were readmitted were screened carefully. For all practical purposes, student opposition to military rule ended until 1969, when the students again rioted and shouted antigovernment slogans over the issue of tickets to the Southeast Asia Peninsula (SEAP) games. Once again the government responded with force and closed the universities. For the remainder of this phase of military rule, the students remained quiet.

The Buddhist monks provided the only other organized open opposition to the government. As was mentioned earlier, the military government had silenced them by 1965.

The underground opposition of the minorities and the Communist parties continued through the entire period of military rule. For purposes of analysis, the two groups will be treated separately, although, as will be seen, elements from both united for short periods of time. When the military seized power, groups from the Karens, Shans, Kachins, Kayahs, and Mons were openly fighting against the government. The Karens and Mons had been in opposition since as early as 1949, the Shans and Kachins since 1958, and the Kayahs since 1959—all were seeking some degree of greater political autonomy. The Mons were eager to obtain a state of their own. The Karens were interested in redrawing their state boundaries to include more of their people and more natural resources. The Shans and Kayahs desired either a redefined federation that would give them parity with a Burmese state or the right to secede from the Union. The Kachins, who had a state, wanted greater power and more autonomy from Rangoon.

While each of these ethnic groups had legal organizations struggling to achieve its desired ends through constitutional means, illegal insurgent groups were battling the government for territory and control of population and sought to be the spokesmen for their particular ethnic constituency. Some of these insurgent groups united at times, and in some areas, as in the Shan State, where they joined forces with remnants of the Nationalist Chinese still in Burma and engaged in the illegal opium and arms trade. The most important coalition of ethnic groups to face the military after the coup was the illegal National Democratic United Front (NDUF), which consisted of the Karen National Union, the New Mon State party, and the Karenni National Progressive party. This coalition allied with the Burma Communist party of Thakin Than Tun, and together they negotiated with the military in 1963. During this period, the Kachin Independence Army and the Shan State Independence Army also cooperated with the NDUF. Following the failure of the negotiations the NDUF fell apart and each unit sought to gain its goal independently. Though the front remained in name, for all practical purposes it ceased to exist as a common opposition force. The various insurgent ethnic groups operated in the hill areas and near Burma's borders with China, Laos, and Thailand. They held large stretches of territory and were able to support the smuggling out of Burma of opium, precious stones, and teak and to bring from Thailand illegally a variety of consumer goods without real interference from the military. The government maintained control over the major trading centers, key villages, and roads so the insurgents never were able to establish a rival government inside Burma, although they controlled substantial territory and people.

To answer the challenge of the ethnic dissidents, the military, as noted, sought to create a unified state exercising central control through the SACs and military authority. At the same time, in 1963 it made an effort to negotiate a settlement with all the dissidents. Although it won the support of a minor fraction of the Karen insurgents—the Karen Revolutionary Council led by Moosso Kawkasa—it failed to end insurgency in Burma.

After the breakdown of negotiations with the leaders of the insurgent minorities, the military chose a new path in 1964 by declaring a new national policy on minority-majority relations, which it hoped would wean the minority peoples from the influence of their insurgent leaders. On Union Day 1964, Ne Win proclaimed the government's policy on relations with the minorities. He declared that while certain tasks such as economic development were the concern of the entire nation, other tasks such as language, culture, literature, religion, and customs were the responsibilities of the individual ethnic groups. He concluded by warning against any activity that threatened national unity.[42] This declaration elevated the Burmese nation above any of its

42. "The Political Report of the Central Organizing Committee of the BSPP, 1971," *Guardian* (daily), June 29, 1971.

component groups and implied that all must strive for the common good, even at the possible expense of their particular rights and without the safety valve of the right of secession.

A major step was taken to implement this policy a year later, in 1965, with the opening of the Academy for the Development of National Groups. Located permanently near Sagaing in upper Burma, in the heartland of Burman culture, the academy sought recruits from all ethnic groups. Those selected lived together, gaining understanding of the diverse cultures and traditions they represented and receiving instruction in leadership and community organization and in basic skills to teach to their people when they returned to their homes. They also were indoctrinated in Burmese socialism and the ideas implicit in the military version of the new Burma. The goals of the academy were never fully realized; the training period and community living experience were too short for the trainees to transcend their ethnic and linguistic background; the new skills were relatively simple, so that most trainees did not learn much more than they already knew. In 1971 a seminar was held to discuss the problems of the academy. The Shan State Council chairman, U Tun Aye, pointed out that the academy was not achieving its mission because the recruits were not drawn from the people living in the less developed and more remote areas, but rather from urban youth and relatives of the armed forces personnel, and they did not return to the remote areas to impart their newly acquired information and skills.[43]

Other efforts were made to overcome racial antagonism, such as nationwide celebration of ethnic national days, publication of the folklore of certain minorities, and historical and anthropological studies of the minorities. These activities were intended to express the idea, as stated by Brigadier San Yu, that "the culture of one nationality was part and parcel of the culture of the whole nation."[44]

Despite these positive steps, the first twelve years of military rule did not see any major changes in the racial attitudes and behavior of the people. One reason was the government's policy of centralized control and domination of the hill areas from Rangoon. A second possible reason was the government's inability to defeat or

43. *Guardian* (daily), January 1, 1971.
44. *Ibid*, February 12, 1965.

materially to weaken the ethnic insurgents who continued to press for greater autonomy and the preservation of indigenous cultures. A third reason was the failure of the government's new leaders among the minorities to be accepted by their people and to displace the loyalty and authority of their leaders who were either in the jungle or the government jail.

The second real source of opposition was the Burma Communist party under the leadership of Thakin Than Tun until his death in 1968. When the military seized power in 1962, the BCP was weak. The party had been in continuous revolt against the government since 1948 and its size had declined, its hold on the people had diminished, and its control had been limited to remote rural areas in central Burma and the northern Shan State. From 1950 onward, the military had been in nearly continuous pursuit and had forced the Communists to retreat to the jungle areas, far from the population centers. The BCP had maintained contact with the urban population through its supporters in the NUF and the university student organizations. When the military curbed legal opposition, the Communists became more isolated than ever. In this situation, the military leaders sought to bring an end to political strife and insurgency through negotiations with both the Communists and the insurgent minorities. On April 1, 1963, the government issued a general amnesty. Prisoners, other than political leaders arrested at the time of the coup, were freed or their sentences were reduced. Having established a favorable climate, the military, on July 11, invited the insurgents to peace talks aimed at ending civil strife. Peace talks were held without preconditions, with a guarantee of free and safe passage to and from the parley, regardless of the outcome, and with an order to field commanders to halt operations against all insurgents. In all, spokesmen for eight groups participated.[45] Discussion began on July 31 and ended in failure on November 14.

During the discussions, leaders of the underground were free to

---

45. Government of Burma, *Party Seminar 1965*, pp. 47–48. The groups in attendance were the Arakanese Communist party, Karen National Unity Organization, New Mon National party, Karenni National Program party, Communist Party of Burma, Burma Communist party, Karen Revolutionary Force, and Kachin Independence Council. Several of these groups were united in the talks as the National Democratic United Front.

meet with the public, talk publicly, and publish their points of view. For many, it was their first return from the underground and an opportunity to renew contact with their followers. Thakin Soe, of the Communist party of Burma (CPB) (Red Flags), basked in publicity, but the real spokesmen for the insurgents were the BCP representatives (White Flags), who spoke both for themselves and as members of the NDUF coalition. The insurgent leaders made three key demands: a nationwide cease-fire, freedom of mobility for insurgent leaders to consult each other, and full publicity for their meetings and all proposals and counterproposals. Discussions broke down over the first issue: cease-fire. The BCP and NDUF demanded the right to continue to administer their areas and collect taxes—to establish, in effect, liberated areas that would be recognized as de facto governments. The military argued that such a demand went beyond a cease-fire and, in effect, divided the nation.[46] Fighting resumed following the delegations' return to the jungle.

But the negotiations strengthened the government's confidence in its popular support and, with the help of people's militias, the military vigorously renewed their attacks on the insurgents. Victories against the Communists and the death in battle of Bo Zeya, the BCP chief of staff, heightened tensions and conflict within the party.

A serious inner party struggle broke out in the BCP almost immediately after the peace talks ended. Those associated with the negotiations and their tactics were branded as revisionists by a group known as the Peking Returnees—party members who had lived in China and were strong advocates of Maoism. The latter group was under the leadership of Ba Thein Tin. The debates led to the expulsion and execution of several BCP leaders—Goshal, a founder of the party, Yebaw Htay, the leader of the negotiation team, and Yan Aung, a member of the "thirty heroes." Their deaths did not halt the purge and, in 1968, Thakin Than Tun was assassinated. The remnants of the party under the leadership of Thakin Zin, a former vice-chairman, Thakin Chit, party secretary,

---

46. For details of the decisions, see: *Internal Peace Parley* (*Historical Documents* no. 1) (Rangoon, 1963) (mimeo).

and Ba Thein Tin, retreated to Kokang, in the northern part of the Shan State on the China border and regrouped, restocked their weapons from Chinese sources, and returned to battle in 1970. With arms and training, the revived BCP gradually expanded its area of control and gained some victories in its battles with the Burma army. By 1972, the BCP held wide areas in the Shan State and had returned to its former sanctuary in the Pegu Yoma and central Burma. Interacting with the ethnic rebels, supported modestly by the People's Republic of China, the BCP presented a greater threat than at any time since 1950 to the one-party state the military sought to impose on the Union of Burma.

Although it failed to end the threat of the BCP, the military was more successful in its contest with the Communist party of Burma (Red Flags). Thakin Soe was captured in the army's stepped-up campaigns in 1967–1968. As the CPB was a one-man party, his removal from his followers was a severe blow.

The third element of the opposition was made up of the individual political leaders who would not support the coup government. Chief among them was U Nu. Imprisoned without trial in 1962, he remained in jail until 1966, when he was released on the condition that he not engage in politics. When a tidal wave struck Arakan in 1968, Nu launched a relief campaign and traveled about the country attracting crowds as he discussed Buddhism.

In 1968, Ne Win sought to draw Nu and other leaders from the past into a committee to plan for Burma's future. The Internal Unity Advisory Body (IUAB) was composed of thirty-three former political and ethnic leaders who were asked to "submit ideas on the means of establishing internal unity that would effectively and directly benefit the working people of the Union of Burma politically, economically, socially and ethnically"[47] and ordered to prepare a report by May 31, 1969. The IUAB report included three different sets of recommendations and a separate report by U Nu. The majority report supported by eighteen participants called for a return to the original constitution and its amendment where necessary; the majority also urged the retention of the federal system with new states added, if the proper criteria could be de-

47. Proclamations no. 72 and no. 74, *Forward*, 7, no. 9 (December 15, 1968), 2.

veloped. The minority report supported by eleven members called for the convening of a national unity congress, the formal adoption of a federal political system, and the creation of a one-party socialist state.

U Nu presented his own views separately. He argued that the real issue was the question of legitimacy. Power had been seized illegally and initially must be returned to him; then the old parliament had to be reconvened to elect Ne Win president of the Union. Following the election, Nu would transfer power to him. The ban on parties would have to be lifted, political rights restored, and political prisoners released.[48]

When his suggestions were rejected, U Nu asked for and received permission to go abroad. In London, he called for a popular revolt against the military which he promised to lead to success. Following visits to several countries, Nu raised money from a Canadian oil company and other sources, and then settled in Thailand, where he organized a rebel army with the aid of Bo Let Ya, a former member of the "thirty heroes," a former minister of defense and a close comrade in arms to Aung San. Nu formed a united front—National United Liberation Front—with several minority dissidents and called his movement the Elected Government of the Union of Burma. He organized a new political party, the Parliamentary Democracy party, as the major constituent unit of the front. His army launched raids inside Burma and, for a while, held territory inside the Burma-Thai border, but his efforts failed to inspire a popular uprising or defections from Ne Win's armed forces. Even a leaflet-dropping air raid on April 7, 1972, over Rangoon and lower Burma failed to arouse the people.

In January 1972, Nu resigned as president of the NULF insurgent group over his differences with the representatives of the minorities on the question of the future of the federal state in Burma. He refused to make any commitment to the right of the minorities to secede. Against his wishes, the right of secession was adopted as part of the NULF manifesto.[49] All his political life he

48. *Working People's Daily,* June 5, 1969.

49. The manifesto listed three points: the union was to be formed on the basis of self-determination with the right to secede; a federal union providing equality, democracy, harmony, and development was in accordance with the interest of the

had fought to hold the Union together, and he refused to agree to anything that contradicted that position. Nu's departure from the insurgent ranks ended his challenge to the military.

Those who opposed military rule were unable to unite, either on goals or tactics, to mount a major challenge to the men in power. The government was never really challenged because the military leaders controlled the means of violence, they remained a cohesive unit, and they retained the loyalty of their junior officers and the men in the ranks. That does not mean that the military exercised authority over the whole of Burma—it did not. It did exercise authority over the centers of population, controlled the means of communication, and was able to protect the bulk of the population from assaults by insurgents; thus it was able to survive in power.

---

nationalities; the duty of all nationalities was to protect the Union of Burma. See Seah Chiang Nee, "Burma's Rebel Force Now Faces a Shaky Future," *Asian*, April 23–29, 1972.

5 | Constitutional Dictatorship: The Second Phase of Military Rule

The men who seized power in 1962 did not see writing a new constitution for Burma as an immediate issue. The military rulers justified having set aside parliament and altered the courts, having arrested the elected government, and having changed the administrative structure in their first publication, *The Burmese Way to Socialism*, which stated that the original constitution was unacceptable because it had defects, weaknesses, and loopholes that kept the nation from realizing its goals of socialism and national unity among all the people.[1] Seven years later, in 1969, General Ne Win announced that the time was ripe for writing a new constitution and criticized the old fundamental law by giving numerous examples of how he thought it favored the private sector of the economy, foreign firms, lawyers, and feudal leaders in the states. He called for a return to the principles of government and the goals for the people set by Aung San before independence.[2] In 1971 the first congress of the BSPP announced that it would be responsible for writing the new constitution and, in 1973, completed its work when the final version was presented and approved by the second congress of the party and submitted to the people for ratification.

1. Government of Burma, Revolutionary Council, *The Burmese Way to Socialism* (Rangoon: Ministry of Information, 1962), para. 6.
2. Government of Burma, Burma Socialist Program Party, *Address Delivered by General Ne Win, Chairman of the Burma Socialist Program Party at the Opening Session of the Fourth Party Seminar on 6th November 1969* (Rangoon: Burma Socialist Program Party, Central Press, 1969).

Just as the Burmese leaders sought a unique road to socialism, so, too, they developed a novel approach to constitution making. The party nominated a State Constitution Drafting Committee, headed by Brigadier San Yu, which included thirty-three military officers among the total membership of ninety-seven. The remaining sixty-four represented the social classes, the ethnic groups, the political leaders who had cooperated with the Revolutionary Council, and legal experts. Although the committee had a nominal civilian majority, its leadership was tightly held by the military representatives of the party, and the final document reflected their goals and interests. The committee was given two years to draw up three drafts and circulate the first two among the people for comment and criticism. The final version was to be offered to the second congress of the BSPP for adoption and then to the people for approval in a referendum.[3] The committee began its work by dividing into fifteen teams, each visiting a different part of Burma to obtain advice from the people prior to writing the first draft. When completed, the initial draft was published in the press, with commentary, and new teams again circulated among the people to listen to their criticism of the document. This procedure was repeated following the publication of the second draft. In this way, the committee both led and listened to the people and concluded that it had obtained the widest popular participation in carrying out its work.[4]

Despite vigorous and outspoken criticism of the initial drafts, there was very little difference between the three versions of the constitution. All contained the same number of chapters and nearly the same number of articles. In all three drafts, the preamble made clear that the Revolutionary Council fulfilled "its historic mission" by adopting *The Burmese Way to Socialism* and creating the Burma Socialist Program Party. As will be seen, the military leaders made certain that their leadership and programs continued into the future.

The 1971 congress of the BSPP adopted six guiding principles

3. *Guardian* (daily), September 26, 1971.
4. *Working People's Daily*, November 8, 1973, reported that 105,000 participated in the first meeting with the committee in preparing the initial draft; over eight million persons were reported to have heard the explanation of the second draft.

for the new constitution: (1) socialism is the goal of the state; (2) a socialist economy shall be adopted and laws for its protection shall be implemented; (3) the state shall be organized as a democratic society; (4) there shall be racial equality and national unity in good times and bad; (5) the people shall have the democratic and personal rights within the framework of a socialist democracy and duties and obligations toward socialism and the state; (6) any other provisions that will contribute to the building of a socialist democratic state will be adopted.[5]

The Locus of Power

No question was left about who has the right to hold and exercise power. Both in the preamble and in the body, the constitution makes clear that power belongs to the Burma Socialist Program Party. The preamble reminds the reader that the party authored the constitution, and it sets forth the proposition, repeated in Article 11, that it shall lead the nation. The same article declares that Burma will be a one-party state and the BSPP is the sole party. The party is charged specifically with the responsibility of drawing up lists of candidates for all offices in consultation with its own mass and class organizations and the electorate (Article 179), and it is empowered to give advice and suggestions to government at all levels on economic planning, the annual budget, and anything else it chooses to discuss (Article 205). With no legal competitors and its leaders in all the dominant positions in the legislature and the executive at the four levels of government, the party rules in fact as well as in theory. As long as the constitution remains in effect, the military controlling the party remain in power. The constitution therefore confirms the military dictatorship.

Other Basic Principles

Although it does not appear until near the end of the constitution, the principle of constitutional supremacy is firmly and clearly stated (Article 202). Only the People's Assembly (Pyithu hluttaw) may interpret the constitution, but its interpretations must be based upon the General Clauses Law promulgated by the military

5. *Guardian* (daily), December 3, 1971.

government prior to the implementation of the constitution (Article 200). Here again, the military assured that during the second phase of their rule, the constitution will not be used against them or interpreted to support any change that does not have their approval.

A chapter devoted to basic principles replaces the directive principles found in the 1947 constitution. The twenty-four articles in this chapter reflect the ideas expressed during the twelve years of military rule. The principles fall into three broad categories—the nature of the state, the economic and social system, and the rights and duties of the people. According to the authors of the constitution, this section is so important that "the remaining chapters and articles . . . are mere detailed enumerations of these fundamental principles."[6]

Consistent with the thinking of the military leaders, the principles begin by restating the idea that the goal of the state is socialism. There must therefore, be a socialist economy (Article 6) with the state as the ultimate owner, extractor, and marketer of the land and the natural resources (Article 18A). The means of production must be nationalized (Article 19). To carry out these economic objectives requires a socialist democracy (Article 7).

In the new state, power belongs to the people and, as has already been shown, is exercised under the leadership of the party. The People's Assembly exercises the sovereign power of the state—it employs the legislative power directly and delegates executive and judicial power to other organs technically responsible to it (Article 13). Power is centralized and hierarchical; the various levels of government are bound together by democratic centralism, collective leadership, and decision making (Article 14).

The people have political rights and duties. They may elect their representatives and, if dissatisfied, may exercise the right of recall (Article 16). All citizens, regardless of race or sex, are equal before the law, enjoy equality of opportunity, have the right of inheritance, and the enjoyment of the benefits of their labor in proportion to their contribution (Article 18).

6. "Report of the Draft Committee," *Working People's Daily*, November 10, 1973, emphasized that sovereignty is not fragmented and does not belong to any one nationality.

All persons whose parents are nationals of the Republic and all persons who were naturalized before the implementation of this constitution are citizens. Citizenship may be acquired or revoked in accordance with the law (Articles 145, 146). The citizenship provisions reflect the policies of the military government during the preceding twelve years in their effort to establish clearly that there is one citizenship and that all who have it are equal, regardless of their residence, their racial origins, or their religion. The emphasis is upon the being a Burmese and not upon place of origin, ethnic background, or religious affiliation—identities that, in the past, divided the people and contributed to national disunity.

The Structure of the State

In name, Burma is the Socialist Republic of the Union of Burma. Emphasis is clearly upon the republic and not upon the union. It is not a federal state, either in the accepted sense of the term or in the unique way it was applied in the 1947 constitution (see Chapter 3). The new constitution created a unified state subdivided both vertically and horizontally. For administrative and political purposes there are four levels of government: ward and village tracts at the base, townships at the second level, states and divisions at the third level, all united under the central government at the national level. The governing principle that links the four levels of government together is "local autonomy under central leadership" (Article 28).[7] In a horizontal sense, the state is divided into fourteen states and divisions. They include the original states—Shan, Kachin, Karen, Kayah—and the former Chin Special Division; in addition, Mon and Arakan states have been created out of territory formerly a part of Burma proper (Article 30). The remainder of Burma proper is divided into seven divisions, politically equal in every way with the states.

As interpreted in the commentary prepared by the BSPP, "the state has not been organized on the basis of the states and Burma

7. In the first two drafts emphasis was placed on central leadership. The wording of the article was, "central leadership and regional implementation are the principles for organizing and building the State" (Article 29, first draft, and Article 28, second draft).

proper, as before; instead, it has been organized hierarchically into people's councils at the three levels below the national government . . . each having equal power and status with another at the same level along Socialist Democratic principles and each serving as a local organ of power with wide self-management powers."[8] The size, the shape, and the name of any state or division can be changed by the People's assembly after ascertaining the wishes of the people living in the particular territory. Thus, the states no longer belong to any ethnic group, but to all citizens residing in the territory. With the supreme authority of the state located in the national parliament and a single political party operating throughout the nation on the basis of centralism, the state is, in fact, unitary and not federal as its formal name implies.

The unitary structure ends all discussion about ethnic states and the right of secession. In theory, it assures cohesion and unity in all the territory of the nation. In fact, it fails to satisfy the desires and hopes of the ethnic minorities who have been in revolt against Burmanization and the total integration of their historic territory into a single political unit. The problem of political unity seems further from solution now than it was at the time of the coup.

The National Government

The new constitution, like the old, creates a parliamentary system. The two-house legislature created by the 1947 constitution has been replaced by a unicameral legislature called the People's Assembly. Its members are elected on a formula based partially on a guaranteed number of seats and partially on the size of the population in the local constituencies and the several states and divisions.[9] Each term of the legislature can last for four years, but may be extended or shortened. By a three-quarters vote the

8. "Report of the Draft Committee," *Working People's Daily*, November 11, 1973. The commentary that accompanied the first draft gave greater emphasis to the unitary, hierarchical state by saying, "the structure of the State is based on socialist-centralism." See "Report of the First Draft," *Guardian* (daily), April 30, 1972, p. 5.

9. Each constituency is based on a township; each township is entitled to one representative; they are entitled to additional representatives according to population. States or divisions with less than ten townships and a population of less than one million also are entitled to additional representatives.

People's Assembly may dissolve itself and call for new elections (Article 62). It also can call itself into session if 34 percent of its members demand a meeting (Article 52). Leadership in the legislature is vested in a panel of chairmen—one from each state and division—who rotate the chairmanship at each meeting. The panel of chairmen have one special power—they may call a special session of the parliament if the Council of State, after receiving a proper request, fails to comply.

The People's Assembly has broad powers that range from creating the several committees of the executive, judiciary, and inspectorate to declaring war and making peace; it may dissolve a People's Council at any of the three lower levels of government,[10] and it has exclusive power to enact laws relating to economic plans, annual budgets, and taxation (Article 47).

The above "power to the people through their legislature" must be read in the light of the fact that leadership is vested in the party and that the party has the chief responsibility for nominating candidates for the legislature and can comment upon any subject before the legislature. An elite minority, without elected responsibility, in fact manages, channels, and directs the people's representatives in carrying out their constitutional tasks.

Executive power is divided between two councils, responsible in theory to the parliament: the Council of State and the Council of Ministers. The symbolic and supervisory roles of the executive are, in the main, located in the Council of State, a body of twenty-nine, all members of the legislature who are elected to serve on this council. Each of the states and divisions is entitled to elect one of its representatives to serve on this body. The People's Assembly elects fourteen others at large. The twenty-ninth member is the prime minister, who is elected by the Chamber of Ministers.

The Council of State elects its own chairman, and he is designated as president of the Republic. The chairman, as president, exercises the symbolic functions as head of state and the practical task of signing and promulgating laws, rules, and resolutions.

The Council of State has a long list of duties, chief of which are

10. Article 63 sets forth five reasons: violation of the constitution; actions undermining national unity; contravening any resolution adopted by the People's Assembly; endangering the stability of the state; and inefficient discharge of duties.

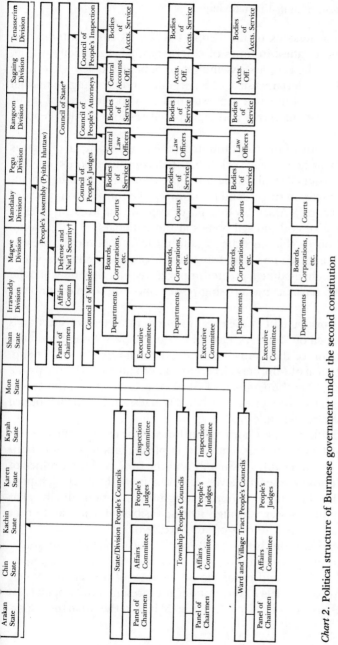

Chart 2. Political structure of Burmese government under the second constitution

* The chairman of the Council of State is also the president. The Council of State has 29 members: 1 each from the 14 states and divisions, 14 elected at large from the People's Assembly, and the prime minister. The prime minister is elected by the Council of Ministers from its members.

† Members on the National Defense and Security Committee are drawn from the membership of the Council of State and the Council of Ministers.

Source: Constitution of the Socialist Republic of the Union of Burma. Adapted from a chart that accompanied the first draft of the constitution, April 1972.

convening sessions of the People's Assembly and ratifying and annulling treaties; in times of emergency, taking military action, and, when the People's Assembly cannot be assembled, governing alone. It can declare a state of emergency and promulgate martial law. In normal times, it can issue orders with the force of law if parliament is in recess and call special sessions of the People's Assembly.

The section of the constitution devoted to the Council of State is silent about how it will work, what shall constitute a quorum, and how the council shall decide if the president and the other members disagree on subject and procedure. The constitution provides for the People's Assembly to make or approve the working rules of all executive and judicial bodies at the national and subnational levels. Conceivably, once the constitution takes root and the present generation of leaders gives way to its successors, such rules within bodies might assume a greater importance than they do while the men who have been exercising power since the coup continue in office.

The working half of the executive under the new constitution is the Council of Ministers, elected by the People's Assembly on the nomination of the Council of State; it has no fixed membership. The Council of Ministers elects one of its members to be the prime minister. Like the Council of State, the Council of Ministers is responsible to the legislature when it is in session and to the Council of State at other times.

In addition to their normal functions as the cabinet, the Council of Ministers is charged with the implementation of resolutions passed by the People's Assembly and the orders of the Council of State. It links the several levels of government through its responsibility for directing and coordinating administration. Finally, it has broad police powers through its responsibility for law and order and maintaining the rule of law (Article 87).

In planning the future of Burma, the Council of Ministers is charged by the constitution with economic planning, drawing up annual budgets, and reporting on the state of the nation (Article 88). Unlike the 1947 constitution, the present fundamental law emphasizes the collective role of the cabinet, rather than the importance of the prime minister.[11] A comparison of the new Burmese executive relationship between the prime minister and the president of the Republic with similar offices in other nations suggests that the DeGaulle model in the present government of France must have been in the forefront of the minds of the constitution's authors at the time of its drafting.

Judicial power in the new constitution is divided between the Council of People's Justices and the Council of People's Attorneys. Members of both councils are nominated by the Council of State and elected by the People's Assembly. Both are responsible to the legislature and when it is not in session to the Council of State.

Consistent with the principle of collective responsibility, justice "shall be administered by collective bodies of judges" (Article 98). The jurisdiction of the Council of People's Justices is limited to the civil population. The armed forces are subject to a separate military system of justice (Article 99). The Council of People's Justices works under a separate set of judicial principles set out in the constitution (Article 101). It is charged with the supervision of all courts and other judicial organs of the state. It conducts its business in Burmese, but local languages may be used and translators shall be provided (Article 102).

The constitution makes no mention of professional qualifications for the members of the Council of People's Justices or for those serving on inferior Judge's Committees. During the period of the Revolutionary Council the military clearly intended to remove the administration of justice from the professional judge or lawyer. Unless the People's Assembly chooses lawyers from among their own members to serve on this council, the idea of lay justice will be its hallmark. At the same time, the principles for the administration of justice imply a knowledge of the law and custom; thus, the Council of People's Justices may be forced to rely upon the advice of professionals.

The constitution provides for a hierarchy of law officers, the Council of People's Attorneys. Their qualifications are not estab-

11. Compare this chapter with Chapter XII in the 1947 constitution entitled the Union Government, for the sharp difference between the two on the question of individual and collective leadership.

lished although their responsibilities and the official interpretation of the constitution indicate that they should have legal training. This council is charged with the protection and safeguard of the socialist system and the rights and privileges of the working people; it also is asked to give legal advice to the councils of state and ministers.

The one really new office created by the constitution is the Council of People's Inspectors. Elected by the People's Assembly from among its members, it is declared the highest organ of inspection of public undertakings (Article 119). Its object is to see whether public undertakings are "beneficial to the interests of the public" (Article 121A). Just what "beneficial" means is not clearly defined nor does the constitution say specifically who are subject to its inspection. According to the official commentary, it can go practically anywhere and survey the several people's councils, ministries, and other bodies of the government.[12] Until the People's Assembly develops guidelines for this council it will remain a sinister office with police and intelligence activity in support of its inspectorate function. The Council of People's Inspectors is yet another organ to concentrate power and to uphold the ideology; for the term, "beneficial to the people" can be interpreted only within an ideological framework and not in purely fiscal terms.

Rights and Duties

The constitution establishes no absolute rights; there is no right of revolution, and the military has no right to seize power and rule by decree. All rights are conditioned by the goals of the state. The constitution makes everyone responsible to strive for socialist goals and to surrender any or all of his rights if they interfere with that objective.

The main emphasis in discussing rights is upon those that flow from the socialist ideas underlying the constitution. All citizens have the right to enjoy the benefits of their labor in proportion to their contribution. They may take up any occupation "permitted by the State within the bounds of the Socialist economy," and they may have the right to rest and relaxation, fixed working hours, and

12. See "Report of the Draft Committee," *Working People's Daily*, November 14, 1973, for an official discussion of this council.

leave in the performance of their labor. All may reside wherever they wish and, although Burmese is the official language, every citizen may use his own language, follow his own customs, and profess any religion he desires, *provided* that in doing any of the above, he does not undermine "unity and solidarity of the national groups, security of the State and the socialist social order." Every citizen has a right to an education, but only basic education for every citizen is compulsory.

In the area of personal and political rights, every citizen may vote or be elected to public office; he has the right of freedom of thought, conscience, and religion; however, the state may enact laws restricting these rights in the interest of the working people and law and order. Every citizen has the right of free speech and publication "unless such freedom is contrary to the interest of Socialism." The state is required to grant personal freedom and security to its citizens and to protect their property, provided it is earned or inherited according to the socialist economic system. Members of religious orders are prohibited from political participation. No citizen can claim a right that is (1) contrary to sovereignty and the security of the state, (2) against the basic essence of the socialist system, (3) against unity and solidarity of the people, or (4) against public peace, tranquillity, and morality.

The duties of citizens are to protect nationalized property and cooperative property and strive for socialist capital accumulation, for strengthening the defense of the nation, and for enhancing the standard of living of the people in accordance with their ability. They have a "noble duty" to protect and safeguard independence, sovereignty, and the territorial integrity of the state. They must take military training and give military service; they must pay taxes and perform duties as prescribed by law.

The detailed language and the elaboration of rights and duties does not disguise the fact that they afford the individual no more protection than the state wishes him to have. The state is the author of the rights and duties, and no one can invoke them against it.

The Structure of the Government below the National Level

As noted earlier, the structure of government is divided into three tiers below the national government: states and divisions, townships and wards, and village tracts. The key institution at each of these levels is the popularly elected People's Council. Its term is identical with that of the People's Assembly, and a single election is held to fill all four levels of government. The several committees of the People's Councils are a reflection of those found in the national parliament. The leaders of the People's Councils are their Executive Committees. Each Executive Committee elects a chairman who serves in a dual capacity, as chairman of the People's Council as well as of the committee. Like the national legislature, each People's Council at the state or division and township level elects various affairs committees to help conduct its business. In addition, the People's Council elects a Judge's Committee. All committees are responsible to the People's Councils at their particular level and are overseen by committees above them. The Council of Ministers directs and coordinates the work of the Executive Committees at the three lower levels. In a lesser way, the Council of People's Judges supervises the work of the Judge's Committee; the inspectorate at the state or division and township levels is governed by laws passed in the national legislature. In addition subunits of the various national executive and judicial bodies operate at the three sublevels of government.

The many and varied duties of the People's Council range from being in charge of public administration and having responsibility for law and order to promoting solidarity among the races and promoting national cultures. They are responsible for providing leadership to the people and protecting the natural environment. These and other duties spell out what the constitution means by local autonomy under central leadership (Article 28). The close supervision of the executive committees and the various other committees suggests that while the national leaders encourage local autonomy and initiative, responsibility always rests with a level of government above the one taking the action. No local area is allowed to stray too far from the national goals and priorities. The linking together in hierarchical fashion of like committees, agencies, and departments assures that orders from the top will pass down, while, at the same time, comment, ideas, and criticism can filter up.

The Constitution in Perspective

The military went to great lengths to publicize the writing and promulgation of the new constitution. As suggested in the above analysis, they fashioned a constitutional dictatorship through the control of the Burma Socialist Program Party, the hierarchical nature of the government, and the absence of any means for legally expressing opposition.

The system is cumbersome and unwieldy. The state of communications and the degree of security suggest that the central government will not be able to exercise as much control as the constitution implies. But that is the result of the political situation and not part of the constitutional design. The constitution continues the goal the military sought following the coup in 1962—direct control over the entire nation through a strong and disciplined administrative structure.

By granting the request of the ethnic minorities that all states should be equal, the new constitution created nine states and divisions out of the former territory known as Burma proper and reduced all to an administrative level beneath the national government. The territorial shape of a particular state can be changed; it can be renamed, and it can be reconstituted. Thus, the states no longer belong to any ethnic group, but to all citizens residing in the territory. Each citizen has equal say with any other in any part of the nation, thus recognizing the principle of racial equality and unity. With no territory of their own, with no cultural protections formerly embodied in the legislative lists, the dominance of the majority of Burmans will expand, and racial enmity, which characterized the first quarter of a century of independent Burma, will continue.

Finally, the hallmark of the new system is its elected bodies and collective leadership. As will be seen in the next section, the election of representatives to four levels of government proved confusing and cumbersome. In emphasizing the role of the voter, it disguises the fact that the candidates were handpicked by the party and the outcome of the election was never in doubt. If the purpose of the constitution was to make a dictatorship appear to be a popular self-governing system, the effect failed because the disguises do not conceal very much.

The National Referendum

The first step in the implementation of the constitution was to obtain popular approval. A national referendum was held during the last two weeks of December 1973. The turnout was large, and the figures were impressive. According to the latest census, taken in 1973, there were 14,760,036 eligible voters. Of these, 14,094,360 or 95.5 percent cast ballots with 13,312,801 or 90.19 percent giving their approval. The government frankly admitted that only 68.84 percent of the eligible voters in the Kachin State, 66.4 percent in the Shan State, and 71.01 percent in the Kayah State cast ballots in favor of the new constitution. It also reported that 168 members of Referendum Commission were killed, injured, or missing.[13] The rebels in the Kayah State captured 62, 20 were killed or captured in the Kachin State, and 7 known killed in the Shan State. The assaults on the government officials in the states where insurgency is most extensive suggest that the insurgents were not prepared to lay down their arms and peacefully accept the new unitary state of Burma. No doubt their disruptive tactics kept eligible voters away from the polls and contributed to the smaller support in those states than elsewhere in the nation.

The official results were hailed by the leaders of the military government as confirmation that the people accepted their leadership. On January 3, 1974, the Revolutionary Council proclaimed that "the State Constitution of the Socialist Republic of the Union of Burma had been adopted by the people."[14]

The National Election

The second and final step in the transition to the second phase of military government was the election of representatives to the People's Assembly and the three levels of People's Councils. On November 5, 1973, the Revolutionary Council promulgated a new

13. *Asia Research Bulletin* (Singapore), 3, no. 9 (February 1974), 2453–2454.
14. Proclamation no. 110, January 3, 1974. See *Guardian* (daily), January 4, 1974, for the full text.

election law[15] that set the number of representatives in the first People's Assembly at 451. Seats in the three lower levels of the People's Councils were allotted on a basis of population with no seats added for underpopulated areas, as was the case with the People's Assembly.[16] Accordingly, seats in the four levels of government were allotted as shown in Table 6.

Table 6. Distribution of seats in the People's Assembly and People's Councils

State/Division	People's Assembly	State/ Division People's Councils	Township People's Councils	Ward and Village People's Councils
Arakan State	24	73	1,423	18,459
Chin State	13	35	541	5.785
Kachin State	20	51	824	8,146
Karen State	14	55	551	7,423
Kayah State	8	30	201	1,540
Mon State	18	67	849	8,590
Shan State	57	86	3,068	29,339
Irrawaddy Division	50	93	2,589	37,803
Magwe Division	38	82	2,029	27,303
Mandalay Division	51	91	2,538	31,390
Pegu Division	47	88	2,258	28,738
Rangoon Division	52	89	2,558	21,560
Sagaing Division	47	86	2,610	32,530
Tennasserim Division	12	50	622	5,847
Totals	451	976	22,663	264,453

The distribution of seats by population guarantees a majority in the legislature to the delegates from the seven divisions, the territory formerly known as Burma proper, with 297; the states have 154 delegates. Indeed, if all the delegates from the divisions vote together they represent 65.8 percent of the membership, and, if the delegates from the Mon and Arakan states—also parts of the old Burma proper territory—vote with them, they represent 75 percent of the membership of the People's Assembly, and they could alter the constitution or take any other legal steps that re-

15. The law was entitled "The First People's Assembly and People's Councils at Different Levels Election Law, 1973." The complete text was published in the *Guardian* (daily), supplement, November 13, 1973. It is hereafter referred to as "Election Law 73."

16. "Election Law 73," Chapter III.

quire an extraordinary majority. This assumes, of course, that the members of the People's Assembly are free to follow their consciences and are not controlled by the party whips.

The voting procedure was made relatively simple. After being checked, each voter received voting tokens to deposit in the boxes of the candidates of his choice. There were four separate voting rooms—one for each level of election. Inside each were boxes equal to the number of candidates; if only one candidate was running, there were two boxes—one for and one against. In this way the voter was given a negative choice.[17]

The law stipulated that all elections should be held on the same day throughout the nation. Because of security problems and the need to move election personnel about, however, the election lasted for fifteen days—January 27, 1974, through February 10, 1974. The law excluded four categories from voting: members of religious orders, noncitizens, persons legally declared insane, and persons in jail.[18]

The candidates were chosen as required; the Burma Socialist Program Party held "coordination meetings" with representatives of class and mass organizations as well as with eligible voters in the constituency. Among those selected were the men who seized power in 1962 and led the nation during the twelve years that followed; also selected were rising figures in the party.[19]

Elections were held in every constituency except one—Palewa in the Chin State. Of the 450 members elected to the national legislature, 10 percent were active senior military officers, just under 2 percent were women, and the remainder were male civilians and recently retired military officers.[20] The Election Commission re-

17. *Ibid.*, Chapter VIII.
18. *Ibid.*, Chapter II.
19. Among those who ran were U Ne Win (Mayangon); Gen. San Yu (Bahan); U Thaung Kyi (Shwebo); U Sein Win (Tavoy); U Than Sein (Pokkoku); Dr. Hla Han (Pyapon); Dr. Maung Lwin (Kyaukse); U Kyaw Soe (Nattalin); Brig. Tin U (Bassein); Brig. Thaung Dan (Sagaing); U Lwin (Moulmein); Commander Thaung Tin (Twante); Dr. Maung Maung (Amarapura). Among the candidate members of the party's Central Committee were U Maung Maung Kya (Hlaing); U Ko Ko (Yankin); U Aung Pe (Sagu); Col. Kyaw Htin (Mingaladon). Other important party officials who ran were U Tun Lin (Yawnghwe); U Than Sein (Myonaung); U Kyaw Zaw (Kyaunggon); Col. Kyi Maung (Myanaung); U Zaw Win (Kayan); U Ba Nyein (Mongwa); U Ba Nyein (Yenangyaung).
20. An examination of 422 elected members revealed that 366 were designated civilians, 8 were women, and 47 senior military officers.

ported that 10,608,267 persons voted and the winning candidates averaged 85.08 percent of the vote in their constituencies. The total vote was just under four million less than the national referendum. No reason was given for this decrease, and, as will be noted later, it troubled Ne Win. Some possible reasons might be the short period between the two elections; the need to work in the fields to finish the harvest; pressure from insurgents; or lack of voter interest in an act that had very little meaning, despite the efforts of the military government to make it appear that the people really were choosing new leaders.

The last step in altering from direct military dictatorship to the new constitutional dictatorship was the promulgation of laws (Laws 2 and 3 of 1974) that transferred the powers of the Revolutionary Council to the People's Assembly and the three levels of People's Councils. This was completed on January 28. On March 2, 1974— twelve years after the coup—the second phase of military rule began.

Politics under the Constitutional Dictatorship

At the opening of the People's Assembly, U Ne Win declared that all power was transferred from the Revolutionary Council to the national legislature and "declared the abolition of the Revolutionary Council." The other major business of the legislature during its first two meetings was to elect the members of the various executive, judicial, and inspection councils.[21] The election of the Council of State gave the first evidence that very little actual leadership would be transferred to a civilian elite. Of the twenty-nine members elected, eleven, or more than one-third, were carryovers from the now defunct Revolutionary Council. Ne Win was chosen chairman, and, under the constitution, automatically became president of the Socialist Republic as well; General San Yu became secretary and the legal successor to Ne Win. Other well-known former leaders elected to the council were Brigadier Thaung Dan, Dr. Maung Maung, U Ba Nyein, U Kyaw Soe, Dr. Maung Lwin, Dr. Hla Han, U Thaung Kyi, U Than Sein, and U Sein Win.[22]

21. *Guardian* (daily), March 3, 1974, p. 8.
22. The remaining members were U Kyaw Soe, Col. Kyaw Win, U Khen Za Moong, U Khin Maung, U Soe Hlaing, Sao Ohn Hnya, U Tin Thein, U Tun Myint, U Tun Lin, Col. Min Thein, Mahn San Myat Shwe, U Hla Tun Pru, U Tha Din,

The heavy hand of the past also was placed on the elected Council of Ministers. The members of the People's Assembly chose eighteen of the twenty-one candidates offered. Among those elected were four former ministers under the RC, eleven former deputy ministers, and three new members. U Sein Win was chosen prime minister, and a civilian former cabinet officer, U Lwin, became deputy prime minister. The strong influence of the active military leadership was represented in the selection of the senior officers for the key posts of defense, cooperatives, and health.[23] The minister of defense, Brigadier Tin U, also became chief of staff of the armed forces, thus removing all separation between the government and the military.

The councils of People's Justices, People's Attorneys, and People's Inspectors were kept small, and at least one active senior military officer was elected to each.[24]

Finally, the key National Defense and Security Committee included three retired senior military officers, three active military officers, and three civilians who had enjoyed cabinet or other high posts in the government of the Revolutionary Council.[25]

Comm. Thaung Tin, U Than Sein (Arakan), Dr. Thein Aung, Thakin Aung Min, U Dingra Tang.

23. The Council of Ministers and the cabinet posts were as follows: U Sein Win, prime minister; U Lwin, deputy prime minister and minister of planning and finance; U Ko Ko, minister of home and religious affairs; U Maung Maung Kha, minister of industry; Dr. Nyi Nyi, minister of mines; U Tha Kyaw, minister of transport and communications; U Htin Kyaw, minister of construction; Col. Sein Lwin, minister of cooperatives; Col. Kyi Maung, minister of health; Dr. Khin Maung Win, minister of education; Brig. Tin U, minister of defense; U Ye Goung, minister of agriculture and forests; U San Win, minister of trade; U Tun Tin, minister of labor; U Chit Khin, minister of information; U Van Kulh, minister of social welfare; U Aye Maung, minister of culture; U Hla Phone, minister of foreign affairs.

24. Council of People's Justices: U Aung Pe, chairman; U Kyi Mya; Lt. Col. Soe Hlaing; Col. Tun Aung Kyaw; U Thant Sin. Council of People's Attorneys: U Moun Moun Wynn, chairman; Col. Tin Aung; U Aye Maung; U Zaw Win; U Aung Hmi. Council of People's Insepctors: U San Maung, chairman; Col. San Kyi; U Tin Aung Hein; U Tun Aye; U Ba Nyein.

25. Members of the National Defense and Security Committee: U Sein Win (former brigadier and member of the RC) presently prime minister; U Thaung Kyi (former colonel and member of the RC) presently Council of State; U Kyaw Soe (former colonel and member of the RC) presently Council of State; Brig. Thaung Dan (former member of the RC) presently Council of State; Comm. Thaung Tin (former minister under RC) presently Council of State; U Lwin (former minister under RC) presently deputy prime minister; U Ko Ko (former minister under RC)

Once the government was organized, the euphoria of technically returning to constitutional government passed, and the People's Assembly devoted its time to the major questions inherited from the military government—security, national unity, and economic improvement. U Ne Win gave a major speech on the differences between the two governments he headed. Under the new government, he said, the People's Assembly is the source of authority, with the people granted power and encouraged to act with self-reliance and independence. In the present one-party system, he said, there no longer is need for "inter-party strife and struggle for power in the legislature." Time no longer need be wasted, and all can work for the welfare of the people and the country. The one and only goal is the promotion of the country's welfare. He asserted that "there will be no case in which partisanship and love of power will lead to rejection of proposals irrespective of the individual merit of the proposals." He called upon party members to put party interest behind national interest. In debate, time must be used well: "When speaking, time in the Hluttaw must be put to the maximum use for the benefit of the country. What is unnecessary must not be said and there should be no wavering." Elected representatives, he said, must know when to do the people's bidding and when to refuse. Representatives also must not think in local terms only: "If you don't consider it in a wider scope, if you are not farsighted and magnanimous, if you don't consider it on a national scale, unity might be adversely affected." The party, he said, must be vigilant to avoid deviation among younger members and the future leaders. The party, he argued, must also note that the people's enthusiasm waned during the election and there were "undesirable occurrences" in the campaign. He scolded the party, whose responsibility was to select candidates. "In the future the people must be able to elect only those who will be able to work for their benefit."[26]

But moralizing and lecturing the elected elite was no answer to the immediate problems of insurgency, national unity, and economic decay. On March 19, 1974, the government once again—as its predecessor had in 1963—declared an amnesty for

---

presently Council of Ministers; Brig. Tin U, chief of staff, armed forces; U Hla Phone (former deputy minister under RC) presently Council of Ministers.

26. *Guardian* (daily), March 6, 1974, pp. 1, 8, for complete text.

those in revolt and a reduction in sentence for those in jail. The amnesty was proclaimed at the very moment the armed forces were locked in serious battle with 1,500 rebels at Myawaddy on the Thai-Karen State border. Under the leadership of General Bo Mya, Burman and Karen rebels fought the government for six days (March 16 to 22); a combined air and ground response by the Burmese military was required to throw back the insurgents. Colonel Shwe Seing of the combined rebel force hailed the affair as a moral victory because it represented the first united military effort of Karen, Kayah, Shan, and Burman dissidents. On the northern front, the government reported fifteen clashes between its forces and the communist forces.[27]

In mid-March 1975, the government launched a major operation against a Communist stronghold in the Pegu area of central Burma. After several days of fighting, the government forces completely destroyed their opposition. Thakins Zin and Chit were killed along with 172 of their followers; 649 other Communists either were captured or surrendered. The government's losses were set at 135. The victory over the Communists in central Burma shifted the fight to the northeast, where Thakin Ba Thein Tin was elected chairman, and where the remaining forces of the Burma Communist party still enjoyed support and received military equipment from the Communist party of the People's Republic of China.[28] Thus, insurgency, which began during the first constitutional period and continued into the military period, remains an important fact of life for the leaders of the new constitutional dictatorship.

The problems facing the new government do not come only from the insurgents. The failures of the military past—maldistribution, withholding of basic foodstuffs at the source, inefficient management, and corruption among both civilian and military officials—are as much a part of the new as they were of the old. Ne Win told the Central Committee of the BSPP on May 2, 1974, of malpractices in the economy that were hurting the nation. Produc-

27. *New York Times*, March 27, 1974; *Asia Research Bulletin* (Singapore), 2, no. 11 (April 1974), 2608–2609.

28. "Monthly Political Supplement," *Asia Research Bulletin* (Singapore), 4, no. 11 (April 30, 1975), 78; *ibid.*, 5, no. 1 (June 30, 1975), 92.

tion of basic foods was less than planned and what entered the market was not distributed well, resulting in higher prices, hoarding, black markets, and outright shortages. Corruption among officials—managers of state industries, chairmen of SACs, and others—helped to aggravate the situation. Peasants, too, shared the blame by failing to repay government loans and withholding their produce from the legal market. Some of the problems facing Burma were caused by the failure of the trains to run on time and of government officials and workers to do their jobs with spirit and interest. Part of the problem traced back to the failure of the Revolutionary Council to deal effectively with the economy; part of it was due to practices that had a longer and deeper root in Burmese society.[29] In another address to his constituents, delivered a few days later, Ne Win picked up the theme, saying, "the most urgent problem now facing us, is the rise in prices,"[30] which he blamed on some external causes, though he was concerned with its domestic roots and the contributing attitude of the people.

A month later, the problem exploded. On June 6, 1974, a strike over food shortages, rising prices, and bad labor conditions erupted at the railway workshop in Insein and spread quickly to forty-two other state concerns with major conflicts occurring at the Thamaing Spinning Mill and Simbalaik Dockyard. Rioting followed, and the troops were called out to restore order. As in the past, the military-led constitutional government called out the troops; twenty-two persons were reported killed and more than sixty injured in the riots. The government claimed that the protests and strikes became riots because of the work of outside agitators. The laborers protested both economic and political issues. On the appeal of the prime minister, backed by the military, the riots ended; hundreds were arrested.[31]

Several weeks after the riots were put down, Ne Win addressed the public to give his assessment of their causes and suggest some ideas about their solution. He began by admitting the well-known fact that Burma was producing sufficient rice, but that farmers were withholding their produce from the legal market, with result-

29. *Guardian* (daily), May 3, 1974.
30. *Ibid.*, May 12, 1974.
31. *Times* (London), June 10, 1974.

ing maldistribution. Private rice dealers also withheld stocks in the hopes of driving up prices. Government holdings were not distributed evenly to the public. Normally, he said, the government sold between sixty and one hundred thousand tons a month; in 1974, it could not buy enough and was able to sell only forty thousand tons a month, thus helping to create a national shortage. Labor unrest, Ne Win said, also stemmed from workers being deprived of their rights, worker and manager disagreement, and other work-related causes. The problems this time, he reminded his listeners, were not too different from the problems at the time of the coup in 1962; despite the efforts to lead the nation to socialism, the military did not give enough attention to economic issues, and they remained unsolved. "The worst part of the labor problem is the stomach problem. Rice is the root cause of this problem."[32] Ne Win said that as president he could request the authorities to be lenient with the dissident workers and rioters but could not order them to do so. The rule of law, he reminded his listeners, must prevail over personal inclinations, and the responsibility for solving this and other problems rested with the Council of State, acting for the People's Assembly which was in recess.

In December 1974, the society exploded once again, this time over the manner in which the government sought to deny any honors to U Thant when his body was returned to Burma for burial. U Thant died in New York in November, and his remains were flown home after the representatives of the United Nations paid their respect to the organization's third secretary general. Because of a long-standing political feud between Thant and Ne Win, the Burma government sent no official delegation to receive the coffin and planned to inter it in an obscure cemetery in Rangoon. As the funeral procession moved toward the proposed burial site, the university students and Buddhist monks seized the coffin and took it to the campus where the remains were given the Buddhist rites for someone who had achieved distinction; they then buried the remains on the site of the student union building before its destruction by the military in 1962. The government responded by sending troops to the campus, reclaiming the coffin,

32. *Working People's Daily,* July 12, 1974.

and reburying it at a cemetery near the Shwedagon Pagoda. The military also arrested large numbers of students and monks, provoking a citywide riot, in which students attacked the police and military. Several sources reported that the students were cheered by the people in the streets. The government met these disorders by declaring martial law and using force to restore order. At least sixteen persons were officially reported killed, hundreds were wounded, and forty-five hundred were arrested before the rioting ended. The government quickly brought those under arrest to trial and sentenced those found guilty to three years imprisonment. Observers who witnessed the events reported that the students were using the Thant incident as a means of expressing their general antagonism and hostility to an incompetent and repressive government. The students singled out issues of corruption among government officials, basic food shortages, economic decline, loss of freedom, and the absence of jobs for university graduates.

In June 1975, a year after the workers' riots, students joined workers in a new demonstration protesting high living costs and demanding the release from prison of students who had been jailed following the U Thant riots. Sit-down strikes, labor demonstrations, and other forms of protest by workers and students lasted for one week. Again, the government closed all universities and used force to break up and end the demonstrations; 213 students were arrested. In July, 203 of those arrested were found guilty and given prison sentences ranging from four to nine years.[33]

In 1976 the political malaise spread to the guardians. On March 6, following yet another demonstration on the campus of Rangoon University, Ne Win surprised the nation by dismissing the minister of defense, General Tin U, who had been considered the third-ranking member of the ruling oligarchy and had a strong following in the armed forces. In July, a serious threat to the government occurred when a plot against Ne Win, San Yu, and the chief of intelligence, Colonel Tin Oo, by eleven captains and three majors was uncovered. The trial of the plotters in the fall of 1976 was reported in the daily press, and the decision of the judge was

33. *New York Times,* June 9, 12, 13, 1975; *Straits Times* (Singapore), July 17, 1975.

published in full. To the surprise of most Burmese, General Tin U was accused of knowing about the plot but not reporting it to the authorities. On January 12, 1977, the leader of the plot, Captain Ohn Kyaw Myint, was found guilty and sentenced to death; General Tin U was given a sentence of seven years imprisonment with hard labor and the rest of the accused were sentenced for periods ranging from life imprisonment to several years. At the trial, it was brought out that the plotters were moved by their dissatisfaction with the government's one-party system and the failures of the economic policies of the government.[34] The trial highlighted the fact that it was the younger officers, men who had been recruited and trained under the rule of the Revolutionary Council and had enjoyed a privileged way of life as part of the new elite, who turned against the regime and sought to bring it down. Although General Tin U was senior to the plotters and his military career began before the 1962 coup, he was seen as outside the group of military officers who have controlled Burma since 1962 and was a hero to the younger officers rising to seniority. His disgrace and imprisonment removed him from the political scene and eliminated him as a possible rival to Ne Win and San Yu, both in politics and the armed forces.

The riots, the attempted coup, and the trial were storm warnings to the party leadership that something very basic was wrong with the system. In November 1976, the party called a special congress and there, the secretary general, San Yu, admitted that the party program, adopted in 1974, was a failure and a new one had to be drawn up and adopted. He also acknowledged the shortcomings of the leaders and members in the party and announced that 54,193 members and leaders had been purged.[35] Those dropped from the party lost their seats in various state organs, party and mass organizations, and cooperatives.

In February 1977, the Third Congress of the Burma Socialist Program Party met at the Central Institute of Political Science, located outside of Rangoon. There were 1,311 delegates represent-

---

34. "Monthly Political Supplement," *Asia Research Bulletin* (Singapore) 6, no. 9 (February 28, 1977), 297.

35. M. C. Tun, "Diversion on the Road to Socialism," *Far Eastern Economic Review*, December 3, 1976, p. 18.

ing a party membership of 885,460; of that total, 181,617 were full members. The congress had two goals, discussing the political report of the Central Committee and choosing a new Central Committee; it had been decided, just prior to the congress, that 55 percent of the old Central Committee would resign and new members would be chosen to replace them. Among the topics covered in the report was the status of the party. The party, it noted, was defective on a number of grounds. Too many people had been admitted who did not abide by its rules. Factions had formed within party units; the technique of criticism and self-criticism was not practiced, and disruptive elements had infiltrated at all levels. The party leaders at all levels were singled out for criticism. They had failed to speak out, practice self-criticism, take corrective action when errors and failures were noted, and perform up to the standards expected of them. Following the reading and discussion of the report, several of the most prominent leaders during the military period voluntarily withdrew from candidacy for membership on the Central Committee; among them were the prime minister, U Sein Win, the finance minister, U Lwin, the home minister, U Ko Ko, and the former socialist theorist and adviser, U Ba Nyein. When the new Central Committee was elected on February 27, Ne Win, once again, was chosen as its chairman and San Yu was chosen as secretary general. New names replaced old ones on the committee, but the leadership was firmly in the hands of the man who made the coup fifteen years earlier.[36]

Following the close of the congress, the People's Assembly met and Sein Win resigned as prime minister; other ranking ministers who had been dropped from the party's Central Committee also resigned their positions. In their place, U Maung Maung Kha was chosen prime minister, U Than Sein was selected to head the Ministry of Finance and Planning; U Tun Lin was chosen to head the Ministry of Transport and Communication, and Colonel Sein Lwin was named to head the Ministry for Home and Religious Affairs. All were members of the new Central Committee of the party, but none ranked higher than eleventh. The change in government represented a change in administrators and not in policy

36. *Guardian* (daily), February 22 through 28, 1977.

makers. If the problems of the past were the result of poor administration, then these changes might lead to improvements; if the
problems were the result of bad policies, then no real change
occurred, despite the drama of the party congress and the criticism
and self-criticism of the report of the Central Committee.

One other aspect of the third congress is important to note. In
two of the resolutions passed at the close of the meeting, pragmatism in approaching political and economic problems was emphasized. In discussing changes in the party constitution, one
resolution said that if an amendment was necessary it should be
in accordance with changing times and local conditions. In the
second, it said that if guidelines for the new four-year economic
plan, that had just been adopted needed to be changed, the Central
Committee was authorized to do so in order to make timely improvements and to overcome the economic hardships encountered
in the state. This recognition that everything is impermanent and
subject to the law of change finds its antecedents both in the
Buddhist tradition and the fundamental ideology of the party. The
flexibility implied in the resolution suggests that the men in power
want to move away from the rigidity of their predecessors without
seeming to have departed from the basic ideas in their ideology. If
the new leaders prove to be more sensitive to changing conditions
and demands and to respond to them, they may dampen the unrest
demonstrated by segments of the population and the military
during the past few years and even win some popular support.

But flexibility is not enough. Given the repeated failures in
judgment, planning and execution over the past decade and a half,
the problem also finds its roots in the personnel who have been in
command. Neither the decisions at the congress or in the People's
Assembly, held immediately afterward, suggests that responsibility
for planning the future has shifted to new leaders. As long as Ne
Win, San Yu, and a few others continue to hold real power and
make the important policy decisions, the pragmatism and flexibility
in the new plans may prove to be no more than empty promises and
meaningless guidelines. All the political, economic, and social problems of the past are still there; it remains to be seen how the new
administrators and the old planners deal with them.

6 | The Economy before and after the Coup and Some Political Implications

One measure of political systems is their ability to create the means for the achievement of society's goals. According to *The Burmese Way to Socialism*, the aim of the socialist economy that coup leaders intended to create was the "establishment of a new society for all, economically secure and morally better, to live in peace and prosperity." The basis for such a society was not be to equalitarian; men, the *BWS* stated, are unequal in physical as well as intellectual abilities. The first step, therefore, was to reduce the gap between individuals in their wealth and power and to see that each worked according to his ability and received according to the quality and quantity of his labor. The new leaders would have to restructure society—to carry out an economic as well as a social revolution. They would have to alter institutions, values, and behavior patterns that had carried over, not only from the constitutional period, but from colonial and precolonial times. To discuss and analyze the military's economic policies and some of their social implications, it is necessary to look briefly at conditions the soldier-rulers inherited when they seized power and the programs and policies in force at that time.

An Outline of the Society and Economy Prior to the Coup

From the 1930s onward, Burmese leaders were committed to altering the nation's economy from dependence, primarily upon the export of rice and other agricultural and mineral products, to a balance between agriculture and industry. Prior to the coup government policy had been to try to transform Burma by using its own financial, intellectual, and technical resources. Thus, from independence on, economic plans were based on using revenue earned from the sale of rice and other primary products to create an industrial sector. Economic development was assumed to be the responsibility of the government, assisted by the private sector. Between 1947 and 1962, several plans were drawn up, altered, and replaced by new ones.[1] All assumed the quick recovery of agricultural production from the devastation of World War II and an expanding world market for Burma's products.

A second characteristic of the economic policy was dependence upon the individual farmer to make technical decisions about planting and harvesting and to do the work, assuming that the state and private moneylender would provide the necessary capital and that the state would market the main product—rice. Although the constitution declared that the state was the ultimate owner of the land, it was held primarily by private owners, who bought and sold and all too often pledged it as security against a loan. The agricultural technology of this period differed little from that of previous generations, with water buffalo to pull a simple plow, hand transplanting of the rice shoots, and natural fertilizer to enrich the soil. Compared with other rice-producing nations, the output was low—approximately thirty baskets per acre.[2] The government, through the State Agricultural Marketing Board (SAMB), purchased the product from the farmer at a low fixed rate—with no differential for quality—and sold it abroad at world market prices.

1. In 1947 the Burmese leaders wrote a *Two Year Plan for Economic Development for Burma* (Rangoon: Superintendent, Government Printing and Stationery, 1948). In the early 1950s the government hired several foreign advisory groups to draw up an eight-year program of development. See Knappen, Tippets, Abbett, and McCarthy, *Comprehensive Report: Economic and Engineering Development of Burma, Prepared for the Government of the Union of Burma*, 2 vols. (Aylesbury, England, 1953). For a discussion of the *Report* and its implementation, see Louis J. Walinsky, *Economic Development in Burma, 1951–1960* (New York: Twentieth Century Fund, 1962). In 1956 a new four-year plan was implemented. See Union of Burma, Ministry of National Planning, *Second Four-Year Plan for the Union of Burma 1961–2 to 1964–65.* (Rangoon: Superintendent, Government Printing and Stationery, 1961), for an assessment of the original 1956 four-year plan and the outline of the second four-year plan.

2. A basket weighs approximately forty-six pounds.

Between 1950 and 1954 the government netted large profits that were invested in the industrial sector, and relatively little was put back into agriculture.

From 1945 until the Korean War truce (1953), world demand for rice and other grains was strong; prices were good, and buyers were not too discriminating about the quality of the product. By the end of 1954, the situation changed; as demand fell, competition increased and the quality of the product became an important consideration. During the boom years, Burma increased its agricultural output and when demand tapered off found itself with ever-increasing stocks of poor quality, due in part to poor milling practices.

The farmer throughout this period received little inducement to improve the quality of his product even though the government tried to encourage the sowing of high-quality seed. The cultivator had few needs and was able to purchase consumer goods at relatively stable prices. He protested the restrictions placed on the sale of his crops, but not vigorously. He found himself standing alone against predator insurgents and dacoits as well as against a government that did not listen closely to what he said. He responded by growing his crops in the traditional way and resisting most of the efforts to get him to modernize his practices. Conservative by nature, he wanted little beyond what he grew and, most of all, to be left alone by government and insurgents. His cash income together with monies he borrowed satisfied his needs, and when he had a little left over, he invested it in festivals and religious activity—giving a feast or decorating a pagoda.

The urban sector was relatively small with a mixed population of alien and indigenous members. While the professions, law, medicine, and engineering, were populated by both groups, the business community was dominated by foreign entrepreneurs and business firms. Despite the government's policy of seeking to assist the growth of an indigenous class of businessmen, its method— parceling out export and import licenses primarily to Burmese businessmen—encouraged corruption and failed in its objective. The business and professional elites were vocal and critical of government policies and practices, especially as they affected the interests of these two groups, but they lacked power in the political parties and government and therefore were unable to obstruct or alter the actions of bureaucracy or of the elected officials. They looked abroad for ideas and models and sought to create a Westernized enclave in a traditional society. The laboring sector was mobilized by government-dominated trade unions and mass organizations and participated as directed in political campaigns and demonstrations. Despite their number and organization, laborers were ineffective in furthering their own interests. Unlike the urban elite, they were traditional in their values and behavior and did not look abroad for alternative ideas and models.

After 1954, the government discovered that as the chief marketer of rice, its vehicle—SAMB—was inefficient and staffed with unqualified personnel at all levels. It lacked a proper accounting system and didn't know exactly how much rice was on hand, where it was stored, and what condition it was in. Storage facilities were inadequate and the rice in various stages of deterioration. At this point, the government sought outside advisers to help correct the situation.

The declining market forced the government to seek new customers. Between 1955 and 1960 it traded rice to socialist states on a barterlike basis,[3] thus disposing of surplus stocks, but forcing it to accept manufactured goods that often were substandard and, in many cases, not suited to its needs. Further, the government discovered that some of the traded rice was resold for cash or retraded to countries that were formerly Burma's cash customers.[4] Despite these disadvantages, this form of trade was not abandoned when the market changed, as the Burmese government felt that retaining these contacts would enable it to offset the effects of a fluctuating free market. From 1956 onward, the Burmese were able to purchase needed agricultural products such as powdered milk,

3. See Robert L. Allen, "Burma's Clearing Accounts Agreements," *Pacific Affairs*, 31, no. 2 (June 1958), 147–164, for a comprehensive analysis of the trade during this period between Burma, the Soviet Union, the People's Republic of China, and the East European states.

4. On several occasions between 1956 and 1959, it was reported that the Chinese bartered the rice they obtained from Burma for rubber and other products offered by former rice customers of the Burmese. On September 18, 1962, the *Nation* reported that a shipload of rice purchased by Yugoslavia was unloaded in Singapore and resold at a considerable profit.

tobacco, and cotton from the United States under special conditions that did not consume Burma's limited foreign exchange.[5]

During the constitutional period, the industrial sector never developed as planned. At its base were small manufacturers primarily of consumer goods. The methods and equipment were labor-intensive and antiquated. When the government began to invest in the industrial sector, it followed no clear plan either for investment or in the type of industries established. With no assurance of a steady flow of raw materials, it built a textile mill, a cold-rolled steel mill, and a pharmaceutical plant. In addition, it sought to revive its oil fields and refineries, expand its timber mills, and create a wood products industry. Hampered by a lack of managers and technicans, shortages of raw materials, poor products, and lack of an adequate transportation system and power resources, it neither fully satisfied internal needs nor made products that could compete in the world market.

To solve some of these problems, especially in the area of personnel, it embarked upon a rapid program of education by expanding the number of schools and teachers and sending some of the most promising candidates abroad for higher and technical education. Mass education was the goal, but it could not be achieved without a pool of trained teachers and well-equipped facilities. One result was that thousands of students went through the system without obtaining a thorough education. As most schools were constructed in the urban or nearby rural areas not directly threatened by insurgency, education was concentrated in the urban population—the smallest sector of the society.

Socialism has been the goal of every government in Burma since independence. The problem has been how to attain it. In 1947, a two-year plan was drawn up to lay the foundation for a planned economy. Its objectives were to redistribute the land, secure a fair share to the cultivators, and restore agriculture so that the nation

5. Under U.S. Public Law 480, surplus agricultural products could be sold abroad for local currency to nations that normally could not afford their purchase using their foreign exchange for payment. The U.S. agreed not to demand foreign exchange for local currency. In 1966, the U.S. returned K82.3 million (U.S. $17.29 million) to Burma; K57.6 million (U.S. $12.1 million) were given for school and hospital construction, while the remaining K24.7 million (U.S. $5.19 million) was to be a loan repayable in dollars over a thirty-year period at 3 percent interest.

regained its prewar position as a rice exporter and became self-sufficient in other agricltural products. The plan also called for the nationalization of the timber industry, restoration of transportation and communications to pre-World War II levels, and development of an industrial sector on the basis of state ownership. The plan never was realized because no financial policy was developed to underwrite it and it was not fitted into the annual budgets. Problems of law and order, insurgency and civil war, deflected the government's energies between 1948 and 1951. When that threat to the nation began to recede, the leaders turned again to economic planning.

Starting afresh, the Burmese government, with the aid of the United States Economic Cooperation Administration (ECA), engaged American economists and engineers to make an economic and engineering survey of the nation and help draw up an eight-year plan. The KTA plan, as it became known, sought to double gross national product between 1951 and 1960. This meant a 31 percent increase over the prewar gross domestic product, or a rate of growth of about 4 percent per year.[6] The plan called for investment from both the public and private sectors. Rising prices and failure to meet the targets forced the government to turn to foreign loans and aid as sources for capital formation. Between 1951 and 1956, no more than 10 percent of new capital was expended in agriculture and irrigation, while industry, power, and transportation claimed approximately 20 percent of capital funds. A fall in the price of rice meant there was no financial surplus to fund the plan, and Burma was forced to engage in deficit financing and the expenditure of foreign exchange reserves built up during the boom years.

As the nation's leaders became aware of the problems of transforming a backward agrarian society into a modern state with a balanced economy, they began to change their priorities and reallocate the meager resources. Socialism remained the goal, but as U Nu, then prime minister, said on June 8, 1957, it was a major blunder to launch "our plans without first preparing the ground

6. For a summary of the KTA, see Ministry of National Planning, *Second Four-Year Plan*, pp. 2–11.

systematically." Three negative consequences resulted: buildings
and machinery were ordered and built before plans were made for
the production and supply of the raw materials; machinery was
delivered before the buildings to house it were completed; no
modern accounting system was developed to compute costs and
measure the efficiency of state enterprises. The KTA plan was set
aside and a new four-year plan was drawn up in 1956 for implementation a year later. It recognized that the government could
not undertake responsibility for everything that needed to be
done; therefore, cooperative societies and the private sector were
expected to share more fully in Burma's development. This did not
mean total freedom for private entrepreneurs; they were to be
encouraged to contribute under the direction of the state, but this
was clearly a temporary measure in the creation of the economic
basis of a future socialist state.[7] Under the first four-year plan
(1957–1961) investment in agriculture, forests, and mining
doubled, while investment in industry and power was the same
as before. Investment in transportation and communications remained about the same because of the need not only to rebuild the
destruction caused by the insurgents, but to expand them in order
to reach more people. Expenditures in law and order continued as
the government sought to bring insurgency to an end.

From 1958 to 1960, the caretaker government of General
Ne Win was in power and the state-controlled sector of the
economy broadened to include the economic enterprises launched
earlier by the military to satisfy its own needs and new ones started
by the military managers during this period. Under the Defense
Services Institute, military-managed enterprises grew rapidly and
entered a wide variety of commercial fields in competition with
existing domestic and foreign firms. In all, the DSI controlled
fourteen enterprises, ranging from shipping and banking to hotels
and the sale of local products such as *ngapi* (fishpaste) to firewood.
It introduced new business practices and demonstrated the business capability of Burmese managers when backed by sufficient

---

7. U Nu, *Premier's Report to the People on Law and Order, National Solidarity, Social
Welfare, National Economy, and Foreign Affairs* (Rangoon: Director of Information,
1957).

capital and given sufficient authority to do their jobs.[8] The experiment in caretaker government revealed that a small pool of able administrators existed in the military who had the capacity to apply their talents to economic and commercial matters.

Some idea of the state of the economy when Burma returned to elected government and prepared to embark upon the second four-year plan in 1961 can be derived from Table 7.

Table 7. Comparison of some economic indicators, prewar and 1960

	Prewar	1960	1960 as a percentage of prewar
Paddy, sown acres (thousand)	12,832	10,667	83
Paddy production (thousand tons)	7,426	6,916	93
Rice exports (thousand tons)	3,303	2,080	64
Total sown acres (thousand)	19,166	17,515	91
Agricultural exports, other than rice (thousand tons)	249	311	125
Teak production (cubic tons)	453,481	332,900	73
Teak exports (cubic tons)	215,000	89,800	39
Other timber products (cubic tons)	501,866	611,000	122
Other timber exports (cubic tons)	40,600	10,000	25
Petroleum products (thousand gals.)	275,673	143,342	52
Mineral products (tons)	188,992	56,204	30
Mineral exports (tons)	139,402	46,760	34
Electric power installed capacity (KW)	33,800	191,000	565
Railroad passengers (passenger miles in millions)	449	969	216
Railroad freight (ton-miles in millions)	579	469	81
Inland water transportation passengers (passenger miles in millions)	8	4.9	61

Source: Ministry of National Planning, *Second Four Year Plan*, pp. 17–18.

The trends noted in Table 7 continued for the next two years until the military seized power. Paddy acreage increased by 5.5 percent but production of rice dropped by 2.5 percent and exports dropped from 2.080 to 1.841 million tons. This level of exports was never again achieved throughout the military period. For agricul-

---

8. Government of the Union of Burma, Ministry of Information, *Is Trust Vindicated?* (Rangoon: Director of Information, 1960), pp. 223–250.

ture as a whole, acreage increased by 9 percent to equal the prewar high; exports of agricultural products other than rice rose from 311 to 383 thousand tons. Both teak and other wood exports grew appreciably, and petroleum products continued an upward trend. Mineral production and exports continued to lag far behind the agricultural sector and neither approached the modest figures of 1959–1960. Both power and transport also showed significant gains. Despite the coup leaders' published views and those of many writers about Burma, the economy in 1961–1962 was growing. Peace in the countryside meant that more land was being cultivated and more crops brought to market; more forest products were being extracted and marketed and the power base for industrialization and transport was growing.

The most notable change in the economy in 1961 was in the area of ownership. Before the war, half the land of lower Burma was owned by nonagriculturalists; rice milling and external marketing, exploitation of forest reserves and marketing of timber products, mining and banking, insurance and shipping and foreign trade were in the hands of foreigners or resident aliens. In 1961 the land was still in the hands of the cultivators, although technically it belonged to the state; rice milling and external marketing of rice and teak were government enterprises. The government was a major partner in mining; it controlled the Central Bank and through its Commercial Bank and Agricultural Bank, provided more than half the commercial credit offered to business and a large portion of the loans to the farmers. Through joint ventures with private and domestic entrepreneurs and the encouragement of cooperative societies, it was moving positively toward complete national control of the economy and laying the basis for its ultimate socialization.

The Economy under the Military

Although socialism became the watchword of the coup government from its first days in office, not until January 1963 were serious steps taken to carry out the ideological goals. In that month, General Ne Win announced that the government had adopted a new economic policy. Henceforth, the functions of production, distribution, import, and export would be taken over by the state.

No new private industries would be started. The Union of Burma Agricultural Marketing Board (UBAMB), the successor to the SAMB, would make all purchases of paddy and all foreign sales. Eventually, all rice milling would be taken over by the government.[9] On February 23, the government seized all private banks, foreign and domestic. The blow against foreign banks was softened by the decision of the government to allow them to repatriate their original capital and some assests after the value had been determined and all debts had been paid.[10] Later that year the government moved against private firms in the areas of exports, imports, and sales. It also nationalized all gasoline filling stations, the pearl and marine fishing industries, and several large and small manufacturing and assembly plants. Under the new Trade Disputes Amending Law (1963), the government seized businesses where labor disputes were in progress and suspended their operations. The military rulers also forced the liquidation of all joint ventures between government and private capital and put their activities directly under government control.

To manage its mushrooming empire, the Revolutionary Council hastily created several overlapping administrative and managerial agencies. Importing was divided between several new government corporations. Exporting was unified under a state-controlled office. The rapid action of nationalizing and socializing the commercial and industrial sectors of the economy produced shortages, rising prices, and black markets. Because there were no trained personnel to assume the management functions of so many state enterprises, the government gave added responsibilities to the proven managers within the military ranks and appointed junior officers as their subordinates. The assault upon the private sector gave clear indication that the military rulers had taken the first steps toward socialism without regard for the effect upon the population—the ultimate beneficiaries of the government's action.

In contrast to the great haste shown in nationalizing business,

---

9. *Nation*, February 16, 1963.

10. One of the banks seized belonged to the People's Republic of China. The People's Republic did not seek either the repatriation of its capital or its assets; instead, it gave them to Burma as a gift of friendship between the two nations. See *Nation*, June 18, 1963, for details.

trade, and industry, the government moved cautiously in the agricultural sector. There, the military rulers, who were eager to win popular backing and establish a broad base of support among the peasants, moved to restrict landlords and free the farmers. In April 1963, they promulgated the Peasant's Rights Protection Law, which prohibited the courts from attaching and seizing land, animals, and implements in payment of outstanding debts and protected the farmer's right to sell his land or personal property as he desired. During the same year, the government also promulgated the Tenancy Act, which declared that rent could be paid in either cash or kind and fixed the rate of rent according to the particular crop grown. The government also created land committees in every village to decide land use and sales and to settle disputes in ownership. Finally, the government appropriated K700 million for loans to farmers so they would not need to seek financial aid from private money lenders. Two years later, General Ne Win declared, "We have one unfinished business which mocks our declaration that we will not . . . permit the exploitation of man by man. It concerns the continued exaction of tenancy rent by the landlords." On April 5, 1965, the omission was corrected when the RC promulgated an amendment to the Tenancy Act abolishing rent on farmlands. The act marked "the destruction of the last line of landlordism."[11]

All these acts were calculated to secure the peasant against his traditional human enemies. He now was free to farm his land as he chose and to market as he desired. The backing of the local land committee protected his tenure. Most important, the fruit of his labor belonged to him. In turn, the military government expected that he would feel indebted to it for his new freedoms and would produce more, pay back the money it lent to him, and sell his product to the state at the prices it set. It also hoped that the farmer would adopt more modern methods of farming, support the socialist objectives of the leaders, and begin to develop cooperatives and other socialist institutions in place of the traditional modes of

11. Government of Burma, Burma Socialist Program Party, *Party Seminar 1965* (Rangoon: Burma Socialist Program Party, 1966), p. 82. When this act was passed there reportedly were 1.1 million tenants paying K13 million to about 350,000 landlords; about one-third of the landlords were nonnationals. See *Forward*, 3 no. 18 (May 1, 1965), 2.

economic and social organization. The peasant did not respond exactly as desired; chaotic purchasing and grading policies of the new rulers and the need to travel long distances between the farm and the puchasing centers often to find an inexperienced buyer grading the product according to the rules rather than on a basis of expertise and experience alienated the farmer from his benefactor.

Further, the government's failure to distribute basic consumer goods efficiently gave the farmer no incentive to produce more than he needed for his family. The government's effort to purchase paddy from the producer at low nationally uniform prices, so that the price to the consumer could be held down throughout the country, caused some peasants to shift from paddy to other crops that offered larger margins of profit and less government regulation. The emergence of a black market in imported goods from Thailand caused more of the annual crop to be withheld from government purchasers and illegally disposed of in exchange for consumer goods. Finally, the market in Thailand for cattle depleted Burma's scarce supply as animals were sold out of the country. Only in July 1974 did the government finally recognize the need to give the farmer monetary incentives if it wished to purchase his crop, and it set the price of paddy 50 percent higher than in previous years—from K600 to K900 per 100 baskets.

While the rural population was able to eat sufficiently during the period of military rule, the smaller urban sector faced serious shortages, extreme inflation, and black markets for the basic commodities necessary for daily life. Between faulty government policies and natural disasters, Burma's economy entered a vicious downward spiral—lower exports, less foreign exchange earned, less consumer goods imported. Despite the expectations of the leaders and their belief in their Burmese way to socialism, the economy gradually declined as its growth slowed down.

Using the government's own figures, the performance of agriculture is easy to chart. Paddy acreage increased to over 12 million acres from 1963 onward, but it never exceeded prewar planting of 12.8 million acres despite the opening of new lands and the reactiviation of land long out of production. During the first two years of military rule, production continued its upward trend only to descend in 1965 and reach a low point in 1966–1967.

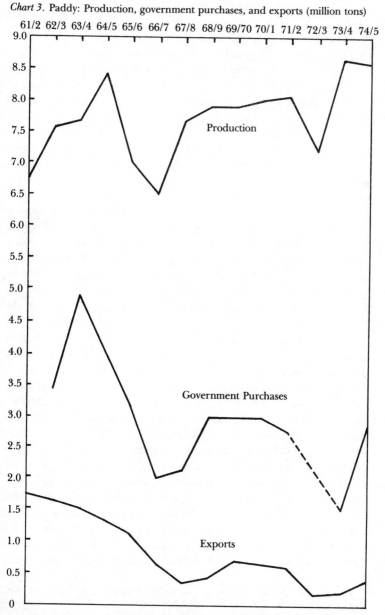

Chart 3. Paddy: Production, government purchases, and exports (million tons)

Note: Data on government purchases for the year 1972–1973 not available.
Sources: *Report to the People*, 1970–1971; ibid., 1971–1972; *Report to the Pyithu Hluttaw*, 1975–1976; Far Eastern Economic Review, *Asia Yearbook*, 1972, 1973, 1974, 1975, and 1976.

Recovery followed the improvement in the weather, and when the climate turned bad again in 1972, production declined (see Chart 3). The next year it increased to over 8 million tons. Production, however, does not give an accurate picture of the success or failure of government policies. State purchases and exports are a more reliable measure. During the first two years of military rule, state purchases were strong and improving; after 1964, the state never reached the levels of the preceding constitutional period. Finally, rice exports, the measure of the ability to earn foreign exchange for both consumer and capital goods, declined steadily from the high levels under civilian rule.

Trends similar to these in paddy production and rice exports existed in other agricultural crops. Planting in sugar cane, Virginia tobacco and groundnut, pulses and cotton expanded under military rule, and production, too, showed significant increases when the weather was good. As with paddy, however, state purchases did not increase significantly over the amounts recorded during constitutional rule and exports, following a limited rise at first, declined steadily.

In their drive to nationalize the economy, the military rulers took a third step during this period; they sought to eliminate foreign firms and alien capitalists active in the economy. On January 1, 1963, they ended their joint venture with the Burma Oil Company by taking over the outstanding shares and, two years later, on January 18, 1965, they ended a similar joint venture with the Burma Corporation (mining) in the same way. Other foreign firms such as Unilever were nationalized because they failed to repay government loans or did not maintain production. To get at the small businessman and indigenous capitalist who was suspected of supporting the black market and hoarding goods, the government, on May 17, 1964, recalled all fifty- and one-hundred-kyat notes and demanded explanations of those who held them. This law fell most heavily upon alien Indians and provoked a mass exodus among those living and working in urban areas (see Chapter 7).[12]

12. The Burmese government did not make restitution to the Indians who left Burma in 1964 until 1974. Specifically, it made provision to pay for buildings used by the government and returned title to buildings not used by the government. It paid compensation from the date of nationalization to the date of return of title and paid

The economic moves described above and others taken between 1963 and 1965 followed no clear plan, and the result, as noted, was economic dislocation, inflation, and confusion.

The burden of socialist endeavor fell hardest upon the urban population. Caught between the millstones of low and fixed wages and high prices and commodity shortages, they had few options open as a means of escape. In a nation where skilled labor received K180 per month (about U.S. $30) and unskilled labor received as little as K82 (about U.S. $16), necessities had to be purchased from the People's Stores where prices for food and ordinary cloth *longyi* doubled between 1962 and 1966, and the buyer often found that the desired item was out of stock or in very short supply.

By mid-1966 the deterioration of the economic situation provoked General Ne Win to make a personal investigation. Following a study from May 30 through June 8, he ordered the Trade Council to make a thorough review and to recommend changes. On September 28 the council rescinded some of its nationalization orders issued the preceding January and restored a portion of private trade in locally produced goods.

The reforms were not sufficient to alter the situation for the average urban dweller. A poor harvest produced serious shortage of such basic items as rice, cooking oil, and *ngapi* in the larger towns and cities of Burma. In Rangoon, many Chinese merchants openly black marketed these items, creating strong anti-Chinese feelings for the first time since independence. When anti-Chinese rioting erupted, following the Red Badge incident in June and July 1967 (see Chapter 7), many Chinese shops and restaurants were looted and demolished in an expression of patriotism in the support of their nation against China and hostility against those who profited from their plight. From interviews with residents of Rangoon, held less than a year after the affair, the author learned that the shortages in the spring of 1967 were so severe that the people were near revolt; the Red Badge affair, however, deflected their rage from

---

for furniture and equipment. There could be no appeal from the government decision and no compensation was paid before all taxes and debts had been cleared. Finally, the government limited itself to compensation payments of K10 thousand per year with K1 thousand in cash and the remainder in noninterest-bearing bonds. See *Asian Recorder*, 20, no. 10, (March 5–11, 1974), 11881.

their own leaders to the Chinese. When tempers finally cooled toward the end of the year, the new harvest was beginning to enter the market, and shortages began to disappear, the government quietly repaired Chinese restaurants and some shops, and communal tensions diminished.

From 1968 through 1971, good harvests and some improvements in state purchasing and distribution gave the urban population sufficient goods at reasonable prices. For the next two years poor harvests brought a return of hoarding, rising prices, and black markets. The government, through inaction against private trading and black marketing and the decontrol of basic consumer goods, in effect, admitted its inability to halt the illegal trade or to provide the wanted merchandise through their own channels. By 1972, Bogyoke Market—the largest in Rangoon—was filled with private traders offering both domestic and foreign goods at prices most people could not afford.

Planning under the Military

In 1967 the military quietly wrote and began to implement an economic plan. U Ba Nyein, a key economic adviser to the government, gave a rare interview in 1969 that shed light on the economy and plans for the future.[13] He admitted that to date government economic policies generally were not popular with most of the people. He confirmed the widely known fact that all production, per capita income, and foreign trade had declined drastically. His only news was that an unpublished four-year plan existed and was in its second year of operations. Although he did not reveal many details, he did report that the plan called for concentration on agriculture, increased rice production, expansion of irrigation, mechanization, and the use of fertilizers. In the industrial sector, it emphasized consumer goods, chemicals, fertilizers, oil refineries, and hydroelectric power. After agriculture, consumer goods had the highest priority. To finance the plan, the government planned to invest U.S. $120 million annually. But, because of an external

13. Carol Goldstein, "Human Errors," *Far Eastern Economic Review*, 63, no. 1 (January 2, 1969), 13–14.

debt of U.S. $180 million and a deficit in the current year of U.S. $28.8 million, there was little likelihood that the investment could be made on a sustained basis; more important, there was no evidence that the men in power had the experience and talent to translate the plan into reality.

Little more was heard of the plan, and in 1970 the country was drawn into a discussion of the first official and public plan of the Burma Socialist Program Party, which was to begin in 1971–1972 and run for four years. Much attention was given to the fact that there was to be consultation with all sectors of the economy and all areas of the nation as the leaders developed and implemented the program. The results of the first year of the plan were disappointing. According to the government's own analysis, there was a net increase in output of only 2.7 percent over the preceding "unplanned" year. Thus, the people's level of living had not improved. The chief reason given was "the incapability of the productive sectors to perform according to the plan."[14]

Production during the second year of the plan was even worse. Total net output increased by 2.2 percent. Measured against a rising birth rate, the economic status of the individual decreased again. This time, agriculture along with the other productive sectors of the economy failed to meet its target. The government summed up its failures after the second year as the result of "natural hazards and weaknesses in the implementation of the plan."[15] The third year of the plan, 1973–1974, even more modest targets were set, but again the goals were not met.

The first twelve years of military rule by the socialist-soldiers saw the economy decline steadily as dogmatic pursuit of ideology displaced common sense and inexperienced administrators displaced the civilian politicians and bureaucrats. Those who have argued that the military are modernizers will find that a careful study of Burma under military rule will bring that proposition into serious question.

14. Revolutionary Council of the Union of Burma, Ministry of Planning and Finance, *Report to the People by the Government of the Union of Burma on the Financial, Economic and Social Conditions for 1973–74*, Book I (Rangoon: Ministry of Planning and Finance, 1973), pp. 4–5.

15. *Ibid.*

The Economy under Constitutional Dictatorship

Implementation of the new constitution in 1974 brought little or no change to Burma's economy. Following the cosmetic political changeover, the government abandoned the first four-year plan one year short of completion and began the implementation of a second four-year plan. Speaking to the People's Assembly in March 1974, the finance minister, U Lwin, noted that the target for investment for this plan would be K5.91 billion (U.S. $1.2 billion); it was anticipated that K4 billion would come from the public sector with foreign aid and loans providing 29 percent or K1.15 billion. The private sector was expected to provide the remaining K1.9 billion. The plan's objectives were modest: for the first year, 1974–1975, it anticipated that agriculture would increase by 5.5 percent; forest industries by 4.7 percent; manufactures by 12.8 percent; power generation by 26 percent; transport by 4.4 percent; trade by 6.6 percent; and construction by 2.2 percent. Per capita income was to be raised by 6.4 percent and consumption by 3.5 percent. But, by year's end, it was clear that the export target of K1.58 million (U.S. $328 thousand) would not be reached because rice exports had to be curtailed to meet domestic needs. With the exception of mining, production in all areas was below target.

The first budget proposed by the government under the 1974 constitution reflected the deepening economic problems facing Burma. It assumed a deficit of K581.9 million (U. S. $121 million). The major items of expenditure were for government and administration, K276 million, and for defense, K675 million. To pay these and other costs, it was anticipated that taxes would produce K1.268 billion and government enterprises would produce a surplus of K974.3 million. Even as the minister was explaining the budget, he was forced to acknowledge that the government overestimated revenue from income tax and saw no alternative source contributing the needed revenue. The budget for 1975 and the economy showed little or no improvement.

1976 was the midpoint of the second four-year plan and a time for decision. The targets set forth in the plan were not met, and there was little likelihood that they might be reached in the next few years. Further, the social unrest of the previous years together with the abortive coup by the young military officers suggested to those in charge that some changes were necessary. The first hint that a rethinking of economic goals and methods was under way was the announcement by the government in September that the World Bank was forming a consortium of Western nations—Australia, Canada, France, West Germany, Japan, Britain, and the United States—to provide aid and loans to Burma. Before the year ended, the World Bank sent a survey mission and held preliminary talks with government leaders about changes in the economic structure and opening the economy to foreign investment. Also, a preliminary meeting between Burma and the consortium was held in Japan where the Burma officials reviewed their plans and needs with representatives from the West.

At the third BSPP Congress in February and the meeting of People's Assembly in March 1977 the party and government officials revealed how bad things really were and outlined the new direction the economy would follow in the future. According to the report of the party's secretary general, San Yu, the rate of growth of the economy was only half of its expected target, 2.6 percent instead of 4 percent per year. Exports in 1975–1976 had fallen below those of 1974–1975—from K511.3 million to K504.6 million—or approximately half of the projected goal. Productivity in the state and cooperative sectors increased at an annual rate of 1.2 percent, instead of the projected 2 percent. To remedy these and other defects, the secretary general announced that in the future, state and cooperative enterprises will be run "on commercial lines" and an incentive scheme will be devised to encourage successful operations. The report also raised the question of whether the "present situation resulted either from weaknesses in the policies or in the people who implement, particularly leading party cadres."[16]

The social effects of the nation's economic shortcomings were also cited in the secretary general's report. Inflation had risen from 100 in 1972 to 295 in October 1976. Deterioration in morals was noted among workers and servicemen. "Taking advantage of these difficulties, attempts have even been made to do away with the party and the socialist system and even to assassinate leaders of the

16. *Working People's Daily*, February 23, 1977.

Burma Socialist Program Party."[17] To correct these and other problems, the BSPP Congress was charged with responsibility to discuss, criticize, and pass decisions on all matters so that by 1981–1982, the country would be back on the path of the twenty-year plan—the comprehensive plan for modernizing and socializing Burma established when the new constitutional system began; the present four-year plan is the second stage of the total plan. In striving for this goal, investment must increase. To obtain the necessary capital to exploit all the nation's resources, technical assistance and equipment must be obtained from abroad, and joint ventures with foreign capital will have to be formed. It is here that the new directions for economic development in the previous September obtain ideological sanction.

It is too early to tell how far Burma's socialist-military leaders will go to achieve their long-term objectives. The party congress opened the way both to elevate new leaders and to liberalize the ideology. Whether these changes are enough to cause the World Bank and the consortium of Western nations to rescue the Burmese economy cannot be answered at this time. But a question must enter the mind of the worker or peasant in Burma who has suffered for fifteen years following the military-designed Burmese way to socialism; can the soldier-leaders who have failed thus far following their own ideology be more successful following the economic ideas they denounced at the time they seized power? Given the unrest among soldiers and civilians alike, it appears as though the men in power will not have another fifteen years to prove that they are on the right road this time.

17. *Ibid.*

7 | Foreign Policy and
Foreign Relations

Burma's relations with the rest of the world provided the one major area of continuity between the constitutional and military governments. When the coup occurred, the Revolutionary Council reaffirmed publicly "the policy of positive neutrality pursued by the Union of Burma ever since her independence,"[1] a significant shift from the ideas and goals set forth by Aung San during the period immediately preceding independence. When Aung San spoke about an international role for Burma in concert with other nations of Asia and sought to prepare the Burmese for their eventual participation in some sort of regional association,[2] memories of World War II were still fresh in the minds of the people and the ideas of collective security current in the writings and speeches of leaders in the newly formed United Nations. His assassination precluded the implementation of his ideas, however, as new leaders who lacked his vision took over. Ethnic and political disunity erupted into rebellion shortly after independence was achieved, and the nation's new leaders had to devote all their attention to saving the Union. The Cold War extended into Burma as the opposition political parties sought to make it a domestic issue. The government's response to these and other domestic and international challenges was to adopt neutralism. The driving force behind that policy, according to James Barrington, Burma's first

1. "Communique No. 3, March 2, 1962," *Burma Weekly Bulletin* 10, no. 45 (March 8, 1962), 388.
2. "Introduction," Josef Silverstein, ed., *The Political Legacy of Aung San* (Ithaca: Southeast Asia Program, Cornell University, Data Paper, no. 86, 1972), pp. 10–11.

permanent secretary of the Foreign Office, was the preservation of its newly won independence. "It furnishes the explanation for most of the attitudes which Burma adopted on international issues."[3] The leaders of this nation that had just recovered its freedom after more than a century of division and colonial rule had to do everything possible to protect their state from conquest, dismemberment, and political domination by foreign powers. Neutralism, as it developed in Burma, served all those purposes well.

Neutralism

The Burmese idea of neutralism often has been misunderstood. It was neither neutrality in the purely legal sense nor isolation in the manner practiced by the United States during the decade of the 1930s. Nor was it "fence-sitting" to find and eventually join the winning side, as many critics suggested. Instead, it was a policy that allowed its proponents to weigh issues, study facts, and arrive at decisions based on legal as well as moral principles and that permitted the nation to serve its own interests. In the context of the Cold War, it provided a means for being friendly with both sides while avoiding the pressure to join one or the other permanently. The policy permitted Burma to stand with the United States on some issues and with the Soviet Union on others. More often than not, Burma stood with other nonaligned nations or by itself. U Nu, in defending Burma's policy in the United Nations at the time of the Korean War, told his parliament that "if we consider a right course of action is being taken by a country we will support that country, be it America, Britain, or Soviet Russia. If wrong, we must object which ever country it be, in some way or other. Although a small country, we will support what is right in the world . . . in order to be able to do right we cannot allow ourselves to be absorbed in any power bloc."[4] Neutralism was a demonstration of Burmese inde-

3. James Barrington, "The Concept of Neutrality," *Atlantic Monthly* 201 (February 1958), 127. For a different interpretation, see Maung Kyaw Thet, "Some Burmese Views on the Neutralization of Southeast Asia," in Lau Teik Soon, ed., *New Directions in the International Relations of Southeast Asia*, 2 vols. (Singapore: Singapore University Press, 1973) I, 146–155.

4. U Nu, *From Peace to Stability* (Rangoon: Ministry of Information, 1951), p. 101.

pendence in world affairs as self-government was in domestic affairs.

The policy of neutralism was based on certain realities that imposed themselves on either a civilian or a military Burmese government. Among them were Burma's small size and population; its location between China and India; its economic underdevelopment; its memories of World War II and the suffering and destruction inflicted upon its people and the land; its internal political instability; and its ethnic and political disunity.

Burma's leaders made a number of assumptions from these realities. Wars do not solve problems between nations and the neutrality or alignment of any small state to a power bloc will not have a real bearing upon the balance of power between the major nations, but will compromise the independence of a small state. Underdeveloped nations must depend upon outside technical and material aid for rebuilding and modernizing their societies, therefore, if a nation accepts aid it should do so on the clear understanding that acceptance does not imply commitment to the power bloc of the donor; aid must be offered and accepted only on a basis of mutual equality with no strings attached. Security could be found in the United Nations and through support of its efforts to maintain world peace. Because Burma was a small Buddhist nation, its leaders assumed that small neutral nations could contribute to world peace through the moral force they represented. While the military leaders in the Revolutionary Council sought to drop their predecessors' moralistic approach to world politics, in almost every other way they continued the foreign policies of the government they displaced.

Burma's adherence to a policy of neutralism has not meant a lack of concern for its self-interest in relations with other states, particularly its immediate neighbors. Five states of unequal size, population, and interest share a long frontier with Burma. The border passes through difficult terrain and, in places, is poorly defended and nearly unguarded. Despite its own weaknesses, the involvement of neighbors in wars and ideological competition, and the pressures exerted by others, Burma has remained independent, its territorial integrity intact, and its relations with neighbors both near and far reasonably good.

Burma's Relations with China

Any discussion of Burma's relations with its neighbors must begin with China. Sino-Burmese relations provide a good example of how a small, weak nation has worked to preserve its independence and pursued its interest in dealing with the largest and most powerful nation in Asia. The relations between the two at the time Burma gained independence were troubled by a disputed border, illegal immigration, and smuggling. After 1949 the possibility of war arose over Burmese inability to control the unlawful entry of Nationalist Chinese forces into its territory and to prevent them from raiding into China. A brief review of Sino-Burmese relations during the constitutional period will provide a good frame of reference for examining and understanding the later period and will demonstrate the strength of continuity in Burma-China relations regardless of who held power in Rangoon.

Until 1954, Sino-Burmese relations were colored by the past—China's invasion and destruction of Pagan in the thirteenth century and Burma's stout defense and resistance to four invasions by the Chinese in the eighteenth century.[5] During that long past China considered Burma to be a vassal state and at various times in precolonial history Burma sent tribute missions to the emperor of China—though this never actually connoted political subserviency, being actuated by the desire for trade and the increased political legitimacy that such recognition by the mightiest kingdom in Asia bestowed.[6] In a historical sense, China had been the traditional home of many of the indigenous minorities in Burma, and language usage indicates that Burmans considered Chinese as *tayok*

5. As late as 1954, U Nu made pointed reference to these events during his first official visit to the People's Republic of China. He reminded his listeners that they occurred only when China was under foreign rule—Mongol and Manchu—and not while the Han Chinese were in control of their foreign affairs. See *Burma Weekly Bulletin*, 3, no. 36 (December 8, 1954), 276; *ibid.*, 3, no. 37 (December 15, 1954), 282.

6. In 1886 the British thought that the tributary relationship between China and Burma was still active and included a provision in the treaty of that year stating, "In as much as it has been the practice of Burmah to send decennial missions to present articles of local produce, England agrees that the highest authority in Burmah shall send the customary decennial missions, the members of the mission to be of Burmese race." For the text of the treaty see *British and Foreign State Papers 1885–86*, LXXVII (London: H. M. Stationery Office, 1893), 80–81.

or *pauk paw*—distant cousins—while they considered all others as
kala—foreigners.

The fact that several minority groups straddled the generally
undefined frontier between areas of Burmese and Chinese power
complicated any mutually satisfactory definition of the boundaries.
As early as 1886, the British sought to impose formal and acceptable boundaries, but, although several treaties were drawn up, the
full length of the common boundary never was agreed upon nor
actually demarcated. As late as 1946, the Nationalist Chinese
forces, which had entered Burma in 1942 as part of the Allied
military forces fighting the Japanese, refused to withdraw from
territory in northern Burma claimed by Chiang Kai-shek's government, and only the threat of military action by Great Britain
persuaded them to leave.[7] When Burma recovered its independence in 1948, the border issue became one of its first problems
because of the refusal of the Kuomintang (KMT) government to
continue to accept an annual rent for the Namwan border tract,
which the British had leased in perpetuity from Imperial China in
1897.[8] From that moment until the boundary settlement in 1960,
the question of how to resolve the problem without resorting to war
or to the surrender of large areas the Burmese considered as part
of their land dominated Burma's relations with both the governments of Chiang Kai-shek and Mao Tse-tung.

The border negotiations must be seen in the light of Sino-
Burmese relations during the period between 1948 and 1960. The
Nationalist government of China was one of Burma's original
sponsors for membership in the UN in 1948, but when that government left the mainland, following the victories of the Communist forces, Burma became, on December 16, 1949, the first
non-Communist state to recognize the new People's Republic of
China. From then on, it supported Peking's claim to represent
China in the United Nations. In 1954, U Nu and Chou En-lai met
in Rangoon and agreed upon five principles on which to base

7. In 1947 the Nationalist Chinese published and distributed maps that included
77,000 square miles of Burma in the territory of China. Early in the period of the
People's Republic these maps were reproduced and circulated.
8. *British and Foreign State Papers, 1896–97*, LXXXIX (London: H. M. Stationery
Office, 1901), 25.

relations between their two states: mutual respect for each other's territorial integrity and sovereignty; nonaggression; noninterference in each other's internal affairs; equal and mutual benefit; and peaceful coexistence. The two countries amplified these principles by affirming the right of the peoples of each nation to choose their own state system and way of life without interference from other nations; they agreed that revolution was not exportable and that outside interference should not be permitted.[9] The two leaders did not publicly discuss the border question until later the same year at their second meeting in Peking. At that meeting they declared that "in view of the incomplete delimitation of the boundary line between China and Burma, the two Premiers held it necessary to settle this question in a friendly spirit at the appropriate time through normal diplomatic channels."[10] The "appropriate time" was hastened by military clashes on the border in late 1955 and publicity about them in the local press six months later.

Burma-China good-neighborliness was tested severely during the long negotiations by the intrusion in 1949–1950 of remnants of the Nationalist Chinese military forces following their defeat by Mao's armies. By 1950, the United States Central Intelligence Agency (CIA) began to supply money and arms to these illegal forces and to encourage them to raid into China from Burmese soil. In the environment of the Cold War, Burma found no ally to help rid itself of this added menace to its fragile independence; in 1953, Burma asked the United States to cancel its aid program and took the question of the illegal Chinese forces to the United Nations. Despite the efforts of the world body, only a partial repatriation of the Chinese to Taiwan was effected, and the remaining KMT soldiers settled down in the border areas of the Shan State and became involved with Burmese ethnic and political dissidents and active in the illegal opium trade. Throughout the long border negotiations, the People's Republic showed patience and restraint on the issue of the KMT forces and allowed the Burmese to find their own solution.

Burma-China negotiations on the border question began in ear-

9. *Burma Weekly Bulletin*, 3, no. 14 (July 7, 1954), 97.
10. *Ibid.*, 3, no. 37 (December 15, 1954), 283.

nest on September 22, 1956, when U Nu, who was then out of office, went to China at the invitation of the People's Republic. He returned to Rangoon on November 7 with a tentative plan for settlement that called for the return of the Namwan border tract and three villages in the Kachin State—Hpimaw, Gawlum, and Kangfang (see Map 1)—in exchange for China's recognition of the Burmese version of the remainder of the border.[11] Open discussion of giving up territory provoked discontent among the Burmese of all ethnic groups. Since the constitution required the approval of the component Burma state or states involved in any surrender of territory, the negotiations became more complex. For nearly four years, peaceful negotiations continued; during that time, China and Burma withdrew their armies from the disputed territories. Finally, on the initiative of General Ne Win—who was then serving as prime minister and head of the caretaker government—negotiations were concluded, and a border agreement, together with a treaty of friendship and mutual nonaggression, was signed on January 28, 1960.[12] Burma surrendered three Kachin villages and an area of approximately seventy-three square miles in the northern part of the Shan State in exchange for the eighty-five square miles of the Namwan border tract and China's recognition of the remainder of the boundary. The agreement also called for China to surrender its right to participate in mining in the Lufang Mines (eastern Shan State)—a right acquired in a 1941 agreement.[13] The treaty of friendship and mutual nonagression reaffirmed and the substance of the five principles agreed to earlier

11. As early as 1906, China protested Great Britain's unilateral declaration of the location of a portion of the China-Burma border. The Chinese argued that they had prior rights to Hpimaw, Gawlum, and Kangfang. On April 10, 1911, the British sent a letter to the government of China restating its border claims, but dropping demands for the territory around and including the three Kachin villages and offering to purchase and annex them to Burma. The Chinese refused the offer, and the British seized the three villages in 1913.

12. *Burma*, 9, no. 4 (October 1960), 1–58.

13. *Exchange of Notes between His Majesty's Government in the United Kingdom and the Government of Burma and the National Government of the Republic of China Concerning the Burma-Yunnan Boundary, Chungking 18, June 1941* (London: H. M. Stationery Office, 1941), Command 7246. Note 3 in this document gave China the right to participate in any mining operations undertaken by British interests on the eastern slope of the Lufang Ridge, provided that China's ownership share did not exceed 49 percent of the total capital investment.

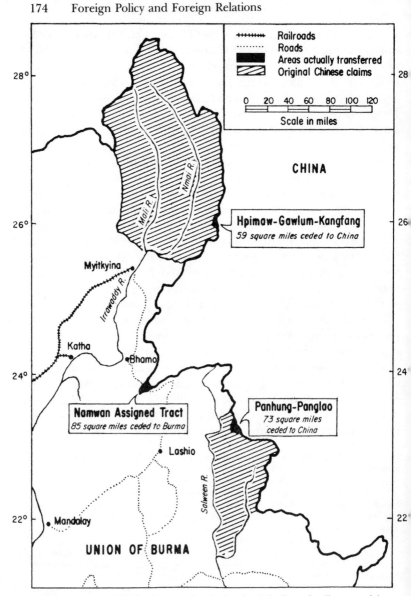

Map 1. Burma-China border area showing lands originally under dispute and those actually transferred according to the 1960 Sino-Burmese agreement. (From George McT. Kahin, ed., *Governments and Politics of Southeast Asia*, 2d ed., Cornell University Press, 1964, p. 165.)

and took a further step by barring participation by either "in any military alliance against the other contracting party," a clause consistent with Burma's position as a neutral and nonaligned nation.[14]

With the border finally settled, in 1961 Burma launched a military campaign to expel the remnants of the KMT on its territory.[15] In February, the Burmese army overran a KMT base where it found new American-made weapons and equipment with their markings intact. In addition, an unmarked plane delivering supplies to the Nationalist Chinese forces inside Burma was shot down in a battle with planes of the Burma Air Force. All this provoked new international tension and returned the issue of illegal Chinese military personnel in Burma to the UN.[16] In April, U Nu discussed the issue with the People's Republic during a visit to Peking; a communique issued at the end of the meeting stated that "since these remnants constitute a serious threat not only to the Union of Burma but also to the People's Republic of China, the Prime Ministers agree that the Chinese and Burmese governments cooperate with each other as required, to solve this problem."[17] When Ne Win seized power in Rangoon in March 1962, the problem of KMT remnants still remained unsolved.[18]

A second aspect to the Chinese problem was that both before and after independence, illegal Chinese immigrants crossed Burma's border. While many were caught and deported, more were able to submerge themselves in established Chinese communities in the cities and towns and there became absorbed into their ethnic kin groups.

14. Article III, "Treaty of Friendship and Mutual Nonagression," *Burma*, 9, no. 4 (October 1960), 26.

15. Unconfirmed reports support the accusations made by the Nationalist government in Taiwan in 1960–1961, that the Burmese had agreed secretly to allow People's Liberation Army forces to enter Burma and attack KMT forces, thus driving them back toward Burmese army units. Neither Burma nor the People's Republic has ever acknowledged this cooperative activity against the KMT.

16. *Burma Weekly Bulletin*, 9, no. 44 (March 2, 1961), 405.

17. *Ibid.*, 9, no. 52 (April 27, 1961), 461. When U Nu returned to Burma he explained this to mean exchange of information and that China had agreed to capture and hold any KMT soldiers driven out of Burma and to disarm them. He said such an agreement existed with Thailand as well. See *Burma Weekly Bulletin*, 10 no. 1 (May 4, 1961), 1.

18. In the spring of 1961, President John F. Kennedy applied pressure upon the Taiwan government to remove its forces inside of Burma. Although he was partially successful, several thousand KMT soldiers remained in Burma.

The problem was complicated by smuggling and the relations between the two nations over the question of the citizenship of Chinese in Burma. Smuggling was a constant irritant to the Burmese. After 1954, when the decline in foreign exchange caused by the drop in export of rice forced the Burmese to limit imports, smuggling grew steadily; following the 1962 coup and the Ne Win policies that limited imports even further, smuggling across all borders at various times became uncontrollable. Illegal trade also was stimulated by the growing world demand for opium and its derivatives. The hill areas of Burma, especially in the Shan and the Kachin states, were an important source of the raw product and Chinese—Nationalist as well as subsequent illegal immigrants—competed with local smugglers in the narcotics trade. Because opium was produced and transported in the remote areas of Burma, the government was incapable either of controlling or eliminating it.

The question of citizenship for Chinese also has a long history in Burma. Prior to 1954, Chinese governments—regardless of ideology—agreed that a person of Chinese ancestry was Chinese regardless of place of birth or acceptance of citizenship in another country. This meant that local Chinese who were legal Burmese citizens were also citizens of China and contributed to anti-Chinese feeling because the immigrants were seen as sojourners who benefited from foreign residence without the full responsibilities of citizenship. After the establishment of the People's Republic in China, many in Burma feared the local Chinese were agents for this government and a threat to domestic stability. Thus, the steady inflow of illegal immigrants was seen as a threat to the non-Communist government of Burma.

The leaders of the People's Republic were aware of the complex problem posed by the overseas Chinese in Burma and elsewhere in Asia. In September 1954, Chou En-lai declared, in a report to the First People's Congress in Peking, that his government was prepared "to urge Overseas Chinese to respect the laws of local government and local social customs."[19] At almost the same time, the Burmese government enacted a new citizenship law that denied

19. Stephen Fitzgerald, *China and the Overseas Chinese* (London: Cambridge University Press, 1972), p. 103.

dual citizenship by requiring all who claimed it either to renounce their foreign allegiance or lose their Burmese citizenship.[20] In 1956, Chou sought to solve this problem by declaring in Rangoon that all "who acquire the nationality of the countries of residence by voluntary decision and accordance to local laws, are no longer Chinese people."[21] This statement went a long way toward easing Burma's fears as it signaled China's intention not to interfere in the relations between Burma and its citizens.

Illegal immigration went in both directions. During the period of civil war in Burma (1948–1951), many ethnic and political dissidents escaped capture by taking refuge in China. Among them were Ba Thein Tin, a leader of the Burma Communist party, and Naw Seng, a prominent Kachin officer of the Burma army who deserted along with men under his command. Many, in and out of the Burma government, felt that the Chinese were supporting leftist rebels while advocating the five principles of good relations between states. The People's Republic never acknowledged granting refuge to Burmese political dissidents, or before 1967 that it permitted Chinese border areas to be used as bases of operations against the government of Burma. Only during the Sino-Burmese quarrels in 1967 did China openly permit Burmese rebels living in China to broadcast anti-Ne Win propaganda and to participate in anti-Burmese demonstrations. To this date, the Chinese have never acknowledged how these Burmese came to China, how they lived, and what they did while they were there. The problems of illegal immigrants, smuggling, and foreign support to Burmese insurgency remain unsolved.

In 1954, Rangoon entered into a clearing accounts agreement with Peking to sell rice, minerals, rubber, and other raw materials in exchange for Chinese exports of coal, textiles, and light industrial products.[22] Three years later, the two countries abandoned this form of trade in favor of cash transactions. In 1958, China provided Burma with a textile factory. On the anniversary of the China-Burma border agreement—1961—the two entered into

20. *Union Citizenship (Amendment) Act, 1954.*
21. Fitzgerald, *China and the Overseas Chinese*, p. 112.
22. Robert L. Allen, "Burma's Clearing Account Agreements," *Pacific Affairs* 31, no. 2 (June 1958), 151.

further aid and trade agreements that provided Burma with a loan of £30 million interest-free for use in technical assistance, material aid, and training. The trade agreement, signed a few weeks later, called for trade expansion.[23]

Between 1962 and 1967, the relations between the two states were cordial and expanding, punctuated by official visits by the leaders of both countries and the reaffirmation of friendship and peaceful coexistence.[24] This peaceable condition was tested in May 1967, as China's Cultural Revolution spilled across the frontier to Burma's Chinese community. Burma initially cooperated with China by rounding up and deporting several hundred Chinese who had entered Burma illegally to escape the political upheaval in their own country. This event coincided with a rising anti-Chinese feeling among Burmese who were beginning to experience the shortages caused by a poor harvest and the rising prices charged by black marketeers—mostly Chinese—who were profiting from the situation. In this environment members of the People's Republic diplomatic delegation in Rangoon, who over the years had established strong contacts with China-oriented members of the local Chinese population, began distributing Mao badges and ordering them worn in the classrooms of Burma's nationalized Chinese-language schools. This violated a Burmese government regulation, and the badges were ordered removed. Clashes occurred following student and teacher refusal to comply and quickly spread throughout Rangoon. Anti-Chinese rioting broke out in Rangoon and elsewhere in the country. The Burmese attacked local as well as known foreign Chinese and burned and looted, killed and maimed. The mobs attacked the Chinese Embassy, and a member of its staff was killed by a Burmese who scaled the wall and entered the compound. The Burma government brought the rioting to a halt through the proclamation of martial law and vigorous enforcement by the military and police.

23. *Burma Weekly Bulletin*, 9, no. 38 (January 19, 1961), 359; *ibid.*, 9, no. 41 (February 9, 1961), 383.

24. Union of Burma, Burma Socialist Program Party, Central Organizing Committee, *Foreign Policy of the Revolutionary Government of the Union of Burma* (Rangoon: Sarpay Beikman Press, 1968), pp. 44–48, 54–55, 61–62 (hereafter cited as *Foreign Policy*).

The incident was followed by mass demonstrations in China and the withdrawal of ambassadors from both capitals. Even more serious, the anti-Ne Win, anti-Burma broadcasts and the public participation at rallies and other demonstrations by Burmese rebels living inside China were given prominent attention by Chinese press and radio in their overseas broadcasts and newspapers, and their voices joined the Chinese in calling upon the Burmese people to overthrow Ne Win's government. In November, China withdrew its technical assistance personnel and halted all projects.[25]

Inside Burma, known Peking sympathizers were arrested, schools and at least one Mandalay newspaper were closed, and the correspondent of the New China News Agency was expelled. The police also arrested those Burmese connected with the attack upon the Chinese Embassy as well as Chinese and Burmese who participated in the rioting and brought them to speedy trials; as the process was under civil law, the trials generally were conducted in a calm and even-handed manner, and those found guilty received moderate sentences.

Despite China's protests over the trials, its call for Ne Win's ouster, and its open support for the Burma Communist party's revolt, the Burmese remained cool and correct. Insurgency rose, but neither the Communists nor the ethnic rebels could gain popular support or territorial control as they sought to capitalize upon the tensions between the two countries. By the end of 1968, the Chinese radio and press muted their call for revolution inside Burma and instead demanded the release of Chinese imprisoned during the riots of the previous year.

Toward the end of 1969, Ne Win reported at the Fourth Party Seminar of the BSPP that eighteen major and minor clashes on the border with China had occurred that year. He nevertheless called for the "restoration of cordial and friendly relations which formerly prevailed between our two countries."[26] With the aid of the

25. *Straits Times*, November 2, 1967. As early as October, 1954, Peking Radio broadcast a congratulatory message on China's anniversary sent by the Burma Communist party, thus giving it recognition and creating a problem in Sino-Burma relations; see also, *New York Times*, November 1, 1964.

26. Government of Burma, Burma Socialist Program Party, *Address Delivered by General Ne Win, Chairman of the Burma Socialist Party, at the Opening Session of the Fourth Party Seminar on 6 November 1969* (Rangoon: Central Press, 1969), p. 36.

Pakistan government, Burma and China finally re-established their previous friendly relations in November 1970, when Burma's ambassador to China returned to his post. An official visit to China by Ne Win and the gradual restoration of commercial, cultural, and diplomatic relations followed.

The rapprochement between the two states was marred when the Chinese government in 1971 permitted a secret radio transmitter, believed to be located in southwest Yunnan, using the call signal Voice of the People of Burma, to broadcast regularly. It reported the activity of the Burma Communist party and called for the overthrow of the "Ne Win-San Yu clique." In 1975 it reported the military defeat suffered by the BCP and the election of Ba Thein Tin as chairman, following the death in battle of his predecessor. From time to time, the official Peking Radio rebroadcast the information sent out initially by the secret transmitter. China's policy toward Burma seems to be conducted at two levels: formally, between governments, which since 1971 has been friendly and correct, and informally, between Communist parties in a revolutionary, anti-Ne Win manner. As long as the government of Burma is able to keep the rival, BCP at bay in the remote areas of the country, it need not greatly fear the support the party receives from abroad. Although this irritant must affect the formal relations of the two states, neither has discussed it publicly and both continue to conduct their formal relations as though it did not exist. Burma has demonstrated that it can live alongside a powerful neighbor and pursue an independent policy in the face of pressures from across the border.

Burma's Relations with India and Pakistan

India served as a model for Burma's policies of neutralism and nonalignment. Even before the two countries achieved independence their nationalist leaders met at a Congress party convention; the younger Burmese leaders admired and borrowed many of its ideas. During Burma's struggle for independence after World War II, Aung San consulted with Nehru both before and after his meetings with Attlee in London. These consultations between leaders in both countries continued through the constitution-making stage and the constitutional period.

Independent Burma inherited a disputed and undemarcated border with India in the northwest and a debt incurred during the colonial period while Burma was a province of India. There was no urgency to solve either problem, and not until 1953 did Nehru and Nu personally inspect the disputed area and acquaint themselves with the terrain. Associated with the border area was a political problem involving a minority people—the Nagas—who lived on both sides of the border. The Nagas sought unity of territory and people and political independence. In 1957 the Indian government created a directly administered territory with some nominal recognition of Naga aspirations, but they were not satisfied.

Burma and India signed an agreement in March 1967 that provided for the creation of a joint boundary commission to demarcate the disputed portion of their common frontier. The Indians felt that China was aiding and supporting the Nagas and that groups of them were being transported across Burma to China to be trained and equipped. At the same time Burma was having trouble with China over the "red badges" and feared China's stepped-up aid to ethnic and political dissidents. The demarcation of the frontier permitted both sides to station troops in the general area and thereby to reduce the freedom of dissidents from both countries to move back and forth to China.

Burma's debt to India proved easier to solve. In 1954 the two states entered into an agreement in which Burma sold 900,000 tons of rice to India at a special low price and agreed to make payment toward the pension fund of civil servants of Indian origin that had been incurred when Burma was a part of India. In turn, India canceled the remainder of the debt.[27] Although some Burmese protested the obligation because it was contracted by the British while Burma was without power to accept or reject it, the settlement generally was approved because it permitted Burma to sell a sizable quantity of rice at a time when the world market was depressed and eliminated an irritant in Indo-Burma relations.

The problem of overseas Indians in Burma had been much greater before World War II than later. Under British rule, migrant Indian laborers were recruited and brought to Burma on a

27. *Burma Weekly Bulletin*, 3, nos. 2–3 (April 21, 1954).

contract basis, and most returned to India upon completing their obligations and were replaced by new migrant workers.[28] Some Indians took up permanent residence in Burma as civil servants and professionals, and many engaged in moneylending and land ownership. During the 1930s serious anti-Indian riots were caused by economic competition for urban jobs and, more important, by controversies inflamed by the local press. World War II and invasion caused countless thousands of Indians to leave Burma, and after the war the Burmese government denied most of them the privilege of returning and reclaiming their property and debts. As early as 1946, Nehru made clear to all Indians living abroad that they must either take up citizenship in their adopted land or return home. There was no question of Indians holding dual citizenship or becoming a problem in the relations between India and its neighbors. Independent Burma ended Indian immigration and encouraged those Indians in Burma who qualified for citizenship to apply for it, although the process was excessively long, and many eligible Indians never received their documents.

Early in the period of military rule, the Burma government decided to recall large-denomination paper currency; Indian merchants and professionals interpreted this action as an effort to drive them out of business and the professions. They petitioned the Indian government for protection and help. The Indian government sent a representative to investigate and concluded that the policy was internal and directed against all residents in Burma—citizens and aliens alike—and refused to interfere. As a result, thousands of Indians left Burma permanently because they saw no future for themselves in the new nationalist-socialist order. Poor Indians who could not afford to repatriate themselves were aided by the Indian government, which sent ships to carry them home. In this cooperative manner both India and Burma solved a problem that could have had serious consequences for their relations.

Although both countries pursued neutralist and nonaligned policies, on many international issues they did not agree. The closeness between Indian and Burmese leaders that existed while

28. For the most systematic official study of the problem, see James Baxter, *Report on Indian Immigration* (Rangoon: Superintendent, Government Printing and Stationery, 1941).

Nehru and Aung San were alive and while U Nu was in power declined after the 1962 coup in Burma and the emergence of the military government. Although Ne Win occasionally visited India and entertained its leaders at home, he did not re-establish closeness with his Indian counterparts. Although Burma-India relations have not been tested in the same way Burma-China relations have, they show Burma's ability to live alongside large and potentially powerful neighbors and to pursue independent policies and relations.

Lodged between India and China on Burma's western frontier was East Pakistan. Unlike its relations with India, which were strongly influenced by the personal ties between leaders, Burma's relations with Pakistan were relatively formal. In 1948, Burma had a minor border dispute with Pakistan in the area of the Naaf River and a political dispute over informal Pakistani aid to and protection of Muslim dissidents from Arakan known as Mujahids. The smuggling of rice into East Pakistan and illegal Pakistani immigration into Burma were further irritants. When Pakistan became a member of the Southeast Asia Treaty Organization and committed itself to the Western side of the Cold War, Burma-Pakistan relations cooled.

In May 1967, shortly after Burma and India agreed on a common border, Burma and Pakistan signed a boundary agreement settling the long-standing differences over possession of the islands in the Naaf River.[29] Two years later, when Ne Win visited Pakistan, it is believed that Ayub Khan, the leader of Pakistan, used his good offices to bring Burma and China together. Thereafter, changes in leadership and civil war in Pakistan caused relations between Burma and Pakistan to decline.

The emergence of Bangladesh met with sympathy in Burma, and Ne Win's government was among the first to recognize the new state in 1972. Burma sent food relief to the stricken areas and entered into an early trade agreement for the sale of rice to Bangladesh, which ruptured relations with the residual Pakistan state and caused the recall of ambassadors. As Pakistan no longer shared a common frontier with Burma, there was no urgency to

29. *Foreign Policy*, pp. 178–180.

restore good relations, and Burma concentrated on its new western neighbor.

Burma's Relations with Thailand and Laos

Relations with Thailand, like those with China, have ancient roots. Both nations have memories of wars, kidnappings, and destruction of cities and religious buildings. The Thais in particular memorialize in song and play the sacking of Ayuthia by the Burmans in the eighteenth century. During World War II, two of the Shan states, Kengtung and Mongpan, were given to Thailand by the Japanese as a reward for permitting them to use Thai territory to launch their invasion of Burma. Although the states were returned to Burma after the war, the episode contributed to the long-standing hostility between the two countries.

Independent Burma encountered difficulty with Thailand during the early phase of the KMT problem. The Burmese believed that Thailand, like the United States, was sympathetic to the operations of Nationalist Chinese forces on Burmese soil. This belief was reinforced at the United Nations in 1953, when Thailand joined with the United States, Nationalist China, and others to water down Burma's complaint against the presence of Chiang Kai-shek's forces and helped to formulate an evacuation plan outside the control of the UN. In 1954 by joining the Southeast Asia Treaty Organization Thailand separated itself further from neutralist Burma.

In the mid-1950s, U Nu took the first steps to secure friendlier relations with Thailand. By moving slowly through the exchange of low-level missions and inviting the Thais to participate in a two-year celebration of the Buddha in Rangoon, he laid the basis for a new relationship. In October 1955,[30] as a gesture of friendship, Burma waived all war claims against Thailand, and a year later the two nations signed a treaty of friendship. But, Thai-Burmese friendship was challenged by the problem of sanctuary for Burmese dissidents on Thai territory. Throughout the constitutional period, KMT, Communists, and various ethnic dissidents took refuge in Thailand and sometimes organized military

30. *Burma Weekly Bulletin*, 4, no. 28 (October 28, 1955), 210.

campaigns into Burma from those sanctuaries. Although the Thai government denied it, the border was like a sieve; Thais living close to it were known to help rebels in Burma. This problem grew in importance in 1959 when several ethnic minorities in Burma openly proclaimed revolt. The military government sought through negotiations to close the border and obtain the right to pursue the rebels across. In March 1963, such an agreement was negotiated, but it rarely was implemented. The border became an active area of illegal and informal export of cattle, timber, precious stones, and other products, while foreign-made consumer goods were smuggled in.

Thousands of ethnic Burmese left their homeland for Bangkok and elsewhere in Thailand because of their opposition to the policies and activities of the military government. This problem became more complex in 1969, when the Thai government granted asylum to U Nu, following his declaration of open revolt against Ne Win's government. Thai-Burma relations were strained, particularly the following year, when Nu began to organize a united front of dissidents and launched a military campaign against Burma from bases inside Thailand. Despite Bangkok's open support for this movement, Burma limited its response to protests and diplomacy and did not take any steps to break formal relations. In the field, Burma's armies contained Nu's movement close to the border. Nu's failure to spark an uprising in Burma finally caused him to give up the leadership of the movement and in the fall of 1973 to leave Thailand. His departure, followed by the internal overthrow of the Thai government that had allowed him to operate, created a new climate for the restoration of good relations between the two states.

The history of Thai-Burma relations must be seen finally as an example of two small states, each seeking to preserve and protect its independence and territorial integrity by different means. Burma chose nonalignment; Thailand joined with the anti-Communist West. The Thais did not have a common frontier with China, but they feared invasion by way of neighboring states. Rangoon was fearful that Thailand's military ties with the United States might involve Burma in a war against China. To reduce possibilities of discord with Thailand, Burma sought to limit the range of controversy to particularly Thai-Burma issues; it neither engaged in ideological competition with the Thais nor publicly condemned them for their pro-Western stand. In this delicate situation, good relations were not always easy to maintain. When, for example, in 1962 the United States sent aircraft and personnel to Thailand to bolster it in the face of increasing military activity in Laos, the Burmese felt they were overreacting; more important, they feared that the sudden influx of weapons and other military supplies might increase the chances of its own dissidents residing in Thailand obtaining and eventually using them against Burma. This fear mounted after 1965 with the rapid build-up of American forces in Thailand in connection with the Indochina war and remained until the war ended in 1975.

Burma quickly extended formal recognition to the newly independent Royal Government of Laos on August 16, 1954, and a year later the two states established diplomatic relations. Although there was no appreciable legal commerce between the two, the opium trade that originated in the poppy fields of the "golden triangle"—Shan State, northern Thailand, and northwest Laos— brought Burma and Laos together in a way that was bound to create difficulties. Burma wanted the trade curbed to keep the product away from its own society and to keep the KMT and ethnic Burmese dissidents from profiting from it. The "golden triangle" became a major center for the supply of the illegal world narcotics trade and was impossible for any one government to control. Throughout the first twenty-five years of Burma's independence, the illegal trade grew and remained an uncontrolled problem in the relations of all nations involved.

Several of the Laotian governments, including that first in power after the conclusion of the first Vietnam war, have shared Burma's attachment to a policy of neutrality. While Burma's was freely adopted and applied according to national interest, Laos's was restricted by the terms of the 1954 Geneva Agreement and limited by the conflicting power interests of intervening foreign states, including the unsolicited protective shield offered by the Protocol of the Southeast Asia Collective Defense Treaty. In April 1961, Burma accepted an invitation to participate at Geneva in a fourteen-nation international conference for the settlement of the

Laotian question. Generally, relations between Burma and Laos have been good, in contrast to Burma's relations with Thailand. Taken together they demonstrate Burma's ability to deal with neighbors who share problems while differing in their ideologies and perceptions of their national interest and continue to live in a relatively peaceful relationship.

Conference Diplomacy

Burma participated in conference diplomacy even before recovering independence, beginning in 1947 in the Asian Relations Conference called by Nehru.[31] A year later, in December 1948, following the second Dutch attack upon the Indonesian nationalists, U Nu urged Nehru to call a second Asian conference. At that meeting, held a month later, Burma proposed recognition of the Indonesian government by all Asian governments and called for the withdrawal of the Dutch and increasing sanctions against them if they did not halt their attack upon the Indonesians.[32]

In 1954, Burma joined the other Colombo Powers—Ceylon, India, Indonesia, and Pakistan—in drawing up proposals that apparently influenced London and Peking in their efforts to work out a formula for ending the conflict in Indochina. At the same Colombo meeting the foundations were laid for the Bandung Conference of April 1955.[33] In 1953, Burma had sponsored the first international conference of Asian socialists. As a result of that meeting a permanent bureau was established in Burma with an Indonesian as leader and a Burmese as one of the joint secretaries.[34] At the second Asian Socialist Conference, held in Bombay in 1956, Burma played a leading role in attempting to mobilize support from socialists and representatives of the nonaligned nations of Asia to use their moral strength to halt aggression and repression in the Middle East and Europe.[35] Burma also participated in the Afro-Asian People's Solidarity Conference in Egypt in

---

31. G. F. Jansen, *Afro-Asia and Nonalignment* (London: Faber and Faber, 1966), pp. 60–61.

32. *Ibid.*, pp. 88–90.

33. *Ibid.*, pp. 413–414.

34. *Report of the First Asian Socialist Conference, Rangoon 1953* (Rangoon: Burmese Advertising Press, 1953), p. 100.

35. *Burma Weekly Bulletin*, 5, no. 32 (November 15, 1956), 255–256.

1957 and attended the four nonaligned nations conferences held in 1961, 1965, 1969, and 1976.

Burma used its Buddhist tradition to reach out to its neighbors who shared that heritage. In 1954, it sponsored a two-year celebration of the twenty-five hundredth anniversary of the birth of Gautama, the Buddha. Buddhists from surrounding states were invited to participate. Among those who attended were political leaders as well as scholars and clergy, and Burma's contact with these visitors helped open relations with several of its neighbors.

Although conference diplomacy declined under Ne Win's rule, his government continued to particpate in meetings devoted to Asian affairs. In 1962, he participated in a conference in Ceylon with other neutral Asian and African leaders to find a solution to the border war between China and India. In 1966, his government called for a peaceful settlement of the fighting in Vietnam on the basis of the 1954 Geneva Agreement and urged all concerned to participate in a new Geneva-type conference to work out a settlement.[36]

Burma's neutralism has not prevented her from participating with other developing nations on issues of anticolonialism, peace, and development. Regardless of which group is in power in Rangoon, conference diplomacy is a tool all have used.

Burma's Relations with the United States

Although Burma maintains twenty-six embassies, four consulates-general, and one consulate in nations around the world, only fourteen are located in countries outside Asia. Her relations with non-Asian states, particularly with the developed states of Europe and America, have focused mainly on aid. At the time of independence, Burma obtained economic, military, and technical aid from Britain. In 1954, Burma abrogated its military training and procurement agreement and concentrated instead on economic and technical assistance. This continued throughout the

36. *Working People's Daily* (Rangoon), March 2, 1966. The local press reported that Ne Win said representatives of the North Vietnamese and the United States had met in Rangoon. "What they discussed and what passed between them we do not know. We were just helping in our small measure to achieve peace in Vietnam by playing host for the representatives."

constitutional period, either by way of bilateral arrangements or through a multilateral program known as the Colombo Plan.

On the eve of Burma's independence, the United States extended diplomatic recognition, and in December 1947 the two nations signed an educational exchange agreement under the Fulbright program. During the next two years relations between the two remained at a low level. The United States generally was unfamiliar with the country even though Americans had fought there in World War II and deferred to Great Britain, which continued to exercise a good deal of influence in the area that long had been its colonial preserve.

The war in Korea set in motion a number of changes in United States policy—among them interest in nations on the frontier of China. In September 1950, the United States began sending aid to Burma under a bilateral agreement that called for the expenditure of $31 million for transportation, public works, communications, commodity imports, agriculture, health, education, mining, and other projects. Although U.S. aid was represented as free of any strings or political commitment, the Mutual Security Act of 1951 seemed to alter this status as Section 511b prohibited the president from extending aid unless it "will strengthen the security of the United States and promote world peace."[37] Uncertainty over the meaning of this provision caused the Burmese to suspend the aid program briefly in January 1952; it was resumed a month later after an agreement that Burmese reaffirmation of support for the principles of peace embodied in the United Nations Charter would satisfy the spirit of the American law. The episode soured the relations between the two countries as the Burmese press, the opposition, and many in government saw U.S. aid as dependent upon the recipient's acceptance of obligations. Because of continued U.S. support for KMT insurgents in Burma, on March 17, 1953, Rangoon terminated the aid agreement although it still had a year to run and approximately $10 million to be spent. Because the United States was closely tied to Taiwan, the CIA was working with the KMT intruders, and the Americans had done little to remove

37. "Public Law 165," *U.S. Statutes At Large*, 82 Cong., 1. sess., 1951, vol. 65 (Washington, D.C.: U.S. Government Printing Office, 1952), pp. 373, 381.

Chiang's soldiers from Burmese territory or to halt the military aid being given to the intruding Chinese forces, the Rangoon government felt they could not continue to receive U.S. aid while making a formal complaint in the United Nations against Chaing Kai-shek's government. The Burmese did not accept U.S. aid again until 1956. For five years thereafter the volume of aid slowly increased. In 1961 relations between the two countries were dealt a sharp blow, following the shooting down of a plane from Taiwan and the loss of two Burmese aircraft in an air battle when the alien plane was in the process of delivering U.S. military equipment to a KMT base inside Burma. This event reawakened memories of 1953 as it seemed to support rumors that the United States again was involved in aiding the illegal KMT forces still in Burma. It provoked a serious anti-American riot in Rangoon, as well as a strong press campaign against the United States.

Following the 1962 coup in Burma, relations between the two countries continued at a low level. Aid and technical assistance that had been contracted before the coup continued, but private aid from the Ford and Asia Foundations was terminated and the educational exchange program under the Fulbright Act was suspended. In 1970 the Burmese resumed educational exchange with the United States. Since 1971, a very small number of Americans have been invited to teach and do research, while only a few Burmese have been sent to the United States for very limited periods of time.

United States military assistance to Burma never has been openly discussed by either side. In 1958 the U.S. entered into two agreements to provide a $10 million loan for Burma to purchase police equipment, to train personnel and purchase military equipment with local currency. During the 1960s, Burma quietly continued to purchase military equipment and arranged for military training of selected Burmese personnel in the United States. In the autumn of 1970 the U.S. revealed that it had provided nearly $80 million in military assistance during the previous twelve years.[38] The Ne Win government did not believe this aid compromised Burma's neutrality and nonalignment and treated it as

38. At a U.S. congressional hearing it was revealed that the United States had an unpublicized military aid program in Burma from 1958 to 1970. It provided arms, other military goods, and services. See *New York Times*, August 25, 1970.

simply a businesslike purchase of goods and services necessary for Burma's survival.

Until 1974, Rangoon was reluctant to cooperate with the U.S. in drug control, fearing that under cover of such a program, the United States might try to become involved with the KMT or seek to use Burma as a base in the struggle against North Vietnam and the secret war in Laos. Once U.S. forces were withdrawn from Indochina the Burmese quietly began cooperating with the U.S. effort to restrict the illegal flow of opium from the "golden triangle." With no publicity, Rangoon purchased six helicopters, valued at $5 million, in 1975 and twelve more, valued at $13.35 million, in 1976. The price included the training of pilots. In addition, Burma sent military and civil chiefs of intelligence to the United States in the spring of 1975 for a month's training in drug control. The helicopters were to be used to suppress the opium traffic. Once they were integrated into the Burma Air Force, they were, of course, available for use against the ethnic and political dissidents, as well as against the narcotics smugglers.[39]

Little or no publicity was given to Burma's receptivity since 1972 to assistance from U.S. private oil companies in the search for and, hopefully, the production of offshore oil deposits. Initially, Burma sought assistance from some of the East European states; after several false starts, however, the Burmese quietly replaced the experts from the socialist countries with Americans and opened offshore oil leases to American firms.

While these developments do not indicate any change in Burma's neutral and nonaligned foreign policy, they may be an indirect means of countering China's support of the Burma Communist party.

Burma's Relations with the Soviet Union

Although Rangoon and Moscow agreed in February 1948 to exchange ambassadors, they did not do so for three years. During

39. A subcommittee of the U.S. House of Representatives Committee on Foreign Affairs visited the "golden triangle" in 1974–1975 and met with Shan insurgents who offered to sell all the opium produced in their area to the U.S. at the Thai border price. See U. S. Congress, House of Representatives, 94 Cong., 1 sess., *The Narcotics Situation in Southeast Asia: The Asian Connection: Report of a Special Study Mission to Southeast Asia, December 27, 1974–January 12, 1975* (Washington, D.C.: U. S. Government Printing Office, 1975).

the immediate postwar period, Burma and its leaders were severely criticized in Soviet publications, which said its independence was spurious and its leaders under the influence of the West. The AFPFL's expulsion of the Communist party from its organization in 1946, and its efforts to put down insurgency and rebellion by ethnic and political dissidents in 1948 and beyond, were criticized in the Soviet press as repression of "progressive" citizens. As has been noted, Burma's internal leftist opposition echoed these and other criticisms. Finally, when Andrei Zhdanov's "two-camp" thesis, which argued that there was no place for neutralist nations in the struggle between "peace-loving and war mongering" nations, became known in Burma, the Burma Communists applied it to their criticism of Nu's government.

In 1951, after the North Korean attack on South Korea had found no support among neutral nations, the Soviet Union began to reverse its policy. The efforts of India and other neutrals in the U.N. to bring the fighting to an end without identifying aggressors created a new climate to which the Russians responded favorably.[40] In search of new friends, Russia exchanged ambassadors with Burma early in that year and toward the end of the year sent a cultural mission to Burma that was reciprocated in 1952. In July 1955, the two countries concluded a trade agreement, exchanging rice for Russian manufactures. A visit by U Nu to Russia was followed by a return visit by Khruschev and Bulganin to Burma in December 1955.

Moscow did not overlook the opportunity to build friendship and goodwill. Following the visit of the two Russian leaders, the USSR offered a number of specific gifts including a hotel, a hospital, and a technical institute. In exchange, Burma sent the Russians a token gift of rice. In April 1956, Anastas Mikoyan visited Burma and concluded a trade agreement that extended a clearing accounts agreement of the previous year for five more years. Burma undertook to sell up to 400,000 tons of rice in exchange for Soviet

---

40. As late as 1951, the Soviet Union was still publishing strongly anti-Burmese material. See V. A. Maslennikov, *Problems of Philosophy* (Moscow, 1951), no. 4, as cited in J. M. Mackintosh, *Strategy and Tactics of Soviet Foreign Policy* (New York: Oxford University Press, 1963), pp. 134–135.

goods and services. The Burmese were never fully satisfied with the trade agreement even when it was extended to include goods from the East European states; the costs were higher than world market prices and the quality was not always the best. Some of the goods were not intended for use in the tropics. Still, trade with Russia and the other Communist states was all that Burma could arrange and disposed of rice surpluses at a time when the markets in the West were glutted. In 1958 the Soviet Union gave a loan of between K20 and 30 million (approximately $4.2 to $6.3 million) for two irrigation dams and K15 million (approximately $3.1 million) for the establishment of a farm implement factory.[41] Modest Russian aid continued after the military coup in Burma.

Ne Win visited the Soviet Union in September 1965, and six years later the president of the USSR returned the visit. Despite the apparent continuity of good relations between the two states, after the coup in Burma their intensity declined. Even when the Sino-Burmese crisis dominated Burmese foreign affairs, Rangoon made no effort to strengthen its position by leaning toward Moscow as a possible counterweight to Peking. Burma showed no interest in the 1969 Brezhnev proposal of an Asian collective security agreement. Although the Burmese continued and in some ways expanded educational exchanges with the Soviet Union and allowed more visitors from the USSR and other East European states, they were careful not to lean too far in any one direction and to remain as free from dependence upon Russia and China as upon the United States. The Russians appeared to appreciate the delicate situation of the Burmese and did not exert pressure.

Burma's Relations with Israel and Japan

U Nu sought to develop good relations with the government of Israel and to use his good offices and friendship with Arab and Muslim leaders to try to find a peaceful solution to the difficult Middle East problems. There were other reasons for friendship

41. U. S. Department of State, *The Sino-Soviet Economic Offensive in the Less Developed Areas* (Washington, D.C.: U. S. Government Printing Office, 1958), no. 6632, European and British Commonwealth Series 51; D. Vasilyav and K. Lvov, *Soviet Trade with Southeast Asia* (Moscow: Foreign Languages Publishing House, 1959).

with Israel, for this new state was seen as an alternative source of technical assistance to the superpowers. It also was a model of a small nation seeking to establish secure borders through resettlement. During the constitutional period, relations between Rangoon and Tel Aviv were good; the leaders exchanged visits and Israel gave technical assistance. Under Ne Win, the links between the two countries began to weaken; no formal visits by heads of state were made, and Israeli technical assistance was phased out. Ne Win felt that U Nu's government had moved too close to Israel, and he attempted to restore the balance by moving in the opposite direction. Thus, while maintaining formal relations with Israel, Ne Win strengthened relations with the Arab and Muslim states. After the coup in 1962, the Burmese military leaders explored new ways to adapt Israeli sociomilitary ideas about armed villages on the frontier and economic ideas about cooperatives.

Burma's relations with Japan are based in part on an informal set of ties. Many of the Burmese military leaders became well acquainted with their Japanese counterparts during World War II. Despite the destruction wrought by the war, initially blamed on Japan, many Burmese regarded the Japanese as friends who had helped them acquire independence. Those Japanese who worked closely with the "thirty heroes" were welcomed back to Burma in the periods of constitutional and military rule. In 1951, however, the Burma government refused to participate in the peace conference at San Francisco because the proposed treaty did not provide reparations for Burma's wartime losses and suffering. Although a year later the two nations entered into a trade agreement, and on April 30, 1952, Burma announced that the state of war with Japan had ended, it was not until 1954 that a treaty of peace was concluded providing Japanese reparations and economic cooperation. Japan agreed to pay $200 million in war reparations and $50 million in investments. By 1960, Burmese attitudes toward Japan began to cool because Japan was making greater reparations payments to Indonesia and the Philippines. Subsequently, U Nu's government reopened the question of further reparations and secured a new agreement that gave Burma an additional $200 million in grants and loans.

Over the years, Japan has become one of Burma's major trading partners. In 1974–1975, Japan was Burma's chief source of imports, providing 30 percent of the total and receiving 11 percent of Burma's exports. In addition, Japan has given Burma aid during the 1970s that was used to replace outmoded machinery and technology and to improve education facilities.

The brief discussion of Burma's relations with Israel and Japan was included to demonstrate the range of contacts it had and to suggest the variety of subjects they included. Whether dealing with large or small, capitalist or socialist states, Burma sought to pursue its interests as it defined them regardless of how other nations interpreted its behavior.

Burma and the United Nations

A careful examination of Burma's record in the United Nations will underscore the independence of her role in the world community. During the constitutional period, Burma's positions on issues and problems reflected the policy of neutralism and nonalignment. In 1950 it joined other nations at the UN in calling for a halt to North Korea's aggression against the South; however, when the United Nations forces crossed the 38th parallel, Burma withdrew support on the belief that the UN had overstepped its original mandate. In 1956 the Rangoon government spoke out forcefully against Russian brutality in Hungary and voted a year later to accept the United Nations report on the Hungarian uprising despite the unwillingness of some neutralist countries, such as India, to do so. Burma voted to condemn the actions of Great Britain, France, and Israel in Egypt in 1956. Burma publicly deplored the violations of the UN Charter implicit in the ill-fated American-backed invasion of Cuba in 1961. In every session of the UN when the question was raised of seating the People's Republic as the representative of China, Burma voted affirmatively. U Nu's government was understandably proud when, following the death of Dag Hammarskjold in 1961, its ambassador to the United Nations, U Thant, was elected as acting and, later, as permanent secretary-general.

On the question of the war in Vietnam, Burma made no public statements supporting either side. Its position was that the Vietnamese people must find a solution themselves without outside interference.

After a decade of military rule, in 1972 the government fairly accurately summed up its foreign policy as follows: "In international affairs Burma has consistently pursued, in and out of the United Nations, an independent policy of peaceful settlement of all problems, peaceful coexistence, disarmament, opposition to all racial discrimination, liquidation of colonialism, participation and strengthening of UN development programs and admission of China into the United Nations."[42]

The same statement could have been made by the leaders of the constitutional government that preceded the 1962 coup, for whom the same conception of neutralism and nonalignment had been basic to their foreign policy.

42. "A Report on the Ten Years of Social Revolution in Burma," *Working People's Daily* (Rangoon), March 2, 1972, p. 9.

8 | Some Concluding Observations

As Burma concludes its third decade of independence, its political record incorporates the experiences of both democratic and authoritarian governments, neither of which has been able to solve the nation's fundamental problems. These problems affect the substructure of Burmese politics; and at least two of them must be solved if the nation is to begin realizing its full social and economic potential.

The Problem of National Unity

Burma is not and never has been a nation in the sense that all or nearly all of its people share a common set of values, beliefs, and goals and acknowledge a primary loyalty to a polity that transcends their loyalty to race, religion, or place of origin. The Burmese nationalist leaders faced this problem squarely in 1947 when in meetings with representatives of the minorities at Panglong they entered into an agreement that provided a basis for unity—in exchange for their loyalty to the state the minorities were granted near autonomy in cultural and local political matters. At the constitutional convention later the same year, this principle was translated into a unique federal system. During the decade that followed, however, the politics of Burmanization ran counter to the agreements of Panglong, provoking revolt among some of the minorities and general discontent among the rest. The military's approach to the problem did not improve this situation. By displacing federalism with central control and employing harsher methods to gain compliance, its parallel effort of cloaking Burmanization with cultural programs and vague pronouncements about the need to incorporate elements of the several cultures of the minorities into a truly national culture did not make centralization more palatable. The minorities' answer to the military was the same as to its civilian predecessors—more revolt, a heightened sense of separate and distinct identity, and a desire for political separation.

During the whole of the independence period, there was only one moment when a solution might have been achieved. In 1962, U Nu convinced the minority leaders to discuss with the Burman leaders the vital issues of statehood and together to take the first step toward finding a lasting solution. Any prospect of success was aborted by the coup and the arrest of many of the minorities' leaders. A year later, when the military tried to establish a dialogue on its own terms, the effort failed mainly because the imprisoned leaders of the minorities were not released from custody and allowed to take their place as spokesmen for their peoples. In addition, the meetings were dominated by the Burman political rivals of the military—particularly the Communists—and no real communication was established.

The military asserted that the 1974 constitution was the result of discussion and criticism by all concerned and that popular ratification indicated public approval. But its emphasis upon centralism and the primacy of the state over the interests both of the individual and of any subgroup was unacceptable to the minorities, and their insurgency continues.

Until a new leadership emerges that is capable of convincing the minorities that it is sincere in wishing to find a solution through mutual consultation, the problem will persist, warfare will continue, economic and social development will not take place in the vast minority areas, and the social distance between the Burmans and the minorities will widen rather than close.

The Problem of the Gap between the Elite and the Masses

Burma also divides between an overwhelming majority of tradition-oriented peasants, and recent migrants to the cities and towns and the Western-educated elite. Despite the efforts of civilian and military leaders, Burma remains a traditional society—physically isolated from the outside world, predominantly agrarian, and strong in its beliefs in religion and man's limited ability to alter his condition. Burma's revolutionary mood immediately following World War II grew out of the suffering inflicted upon the people by a war they did not make and whose outcome they could not influence. They were ready to throw off foreign rule and alien retainers. Those in the society who held a new vision of Burma—as united, industrialized, and modern—were the Western-educated elite who lived in the cities and were involved in politics, journalism, the professions, and the military. But hardly had the country regained independence before it was plunged into civil war and the urban leadership was cut off from the countryside, leaving the masses of peasants to face the rebels as best they could. The peasants looked to the traditional local leaders—the headmen, the Buddhist monks, the village elders—but most of all, they looked to their own resources to cope with the existing situation. Their goals were to hold their land, to farm, and to market as they desired and to live in the manner they inherited from the past.

When the insurgency declined, the Western-educated national leaders sought to re-establish their links with the countryside through their political parties and individuals whom they thought enjoyed standing among the people. But neither the parties not the appointed leaders had the stature to unite the people or the ability to transmit the vision of a new Burma. Most were not committed to work for the people and, instead, used their power and position to improve their personal wealth and status. The coup brought no outcry from the countryside and no rush to the barricades to defend the political system.

The vision and the goals of the Western-educated elite had been at odds with tradition. The democratic ideal, the socialist goals, and the modern values that informed the rhetoric of the leaders were not understood or adopted by those for whom the message was intended. This elite made few converts to its ideas because of the poor state of the roads, radio, and newspapers and the Western idiom of the leaders. When its members spoke in the language of the people, as U Nu did, and when they produced evidence that the adoption of new ways and ideas would result in improvements, they gained some converts. For all too many people in the countryside, however, what was said and done in the cities had no real meaning, and change on a large scale did not follow.

Subsequently, the new ideology, institutions, and approaches to modernization of the military's elite once again affected the urban population primarily, leaving the peasantry largely untouched. The farmers accepted the security of their land, the easy loans, and other benefits bestowed upon them by the soldiers in power, but they did not change their outlook or life style. They farmed and marketed as before, and when consumer goods were not available or government demands seemed unacceptable they sold their produce on the black market, withheld their crops from the government buyers, and continued to live in their traditional unsocialistic ways. Even though the military attempted to displace their traditional local authority with the SACs and the cadres from the BSPP, the new local leaders proved no more successful than the political hacks of the civilian parties they replaced.

The military has not united the people behind its leadership. Its two steps backward in 1974–1975—away from socialism by raising the price to the farmer for his product and borrowing from abroad from international lending institutions—are not convincing the peasant that the Burmese way to socialism offers him a better set of values than those he inherited from his parents and learned in the village. He continues to respond as an "economic man" to economic incentives; he is wary of coercion, having lived with that of insurgents and governments alike; he looks inward to his family and immediate neighbors and not to Rangoon. He attends meetings, participates in rallies and elections. But thus far this participation has not altered his beliefs and activity. Most Burmese peasants view the city as an alien place they visit upon occasion and might have to move to if natural disaster or warfare force them off the land. When the peasant becomes a city dweller he brings his values and beliefs with him, and though he becomes more susceptible to the indoctrination and mobilization of the government, he remains estranged from it. This is the result of the government's failure to provide jobs and lift the standard of living, of the peasants' natural inclination to fear and avoid government, and of their being unconvinced that the leaders are genuinely interested in their well-being.

Neither the indifferent approaches to the problem by the civilian leaders before 1962 nor the authoritarian methods of the military afterward appreciably reached the people in the countryside. The gap between the governing, urban-centered elite and the masses that was evident in the 1950s persists and may have widened in the 1970s. The problem cannot be solved quickly or easily. Patience and understanding are needed, as well as a new leadership sympathetic to tradition and able to use it to get the people to change and to voluntarily accept direction.

Bibliography

Selected Official Publications of the Union of Burma (General and Serial)

1948–1962

Central Statistical and Economics Department. *First Stage Census, 1953*. 4 vols. Rangoon: Superintendent, Government Printing and Stationery, 1957–1958. Covers 252 towns in Burma proper and Chin Special Division; included are detailed data on population, housing, industry, and agriculture.

——. *1957 Sample Census*, Rangoon, 1958.

——. *Quarterly Bulletin of Statistics*.

——. *Report on the Survey of Household Expenditures, 1958*. Rangoon: Rangoon Lithographers and Printers, 1959.

Directorate of Industries and Central Statistical and Economics Department. *Annual Survey of Manufactures, 1957–58*. Rangoon, 1961.

Ministry of Agriculture. *Season and Crop Report*.

Ministry of Information. *Burma*. A quarterly; every January issue was called *Anniversary Number* and contained a survey of events of the past year. Issued quarterly 1950–1962.

——. *Burma Weekly Bulletin*. Official publication of the government covering a wide range of topics. Issued weekly 1952–1962.

Ministry of National Planning. *Economic Survey of Burma*. Issued annually at time that the budget was being considered by parliament. Publication halted in 1962.

——. *The National Income of Burma*. Issued annually, 1951–1961.

Union Bank of Burma. *Monthly Review*.

——. *Quarterly Bulletin*.

1962 to present

Director of Information. *Forward*. A fortnightly that replaced *Burma Weekly Bulletin*.

Revolutionary Council of the Union of Burma. *Report to the People by the Government of the Union of Burma on the Financial, Economic and Social Conditions*. From 1973, issued by the Ministry of Planning and Finance.

Newspapers and Periodicals

1948–1962

Atlantic, Special Supplement, 201, no. 2 (February 1958), 99–170. An excellent cross-section of contemporary political and social life during the first decade of independent Burma. All contributors are Burmese.

Burman. An important English-language daily during the first eight years after World War II. It lost its political significance as it changed its focus and concentrated on Buddhism and local affairs. It ceased publication after the 1962 coup.

Guardian. Both daily and monthly. It was the leading English-language periodical in Burma and drew articles from Western writers as well as Burmese. It was nationalized in 1964.

Nation. Until forced to shut down in 1964, it was the leading daily in Rangoon. It often performed the role of a loyal opposition in mobilizing and influencing public opinion.

1962 to present

Working People's Daily. The official government newspaper, from 1963. There are two editions daily—one in English, the other in Burmese.

Historical and Cultural Background

Adas, Michael. *The Burma Delta: Economic Development and Social Change on an Asian Rice Frontier, 1852–1941*. Madison: University of Wisconsin Press, 1974. A socioeconomic history of lower Burma based on official colonial records.

Ba Maw. *Breakthrough in Burma: Memoirs of a Revolution, 1939–1946*. New Haven: Yale University Press, 1968. The author was Burma's first prime minister under the 1937 constitution, and later, under the Japanese occupation, was the head of state.

Ba U. *My Burma: The Autobiography of a President*. New York: Taplinger, 1958. The first president under the constitution of the Union of Burma. Contains good description about growing up under colonial rule.

Baxter, James. *Report on Indian Immigration*. Rangoon: Superintendent, Government Printing and Stationery, 1941. An official report published just prior to World War II.

Burma, Government of. *Burma during the Japanese Occupation*. 2 vols. Simla: Government of India Press, 1943–1944. A confidential report on Burma drawn from intelligence sources; very useful on this period, especially vol. II.

——. *Correspondence for the Years 1825–26 to 1842–43 in the Office of the Commissioner, Tenasserim Division*. Rangoon: Superintendent, Government Printing, 1929. Indispensable for the study of the beginnings of British rule in Burma.

———. *Selected Correspondence of Letters Issued from and Received in the Office of the Commissioner, Tenasserim Division, for the Years 1825–26 to 1842–43*. Rangoon: Government Printing and Stationery, 1929. Like the *Correspondence*, invaluable for the study of the beginning of British rule in Burma.

Burma Research Society. *Fiftieth Anniversary Publications No. 2*. Rangoon: Sarpay Beikman Press, 1960. Selected articles in history and literature from the *Journal of the Burma Research Society*; reproduced some of the classic literature of Burma.

Cady, John F. *A History of Modern Burma*. Ithaca: Cornell University Press, 1958. Especially good description of the period of colonial rule.

———. *The United States and Burma*. Cambridge, Mass.: Harvard University Press, 1976. A shortened version of his earlier *History*, updated slightly to take account of some new research published since the original appeared.

Chakravarti, N. R. *The Indian Minority in Burma*. London: Oxford University Press, 1971. A useful study of an important minority group in Burma; covers the period up to World War II best.

Cheng Siok-Hwa. *The Rice Industry in Burma*. Kuala Lumpur: University of Malaya Press, 1968. Covers some of the same material that Adas covered, but dwells upon the economic factors and gives little or no attention to the social factors.

Christian, John L. *Burma and the Japanese Invader*. Bombay: Thacker, 1945. A rewritten version of the author's earlier study, *Modern Burma*, with new material about Burma and World War II; excellent bibliography.

Collis, Maurice S. *Last and First in Burma*. London: Faber & Faber, 1956. Drawn from official papers supplied by former Governor Dorman-Smith, it attempts to explain the governor's actions during the 1945–1946 period.

———. *Trials in Burma*. London: Faber & Faber, 1938. A good firsthand account of British rule during the 1930s by a former civil servant.

Crosthwaite, Sir Charles. *The Pacification of Burma*. London: Cass, 1968. A reissue of a classic study of the unification of upper Burma following the third Anglo-Burmese War.

Dautremer, Joseph. *Burma under British Rule*. London: T. Fisher Unwin, 1913. A Study of British rule by a French civil servant stationed in Burma. Useful for its descriptions and comparative references to French rule in Indo-China.

Donnison, Frank S. V. *Public Administration in Burma*. London: Royal Institute of International Affairs, 1953. A brief but useful summary by a former British civil servant of the growth of the administrative system; very pro-British.

Furnivall, John S. *Colonial Policy and Practice*. New York: New York University Press, 1956. A reissue of a classic comparative study of colonialism in Burma and Indonesia.

——. *An Introduction to the Political Economy of Burma*. Rangoon: Burma Book Club, 1931. The first effort to apply an economic analysis to Burma; a strong criticism of British rule.

Hall, Daniel G. E. *Burma*. London: Hutchinson's University Library, 1950. A short, good history.

——. *Europe and Burma*. London: Oxford University Press, 1945. A short diplomatic history of Burma's relations with the West prior to colonial rule.

Harvey, Geoffrey E. *British Rule in Burma, 1824–1942*. London: Faber & Faber, 1946. A short study with a thematic approach to history; an attempt to bring his original study up to date but falls far short in terms of scholarship and detail.

——. *History of Burma from the Earliest Times to 10 March 1824*. London: Longmans Green, 1925. A very good history of precolonial Burma with detailed and well-documented notes at the end of the text.

Htin Aung. *Burmese History before 1287: A Defence of the Chronicles*. Oxford: Asoka Society, 1970. A response to Western scholars who, in reviewing his *History*, were critical of his reliance upon indigenous sources.

——. "First Burmese Mission to the Court of St. James's: Kinwun Mingyi's Diaries 1872–74," *Journal of the Burma Research Society*, 57 (December 1974), 1–196. An abridged translation, with commentary, of the first Burmese to travel to Europe on an official mission and record his experiences and feelings.

——. *History of Burma*. New York: Columbia University Press, 1967. Burmese history from a nationalist point of view.

——. *The Stricken Peacock: Anglo-Burmese Relations, 1752–1948*. The Hague: Martinus Nijhoff, 1965. Diplomatic history from a Burmese perspective.

Khin, U. *U Hla Pe's Narrative of the Japanese Occupation of Burma*. Ithaca: Southeast Asia Program, Cornell University, Data Paper no. 41, 1961. An excellent account of the war years in Burma.

Khin Maung Kyi and Daw Tin Tin. *Administrative Patterns in Historical Burma*. Singapore: Institute of Southeast Asian Studies, 1973. An original study by two Burmese scholars who attempt to apply Marx's Asiatic modes of production theory to Burmese history.

Kyaw Min. *The Burma We Love*. Calcutta: India Book House, 1945. An assessment of Burmese politics and leaders during the late 1930s and early 1940s by a senior Burmese civil servant.

Mahajani, Usha. *The Role of Indian Minorities in Burma and Malaya*. Bombay: Vora, 1960. A comparative study based on documents and official papers.

Masters, John. *The Road Past Mandalay*. London: Michael Joseph, 1961. Autobiography in which the author gives an excellent account of those events of the military campaign to recover Burma from the Japanese in which he participated.

Maung Maung, ed. *Aung San of Burma*. The Hague: Martinus Nijhoff,

1962. A collection of essays, speeches, letters, and articles by Aung San and others.

———. *Burma in the Family of Nations*. Amsterdam: Djambatan, 1956. A short history of Burmese diplomacy prior to British rule. The appendixes contain many documents difficult to obtain elsewhere.

———. *Law and Custom in Burma and the Burmese Family*. The Hague: Martinus Nijhoff, 1963. An essay on Burmese Buddhist law placed in the context of Burmese history and society.

———. *A Trial in Burma: The Assassination of Aung San*. The Hague: Martinus Nijhoff, 1962. A brief but detailed account of the trial of Aung San's assassin along with pertinent documents.

Maung Maung Pye. *Burma in the Crucible*. Rangoon: Khittaya, 1951. A journalist's account of the nationalist movement in Burma; contains some interesting data, which unfortunately are not documented.

Mendelson, E. Michael. *Sangha and State in Burma: A Study of Monastic Sectarianism and Leadership*. Ed. by John P. Ferguson, Ithaca: Cornell University Press, 1975. An important study on the relationship between the two forces that helped shape Burmese politics, society, and the values of the people.

Morrison, Ian. *Grandfather Long Legs*. London: Faber & Faber, 1947. A useful account of the war behind the Japanese lines in Burma. The author is pro-Karen in discussing the conflicts between the Burmans and Karens during the war years.

Moscotti, Albert D. *British Policy and the Nationalist Movement in Burma, 1917–1937*. Hawaii: University Press of Hawaii, 1974. An early postwar study of colonialism in Burma that was used by later scholars with profit. Originally a Ph.D. thesis, it only recently was published.

Mountbatten, Louis. *Report to the Combined Chiefs of Staff by the Supreme Allied Commander, South-east Asia, 1943–45*. London: H. M. Stationery Office, 1951. Official report of the recapture of Burma by the Allies in 1944–1945.

Mya Sein, Ma. *The Administration of Burma*. Kuala Lumpur: Oxford University Press, 1973. A reissue of an early study of pre-Western Burma based on Burmese sources.

Nu, Thakin. *Burma under the Japanese*. London: St. Martin's Press, 1954. A firsthand account of Burmese society and politics under Japanese rule.

———. *U Nu—Saturday's Son*. Translated by U Law Yone and edited by U Kyaw Win. New Haven: Yale University Press, 1975. The memoirs of Burma's first prime minister after independence.

Ogburn, Charston, Jr. *The Marauders*. New York: Harper, 1959. An excellent account of the U.S. military participation in the recovery of Burma from Japanese control.

Pe Maung Tin and Gordon E. Luce. *The Glass Palace Chronicles of the Kings of Burma*. London: Oxford University Press, 1923. A translation of the Burmese royal chronicles describing the period of the Pagan dynasty; excellent example of precolonial indigenous historical writing.

Saimong Mangrai, Sao. *The Shan States and the British Annexation*. Ithaca: South-east Asia Program, Cornell University, Data Paper no. 57, 1965. A history of the Shan states written from a Shan point of view, drawing upon material not previously used.

Sangermano, Father. *A Description of the Burmese Empire*. London: Susil Gupta, 1966. A reissue of one of the earliest histories of Burma by a Westerner, particularly valuable because it was written during the early Konbaung period.

Sarkisyanz, E. *Buddhist Backgrounds of the Burmese Revolution*. The Hague: Martinus Nijhoff, 1965. A controversial study of ideology, religion, and politics that cannot be ignored by serious students of the subject.

Sens, Nirmal C. *A Peep into Burma Politics, 1917–1932*. Allahabad: Kitabistan, 1945. A good short account of Burmese politics during the period of political awakening among the people. The author participated in the events described.

Silverstein, Josef, ed. *The Political Legacy of Aung San*. Ithaca: Southeast Asia Program, Cornell University, Data Paper no. 86, 1972.

——. "Politics, and Railroads in Burma and India: A Problem of Historical Interpretation," *Journal of the Burma Research Society*, 45 (1962), 79–89.

——. "Transportation in Burma during the Japanese Occupation," *Journal of Burma Research Society*, 39 (1956), 1–17.

Slim, William. *Defeat into Victory*. London: Cassell, 1956. A thoughtful and well-written account of the British retreat and return to Burma during World War II.

Smith, Donald Eugene. *Religion and Politics in Burma*. Princeton: Princeton University Press, 1965. An excellent study of this topic treated in a historical manner. Author uses sources not found in other similar studies.

Stewart, A. T. Q. *The Pagoda War: Lord Dufferin and the Fall of the Kingdom of Ava, 1885–1886*. London: Faber & Faber, 1972. An important addition to the political-military history of the third Anglo-Burmese war.

Trager, Frank N. *Burma—From Kingdom to Republic: A Historical and Political Analysis*. New York: Praeger, 1966. Emphasis is not upon the kingdom, but upon the end of British rule and the independence period. Special attention is given to Burma's foreign relations, especially with the United States.

——, ed. *Burma: Japanese Military Administration, Selected Documents, 1941–1945*. Philadelphia: University of Pennsylvania Press, 1971.

Tun Pe. *Sun Over Burma*. Rangoon: Rasika Ranjani Press, 1949. A personal account of World War II in Burma as experienced by one who was there.

Tun Wai. *Economic Development of Burma from 1800 to 1940*. Rangoon: University of Rangoon Press, 1961. An economic history written by a Burmese scholar.

Woodman, Dorothy. *The Making of Burma*. London: Cresset Press, 1962. A detailed history of the amalgamation of the Frontier Areas with Burma proper.

The Contemporary Setting

Andrus, James R. *Burmese Economic Life.* Stanford: Stanford University Press, 1948. Excellent survey of the period prior to independence.

——. *Rural Reconstruction in Burma.* Calcutta: Oxford University Press, 1936. An interesting account of social work as part of student life at Judson College; a useful study for those interested in prewar student life and activity.

Aye Hlaing. *Some Aspects of Seasonal Agricultural Loans in Burma and Agroeconomic Problems in Burma.* Economic Papers nos. 14 and 21. Rangoon: Department of Economics, Statistics, and Commerce, University of Rangoon, 1958. Very useful for the study of the problem of rural indebtedness and its social and economic implications.

Brant, Charles. *Tadagale: A Burmese Village in 1950.* Ithaca: Southeast Asia Program, Cornell University, Data Paper no. 13, 1954.

Brohm, John F. "Buddhism and Animism in a Burmese Village," *Journal of Asian Studies,* 22 (February 1963), 155–167. Excellent treatment of the topic.

Dobby, Ernest H.G. *Southeast Asia.* 2d ed. New York: Wiley, 1951. Chs. 9, 10, and 11 are devoted to Burma.

Economic Research Project. *Village Studies Series: Okpo. Wanetkon, Kyungale, Kyaukanya.* Economic Papers nos. 11, 12, 13, and 17. Rangoon: Department of Economics, Statistics, and Commerce, University of Rangoon, 1957, 1959. Excellent brief accounts of villages in lower Burma; compiled from printed statistical data and field studies.

Hanks, Lucian M. "The Quest for Individual Autonomy in Burmese Personality." *Psychiatry,* 12 (1949), 285–300. Work of a social psychologist based on wartime experiences in the Arakan area.

Khin Maung Kyi et. al. *Process of Communication in Modernization of Rural Society: A Survey Report on Two Burmese Villages.* Rangoon: Department of Research, Institute of Economics. Rural Socio-Economic Research Series (2), 1972. A follow-up study of the two villages surveyed in 1956.

King, Winston L. *A Thousand Lives Away.* Cambridge, Mass: Harvard University Press, 1964. A study of Buddhism in contemporary Burma.

Knappen, Tippetts, Abbett, and McCarthy. *Comprehensive Report: Economic and Engineering Development of Burma.* 2 vols. Aylesbury, England, 1953. A survey undertaken by American engineers and economists for the purpose of developing and recommending an economic plan.

Koop, John C. *The Eurasian Population in Burma.* New Haven: Yale Southeast Asian Studies, 1960. An original attempt to define the problems and place of this minority in contemporary Burma.

Kyaw Thet. "Burma: The Political Integration of Linguistic and Religious Minorities." In Philip Thayer, ed. *Nationalism and Progress in Free Asia.* Baltimore: Johns Hopkins Press, 1956.

——. "Cultural Minorities in Burma." In Hubert Passim, ed. *Cultural Freedom in Asia.* Rutland: Tuttle, 1956.

Leach, Edmund. *Political Systems of Highland Burma.* London: Bell, 1954.

Based upon a field study; provides a detailed and interesting account of Kachin social and political life.

Lehman, Frederick K. *The Structure of Chin Society: A Tribal People of Burma Adapted to a Non-western Civilization.* Urbana: Illinois Studies in Anthropology, no. 3, University of Illinois Press, 1963. A careful study of modern Chin society with emphasis upon the problem of cultural adaptation among Chins living in close proximity to Burmans.

Marshall, Harry. *The Karen Peoples of Burma: A Study in Anthropology and Ethnology.* Columbus: Ohio State University Press, 1922. The best study available on the Karens.

Mi Mi Khaing. *Burmese Family.* Calcutta: Longmans, Green, 1946. A very readable account of Burmese life and customs written by a well-to-do Burman.

Myo Htun Lynn. *Labour and the Labour Movement in Burma.* Rangoon: University of Rangoon Press, 1961. A good survey of the labor movement in Burma during the first decade of independence.

Nash, Manning. *Golden Road to Modernity: Village Life in Contemporary Burma.* New York: Wiley, 1965. An excellent account of village life in upper Burma based on research carried out just before the coup.

Pye, Lucian W. *Politics, Personality and Nation Building: Burma's Search for Identity.* New Haven: Yale University Press, 1962. An appraisal of Burmese political behavior in the light of a national character model developed by the author from various theoretical works in the social sciences.

Shwey Yoe (pseud. of J. G. Scott). *The Burman: His Life and Notions.* London: Macmillan, 1910. A standard work on Burman customs, dress, and society.

Spiro, Melford E. *Buddhism and Society: A Great Tradition and Its Burmese Vicissitudes.* London: Allen & Unwin, 1971. A careful study, based on extensive field research in upper Burma just prior to the coup.

——. *Burmese Supernaturalism.* Englewood Cliffs: Prentice-Hall, 1967. A comprehensive examination of Burmese folk religion and its relationship to Buddhism.

Thompson, Virginia, and Richard Adloff. *Minority Problems in Southeast Asia.* Stanford: Stanford University Press, 1955. Problems of minorities discussed by groups rather than by country and therefore presenting some interesting and revealing comparisons.

Tinker, Hugh. *The Union of Burma.* London: Oxford University Press, 1956. A general survey of politics, economics, and society in Burma from 1948 through the mid-1950s. Subsequent editions have appeared, but the text remains as published originally.

Wohl, Julian, and Josef Silverstein. "The Burmese University Student: An Approach to Personality and Subculture," *Public Opinion Quarterly,* 30 (Summer 1966), 237–248.

Constitutional Government, 1948–1962

Ba Swe. *The Burmese Revolution*. Rangoon: Information Department, 1952. A long speech containing the oft-quoted passage about the harmonious relationship between Buddhism and Marxism.

——. *Guide to Socialism in Burma*. Rangoon: Superintendent, Government Printing and Stationery, 1956. The report of the secretary general of the All-Burma Socialist party, drawn up and approved at the party's first conference in 1946; important to anyone interested in studying the evolution of the socialist ideology in Burma.

Badgley, John. "Burma's Political Crisis," *Pacific Affairs*, 31 (1958), 336–351. Excellent discussion of the split in the AFPFL that led to political ascension of the military to power in 1958.

——. "Burma's Radical Left: A Study in Failure," *Problems in Communism*, 10 (January 1961), 47–55. A brief account of the splits among the leftist leaders and implications in Burmese politics.

——. *Politics among Burmans: A Study of Intermediary Leaders*. Athens, Ohio: Ohio University Center for International Studies, Southeast Asia Series, no. 15, 1970. An empirical study of leaders standing between those at the top and those at the village level. Research was conducted just prior to the 1962 coup.

Brohm, John. "Burmese Religion and the Burmese Buddhist Revival." 2 vols. Ph.D. dissertation, Cornell University, 1957. Vol. II includes the best study available of the early effort by the national leaders to link religion and politics.

Burma, Government of the Union of. *Burma and the Insurrections*. Rangoon: Government of the Union of Burma publication, 1949. An official survey of the various insurgent political and ethnic movements.

——. *The First Interim Report of the Administration Re-organization Committee*. Rangoon: Superintendent, Union Government Printing and Stationery, 1955. An official study of the inherited colonial administrative system and recommendations for ways to improve it.

——. *The Final Report of the Administration Reorganization Committee*, Rangoon: Superintendent, Government Printing and Stationery, 1954. Final recommendations of necessary changes to make the administration of Burma more democratic.

——. *The Pyidawtha Conference: August 4–17, 1952*. Rangoon: Ministry of Information, 1952. The first national conference called to discuss programs and plans for the creation of a "new Burma." Includes speeches and resolutions of the participants.

——. *Reports of the Parliamentary Election Petitions Enquiry Commission (Extracts)* Rangoon: Superintendent, Government Printing and Stationery Office, 1959. Useful in the study of the actual working of the election process in 1952 and 1956.

——. *Report of the Public Services Enquiry Commission, 1961*. Rangoon: Superintendent, Government Printing and Stationery, 1961. A re-examination of the administration with a view to recommending ways to improve it.

——. Constituent Assembly. *The Constitution of the Union of Burma*. Rangoon: Government Printing and Stationery Office, 1948. Also reprinted in A. J. Peaslee, *Constitutions of Nations*, 2d ed. 3 vols. The Hague: Martinus Nijhoff, 1956. Neither copy of the constitution includes any of the amendments.

——. Defense Services. *The National Ideology and the Role of the Defense Services*. Rangoon, 1960. An important document in the political maturation of the military in Burma; originally distributed at the Defense Services conference held in Meiktila, October 21, 1958.

——. Ministry of Information. *Is Trust Vindicated?* Rangoon: Director of Information, 1960. An official account of the caretaker government.

——. ——. *The Nine Months after the Ten Years*. Rangoon: Government Printing and Stationery, 1959. The caretaker government's interim report on its programs and performance.

Butwell, Richard. *U Nu of Burma*. Stanford: Stanford University Press, 1963. A political biography that attempted to evaluate the man and his ideas.

——, and Fred Von der Medhen. "The 1960 Election in Burma," *Pacific Affairs*, 33 (June 1960), 144–157. A good account of the caretaker government and the events leading up to the election.

Christian, Winslow. "Burma's New Constitution and Supreme Court," *Tulane Law Reivew*, 26 no. 1 (1951), 47–59. An early account of the problems of judicial freedom and preventive detention.

Donnison, Frank S. V. *Burma*. New York: Praeger, 1970. A good overview of Burmese politics during the constitutional period and the early years of the military regime that followed.

Dupuy, T. N. "Burma and Its Army: A Contrast in Motivations and Characteristics," *Antioch Review*, 20 (1960), 428–460. An essay on the Burmese military leaders by an American admirer who worked with them while he was in Burma.

Furnivall, John S. *The Governance of Modern Burma*. New York: Institute of Pacific Relations, 1958. A general survey of the political institutions under the 1947 constitution and a personal evaluation of the AFPFL split.

Gledhill, Alan. "The Burmese Constitution," *Indian Yearbook of International Affairs, 1953*, II Madras: Indian Study Group of International Affairs, University of Madras, 1954, 214–224. A good summary of the main provisions in the constitution with special emphasis on the sources of the document.

Hla Aung. "The Law of Preventive Detention in Burma," *Journal of the International Commission of Jurists*, 3, no. 1 (1961), 47–68. The best discussion of the issue available.

Josey, A. "The Political Significance of the Burma Workers' Party," *Pacific Affairs*, 31 (December 1958), 372–379. A good short account of the left wing in Burmese politics by a socialist writer.

Lahiri, Sisur C. *Principles of Modern Burmese Buddhist Law*. 6th ed. Calcutta: Eastern Law House (Private), 1957. An excellent treatment of the subject with cases and examples to amplify the discussion.

Maung Maung. *Burma's Constitution*. The Hague: Martinus Nijhoff, 1959. A popular treatment of the constitution preceded by an essay on the nationalist movement in Burma. Updated slightly in the second edition (1961).

Nu, U. *Burma Looks Ahead*. Rangoon: Ministry of Information, 1953.

——. *Forward with the People*. Rangoon: Ministry of Information, 1955.

——. *From Peace to Stability*. Rangoon: Ministry of Information, 1951.

——. *Premier's Report to the People on Law and Order, National Solidarity, Social Welfare, National Economy, Foreign Affairs*. Rangoon: Director of Information, 1958.

——. *Toward Peace and Democracy*. Rangoon: Ministry of Information, 1949. A collection of Nu's speeches that indicate his political philosophy and trace the first decade of Burma's independence.

Pye, Lucian W. "The Army in Burmese Politics." In John J. Johnson, ed., *The Role of the Military in Underdeveloped Countries*. Princeton: Princeton University Press, 1962. pp. 231–251. Social analysis of the military in Burma based on the 1958–1960 experience when the military saw its political role as temporary and acted under the constitution.

——. *The Spirit of Burmese Politics: A Preliminary Survey of a Politics of Fear and Charisma*. Cambridge, Mass.: Center for International Studies, Massachusetts Institute of Technology, 1959. A preliminary report of the field research that was used in *Politics, Personality and Nation Building*.

Sein Win. *The Split Story*. Rangoon: Guardian, 1959. An account of the AFPFL split in 1958 by the editor of the *Guardian* (daily). Some errors in the narrative; a partisan view of the Kyaw Nyein-Ba Swe faction.

Silverstein, Josef. "Burmese Student Politics in a Changing Society," *Daedalus*, 97 (Winter 1968), 274–292. A survey and analysis of the student movement in historical perspective.

——. "The Federal Dilemma in Burma," *Far Eastern Survey*, 28 (July 1959), 97–105.

——. "From Democracy to Dictatorship in Burma," *Current History*, 46 (February 1964), 83–88.

——. "Politics, Parties and the National Election in Burma," *Far Eastern Survey*, 25 (December 1956), 177–184.

——. "Politics in the Shan State: The Question of Secession from the Union of Burma," *Journal of Asian Studies*, 28 (November 1958), 43–58.

——, and Julian Wohl. "University Students and Politics in Burma," *Pacific Affairs*, 37 (Spring 1964), 50–65.

Subramanian, N. A. "Some Aspects of Burmese Constitutional Law," *Indian Yearbook of International Affairs, 1956*, VI Madras: Indian Study

Group of International Affairs, University of Madras, 1957, 123–155. One of the best essays on the constitution of Burma.

Tinker, Hugh. "Nu, the Serene Statesman," *Pacific Affairs*, 30 (June 1957), 120–157.

Trager, Frank N., "The Political Split in Burma," *Far Eastern Survey*, 27 (October 1958), 145–155.

Von der Mehden, Fred. "Burma's Religious Campaign against Communism," *Pacific Affairs*, 33 (September 1960), 290–300.

Military Rule and Constitutional Dictatorship

Badgeley, John. "Intellectuals and the National Vision," *Asian Survey*, 9 (August 1969), 598–613.

Burma, Government of. *The Constitution of the Socialist Republic of the Union of Burma*. Rangoon: Printing and Publishing Corporation, 1974.

——, Burma Socialist Program Party. *Address Delivered by General Ne Win, Chairman of the Burma Socialist Program Party at the Opening Session of the Fourth Party Seminar on 6th November 1969*. Rangoon: Burma Socialist Program Party, Central Press, 1969.

——, ——. *Address Delivered by General Ne Win Chairman of the Burma Socialist Program Party at the Closing Session of the Fourth Party Seminar on 11th November 1969*. Rangoon: Central Press, 1969.

——, ——. *Party Seminar 1965*. Rangoon: Burma Socialist Program Party, 1966.

——, ——. *The System of Correlation of Man and His Environment*. Rangoon: Burma Socialist Program Party, 1964. A long document that provides the basis for the ideology of the military; attempts to blend idealism and materialism and show why socialism is consistent with Burmese culture and tradition.

——. Director of Information. *Burma: Administrative and Social Affairs, 1962–1963*. Rangoon: Director of Information, 1965. An assessment of the first year of military rule.

——, ——. U Ba Than. *The Roots of the Revolution*. Rangoon: Government Printing Press, 1962. Reprinted from the *Guardian*, March 27, 1962. A brief and partisan history of the Defense Services and the nationalist movement.

——, Revolutionary Council. *The Burmese Way to Socialism: The Policy Declaration of the Revolutionary Council*. Rangoon: Ministry of Information, 1962. The ideological basis for military rule published shortly after the coup in 1962.

——, ——. *International Peace Parley (Historical Documents No. 1)*. Rangoon, 1963 (mimeo). The documents produced during the discussions between the government and several rebel groups, known as the National Democratic United Front, which ended in failure.

Butwell, Richard. "Ne Win's Burma: At the End of the First Decade," *Asian Survey*, 12 (October 1972), 901–912.

Hla Aung. "Burmese Concept of Law," *Journal of the Burma Research Society,* 52 (1969), 27–41.

——. "State and Law on Contemporary Socialist Legal Thought," *Journal of the Burma Research Society,* 50 (1967), 245–262.

Holmes, Robert. "Burmese Domestic Policy: The Politics of Burmanization," *Asian Survey,* 7 (March 1967), 188–197.

Lissak, Moshe. *Military Roles in Modernization: Civil-Military Relations in Thailand and Burma.* Beverly Hills: Sage, 1976. A theoretical and descriptive study with a number of useful comparative insights.

Maung Maung. *Burma and General Ne Win.* New York: Asia Publishing House, 1969. A patronizing study of the general that seeks to establish that he and not his constitutional predecessors is leading Burma in the tradition of Aung San.

"A Report on Ten Years of Social Revolution in Burma," *Working People's Daily,* March 2, 1972. An official assessment of the first decade of military rule. Very useful as it contains data and information not available in other sources.

Silverstein, Josef. "Burma: Ne Win's Revolution Considered," *Asian Survey,* 6 (February 1966), 95–102.

——. "The Burma Socialist Program Party and Its Rivals: A One-Plus Party System," *Journal of Southeast Asian History,* 8 (March 1967), 8–18.

——. "First Steps on the Burmese Road to Socialism," *Asian Survey,* 4 (February 1964), 716–722.

——. "Military Rule in Burma," *Current History,* 52 (January 1967), 41–47.

——. "A New Vehicle on Burma's Road to Socialism," *Asia* 29 (1973), 55–76.

——. "Problems in Burma: Economic, Political and Diplomatic," *Asian Survey,* 7 (February 1967), 117–125.

——. "Political Dialogue in Burma: A New Turn on the Road to Socialism?" *Asian Survey,* 10 (February 1970), 133–142.

——, ed. and contrib. *The Future of Burma in Perspective: A Symposium.* Athens, Ohio: Ohio University Center for International Studies, Southeast Asia Series, no. 35, 1974. A series of essays by Burmese and American scholars that evaluate the period of military rule and look ahead to the period of constitutional dictatorship.

Wiant, Jon A. "Burma: Loosening Up on the Tiger's Tail," *Asian Survey,* 13 (February 1973), 179–186.

The Economy

Ahmad, Nafis. *Economic Resources of the Union of Burma.* Natick: United States Army Natick Laboratories, 1971. An economic survey.

Allen, Robert L. "Burma's Clearing Accounts Agreements," *Pacific Affairs,* 31, no 2 (June 1958), 147–164. A comprehensive analysis of Burma's experience in trading with Russia, China, and several East European countries.

Behman, Jack M. "State Trading by Underdeveloped Countries: Burma," *Law and Contemporary Problems*, 24 (1959), 454–460.

Burma, Union of, Economic and Social Board. *Pyidawtha: The New Burma.* Aylesbury, England: Hazell Watson & Viney 1954. A report on Burma's economic plans.

——, Ministry of National Planning. *Second Four-Year Plan for the Union of Burma 1961–1962 to 1964–1965.* Rangoon: Superintendent, Government Printing and Stationery, 1961.

——, ——. *Two-Year Plan of Economic Development for Burma.* Rangoon: Superintendent, Government Printing and Stationery, 1948. The original economic plan.

Hagen, Everett E. *The Economic Development of Burma.* Washington, D.C.: National Planning Association, 1956.

Lloyd, J. "Planning a Welfare State in Burma," *International Labor Review*, no. 69 (1954), 117–147.

Lockwood, Agnese N. "Burma's Road to Pyidawtha," *International Conciliation*, no. 518 (1958), 385–450.

Mya Maung. "Burmese Way to Socialism Beyond the Welfare State," *Asian Survey*, 10 (June 1970), 533–551.

Richter, H.V. "Union of Burma." In R. T. Shand, *Agricultural Development in Asia.* Berkeley: University of California Press, 1969. 140–180.

Stifel, Lawrence D. "Burmese Socialism: Economic Problems of the First Decade," *Pacific Affairs*, 45 (1972), 60–74.

——. "Economics of the Burmese Way to Socialism," *Asian Survey*, 11 (1971), 803–817.

Thet Tun. "Outline of a Socialist Economy for Burma," *Journal of the Burma Research Society*, 38 (Spring, 1954), 59–76.

Trager, Frank N. *Building a Welfare State in Burma.* New York: Institute of Pacific Relations, 1958.

Walinsky, Louis J. *Economic Development in Burma, 1951–1960.* New York: Twentieth Century Fund, 1962. An account of economic planning and development by one of the senior American private advisers in Burma.

Foreign Affairs and Relations

Bert, Wayne. "Chinese Relations with Burma and Indonesia," *Asian Survey*, 15 (June 1975), 473–487.

Bingham, June. *U Thant: The Search For Peace.* New York: Knopf, 1970. A biography of Burma's former ambassador to the United Nations who became its third secretary general.

Burma, Union of, Burma Socialist Program Party. *Foreign Policy of the Revolutionary Government of the Union of Burma.* Rangoon: Sarpay Beikman Press, 1968. Documents on Burma's foreign policy and relations since the coup.

——. Ministry of Information. *Kuomintang Aggression against Burma.* Rangoon: 1953. Burma's case before the United Nations on the illegal presence of Nationalist Chinese forces on its soil.

Fifield, Russell H. *The Diplomacy of Southeast Asia, 1945–58*. New York: Harper, 1958. Pp. 167–229.

"From Coexistence to Condemnation: The New Chinese View of Burma," *Current Scene: Developments in Mainland China*. Hong Kong: U.S. Information Services 5, no. 17 (October 17, 1967), 1–11. A publication of the United States that seeks to analyze and report events inside China. This is a useful summary of statements from the People's Republic on the Sino-Burma incident in Rangoon in 1967.

Hinton, Harold. *China's Relations with Burma and Vietnam*. New York: Institute of Pacific Relations, 1958. A well-documented short historical account of diplomatic relations that attempts to trace a line of continuity between past and present.

Holmes, Robert A. "China-Burma Relations since the Rift," *Asian Survey*, 12 (1972), 473–487.

Johnstone, William C. *Burma's Foreign Policy: A Study in Neutralism*. Cambridge, Mass.: Harvard University Press, 1963. Interesting account and interpretation of Burma's foreign relations and policies.

Kaznacheev, Alex. U. *Inside A Soviet Embassy: Experiences of a Russian Diplomat in Burma*. Philadelphia: Lippincott, 1962. An account of Russian efforts to influence the Burmese through espionage and propaganda.

Kozicki, Richard J. "Burma and Israel: A Study in Friendly Asian Relations," *Middle East Affairs*, 10 (1959), 109–116.

——. "The Sino-Burmese Frontier Problem," *Far Eastern Survey*, 26 (March 1957), 33–38.

Martin, Edwin W. "Burma in 1975: New Dimensions to Non-Alignment," *Asian Survey*, 16 (February 1976), 173–177.

Thant, U. "Burmese View of World Tensions," *Annals of the American Academy of Political and Social Sciences*, no. 318 (1958), 34–42.

Thomson, John S. "Burma: A Neutral in China's Shadow," *Review of Politics*, 19 (1957), 330–350.

——. "Burmese Neutralism," *Political Science Quarterly*, 72 (1957), 261–283.

Tinker, Hugh. "Burma's Northeast Borderland Problems," *Pacific Affairs*, 29 (December 1956), 324–346.

Trager, Frank N. "Burma's Foreign Policy, 1948–56: Neutralism, Third Force, and Rice," *Journal of Asian Studies*, 16 (November 1956), 89–102.

U.S. Congress, House. 94 Cong. 1 sess. *The Narcotics Situation in Southeast Asia: The Asian Connection: Report of a Special Study Mission to Southeast Asia, December 27, 1974–January 12, 1975*. Washington, D.C.: U.S. Government Printing Office, 1975. An account of a U.S. mission to Shan leaders seeking ways to stem the opium traffic from Burma to the rest of the world.

——. "Proposal to Control Opium from the Golden Triangle and Terminate the Shan Opium Trade," *Hearings before the Subcommittee on Future Foreign Policy Research and Development on the Committee on International Relations, House of Representatives Ninety-fourth Congress, First Session, April*

22 and 23, 1975. Washington, D.C.: U.S. Government Printing Office, 1975. Testimony includes a discussion of the U.S. agreement to sell helicopters to Burma for the purpose of controlling the narcotics trade in the Golden Triangle.

Whittam, Daphne E. "The Sino-Burmese Boundary Treaty," *Pacific Affairs*, 34 (1961), 174–181.

Index

Library of Congress Cataloging in Publication Data
(For library cataloging purposes only)

Silverstein, Josef.
  Burma: military rule & the politics of stagnation.

  (Politics and international relations of Southeast Asia)
  An expansion of the author's section on Burma originally published, 1959 and
  1964, in Governments and politics of Southeast Asia, edited by G. M. Kahin.
  Includes index.
  Bibliography: p.
  1. Burma—Politics and government. I. Title. II. Series.
  530.4.S55   320.9′591′05   77–3127
   N 0–8014–0911–X
  BN 0–8014–9863–5 pbk.

69825282
copy 1

Burgess-Carpenter Library
406 Butler
Columbia University
New York, N. Y. 10027

ASIAN STUDIES

Burma
Military Rule and the Politics of Stagnation
JOSEF SILVERSTEIN

This book charts the course of Burma's controlled revolution—a do-it-yourself revolution that, the author contends, has thus far failed. After tracing the roots of Burmese political culture to the precolonial era, Professor Silverstein concentrates on the period of military rule from 1962 to 1974, and the constitutional dictatorship from 1974 to the present. His analysis focuses on the new leadership, ideals, institutions, and political processes that were grafted onto the previous constitutional system. After providing a careful examination of the economy and foreign policy under both democratic and military rule, he concludes with some astute observations on fundamental problems that must be resolved if the nation is to begin realizing its social and economic potential.

JOSEF SILVERSTEIN is Professor, and Chairman, Department of Political Science at Rutgers University.

ISBN 0-8014-9863-5

The Series

POLITICS AND INTERNATIONAL RELATIONS OF SOUTHEAST ASIA
General Editor: George McT. Kahin

This new series, consisting of separate volumes devoted to each of the larger Southeast Asian states, will offer two kinds of studies.

The first category will include concise introductory surveys, reflecting the general format of the contributions to the earlier book, *Governments and Politics of Southeast Asia*, edited by Professor Kahin (second edition, Cornell University Press, 1964). Containing historical sections as well as descriptions of the salient features of the present social and economic setting, these volumes will follow a broadly similar pattern of organization and analysis of the political history, dynamics, and processes of each state.

The second category of books in the series will include longer, more intensive, and more specialized studies of particular aspects of a country.

Cornell University Press
Ithaca and London

COVER DESIGN BY GARY GORE